RIGHT WING REVOLUTION

RIGHT WING REVOLUTION

HOW TO
BEAT THE **WOKE**
AND
SAVE THE **WEST**

CHARLIE KIRK

WINNING TEAM
PUBLISHING

This book is dedicated to my wife Erika Kirk.
Thank you for all you do. You are an incredible mother and wife.
I love you.

CONTENTS

PART FOUR
CHANGING YOURSELF

Intro/Prologue

In more ways than one, this is going to be an offensive book.

You'll find a few anecdotes about *crazy* things those *wacky* liberals have done, but that's not what this book is about. The world has more than enough junk food books filled with stories explaining why libs are bad, and the world doesn't need another.

This also is not a book filled with handwringing and pearl-clutching, desperately trying to conserve whatever pockets of Christian, conservative culture still existing in America. Nor is this a book instructing you to hunker down and ride out the storm until liberalism collapses in on itself. This is not a book for would-be monks and wannabe hermits who hope to hide from the wickedness of a fallen world.

No. This is a book about going over to the counterattack. This is a book about launching a right-wing revolution.

• • •

The Right is no stranger to revolution, despite the Left, in their perpetual arrogance, thinking they have a copyright on it. After all, they don't call it "The Reagan Revolution" for nothing. Ronald Reagan's sweeping reforms and, more importantly, his personal vision for America changed the country for the better. There was a vivid "before-and-after-Reagan" effect on our whole country that endures even now.

But it didn't end there. Trump brought a political revolution in 2016. As of this writing, it is hard to imagine American politics, for better or for worse, ever going back to how it was when he descended the escalator in his hotel in New York to announce he was running for president. Now, pro war conservatism is dead. Pro-open borders "conservatism" is even more dead. The very nature of American retail politics and the nature of politics for the entire planet is radically different in a way that will never be undone.

And that's good. I don't want to undo either of those revolutions. But it's time for another one.

This is above all a practical book. It's a book of things that can and must be done to fix a crisis that is shaking America to its foundations.

The crisis, of course, is *wokeness*. The term itself still feels weird to say. American conservatives have been battling against socialism, Marxism, communism, leftism, progressivism for more than a century. But "wokeness?" Just ten years ago, if you mentioned the term "woke" to a conservative activist, you might get a raised eyebrow and a funny look.

"Woke" has become a bit of a fad term on the right, with the term getting so overused and watered down it seems to only refer to anything liberal. It's unfortunate, because that isn't what the term means. Wokeness represents a unique, more immediate threat to America, more than the liberalism of the past. Stopping it as soon as possible is even more important than most bad ideas emanating from the left, because wokeness is formidable. Almost overnight, it devoured practically every power center in America, became the national ideology taught in our schools, and even found its way to our pulpits. Defeating this threat is going to require an offensive posture. It's going to take a revolution as dramatic as the one that brought us wokeness in the first place.

Revolution can't be approached with a timid, soft touch. It's not the place for gentle words, so it is very possible that in many places, this book is going to be offensive to you, the reader.

I frequently get emails from people that deride me for my tone or my rudeness, saying things like, "I'm a lifelong conservative, but I was appalled by your wording!" If that's you, then I beg of you to just put this book down. You are not prepared for this fight. But if you feel like you're ready to carry on with me, just remember, I warned you.

To quote Christ, I come not to bring peace, but a sword.

Because I'll be honest, the first and most important reason our country is in so much trouble is not due to any outside force. It's not even because of the left. It's because of us. If we were nobler men and finer women, none of the horrible things befalling our country would have happened. We would have stopped it all cold.

But we are not as great as we once were. And so, we are losing.

Far too often, American conservatives reflect the dysfunction that has become more common in America as a whole. Our marriages end in divorce. We fail to properly raise our children. We are increasingly alienated from our neighbors and communities. We are fat, unhealthy, and watch too much TV. We are addicted to pornography. We treat politics as a spectator sport rather than something of enormous importance to hundreds of millions of people and the fate of the greatest country to ever exist. In too many ways we are not categorically different from liberals, differing only in degree and how quickly we adopt the newest moral norms.

In fact, I would go so far as to say that if every liberal activist up and vanished tomorrow, the state of "normal" and even conservative America is still so dire that this would only buy us a few years before the same cancer we call "wokeness" would emerge in new or even identical forms.

This book is going to have more criticism of *you* than of the left, and the truths we will unpack might be hard to swallow. You might even feel offended, but fear not, it's all for the long-term good of the country.

Why does a young punk like me get to diagnose the state of the entire conservative movement and how to fix it? Because more than perhaps *any* other person over the past half-decade I've seen the conservative movement up-close, in the trenches, from every angle, not just from those at the top in Washington DC. I'm not only seeing the conservative movement from those in power in its current state, but I'm seeing how it is evolving in the next generation. My organization, Turning Point USA, established a presence on more than 3,500 college and high school campuses in all fifty states. It is both the largest conservative youth organization, *and* the fastest growing. We have a donor base of 275,000 people. We host well-attended Latino leadership and young women's leadership events, meaning we're in the vanguard of winning over groups conservatives have long struggled with. Turning Point's social media footprint is second to none on the right, certainly a lot better than the RNC's!

Through Turning Point's political arm, Turning Point Action, I've been directly involved in election work for the 2016, 2020, and 2024 presidential election, the upcoming election at the time of writing. In summer 2023, we hosted the first ever ACT Con to rally conservatives for 2024, drawing in more than six thousand attendees. We recruited 2,000 precinct leaders for 2022 and hope to recruit 10,000 for 2024.

By this point, I've spoken privately with thousands of conservative donors, organizers, candidates, and officeholders, and had hundreds of them onto my daily podcast show as well. I've gained an understanding of what makes them tick, what they value, and what they fear.

I think I know the conservative voices rising up in the conservative movement that exists now, at the dawn of the 2024 presidential election is better than just about any of our elected leaders, and certainly better than the RNC in Washington. I don't think that's too shocking. How could people living in Washington DC, a city whose population is 95% Democrats, really understand right-wing America?

I'm anything but perfect. But I've learned a lot running Turning Point— enough to know the ingredients for a sustained, right-wing, anti-woke revolution.

In the first part of this book, I will start things off by simply giving a long list of abhorrent things that are ascendant in America today. I will do it because, even now, far too many conservatives live in a state of denial about what is really happening in their country. The "woke virus" that they mock as a peculiarity of San Francisco and New York liberals is now a nationwide pandemic. Wokeness is also, for all intents and purposes, the official ideology of the federal government. Scratch that, it's essentially the state religion. This new state religion goes beyond mere bad policy ideas. It fundamentally transforms everything about America. Because most liberals see themselves as *ipso facto* irreligious, they have no self-awareness or embarrassment about the fact their worldview is obviously a newly born religion. And so, in Chapter 2 we'll explain what the tenets of this godless faith are.

From there, the book will proceed in three more parts. In Part II, I will look into the reasons we have been losing to wokeness for so long, and why a major change in attitude is essential for turning the tide. The shortcomings of the conservative attitudes the past few years are many, but I will reduce it to a core handful:

Conservatives Care Less: Read the polls and follow the news, and you'll see that it's true. Conservatives don't care as much about saving this country as the left cares about demolishing it. While it is always healthier for your life to revolve around your family or your faith more than politics, but in this time of crisis, that has to change, or we will lose both our faith and our families. We can't remain complacent and focus only on our families, ignoring what is happening to our country if we wish to save it.

Conservatives are Scared: The shadow of "cancel culture" looms large over American conservatism. Deep down, conservatives are scared of a liberal calling them a racist, a sexist, or some other kind of bigot. Winning against woke will require *not* being swayed by these labels, and not being swayed when liberals lob them at other people.

Conservatives are Smug: Far too often, even when we *know* the left is up to no good, conservatives have done little to nothing about it. We assumed wokeness is so silly that it will burn itself out, or that it's the problem of far-away places and will never disturb their own lives. Sometimes, we've simply been lazy, plain and simple. In one red state after another, legislatures have failed to take steps to curb wokeness when they could have easily done so. Now uprooting it will be more difficult but as I will explain, not impossible.

Conservatives are Lazy: Even in their current weak condition, conservatives control many state and local governments and a handful of major institutions. Too often, they're content to stand pat and do nothing rather than actively prepare for the storms emanating from blue America, or, better yet, thinking of ways to turn those storms back aground.

Conservatives are Defeatist: Countless conservatives already assume they're going to lose, and simply allow their very beatable enemies to win without a fight.

Conservatives Are Morally Colonized By the Left: Over and over, conservatives let themselves be controlled by the left's moral framing of the world and America. Instead of rejecting the left's identity politics view of the world, they embrace it, and simply try to argue that the left is hypocritical or unworthy in its use of that view. This is a mental framework that guarantees conservative defeat.

After laying out the attitude shift that will prepare conservatives for a more offensive posture against wokeness, I will show what can actually be done, substantively, to stop it. Some of this will be at the federal level and will require winning presidential elections and appointing pliable judges. But much of this will be at the state and local level, things conservatives in red areas can be doing *right now* to turn the tide against wokeness. At this moment, red states have everything needed in their toolkit to launch an epic rollback of wokeness, they just have to actually do it. Are public colleges, government bureaucracies, and grant programs honeycombed with radicals? Defund them! Are public schools hopelessly left-wing? Empower parents to go elsewhere. Are businesses and organizations engaging in flagrant discrimination in the name of "equity"? Ban it, and punish those businesses.

The final part of the book might be the most important, though. It will certainly be the part that has the highest likelihood of offending, because it will be about all of you. Even after we reject wokeness with our words and our ballots, there is still the matter of rejecting it in how we live our lives. Wokeness is more than a political movement. It's a disease, and just like a strong body will be more resistant to a deadly virus, we will resist wokeness better when we ourselves are better. That means embracing time-tested religious traditions, rather than living with the vacuous nihilism of modernity. It means improving ourselves physically. It means removing modern poisons in our own lives, from pornography to substance abuse to watching too much television. It means protecting our kids by getting them away from propaganda-filled public schools.

Winning is going to require that you, personally, step up. And if you aren't willing to do that, then you are doing nothing but playing your own small role in the death of this great country.

PART ONE

WHAT'S HAPPENED TO AMERICA?

CHAPTER ONE

The Threat

Tradition has it that when the British army surrendered to George Washington at Yorktown, the British army band played the English ballad, "The World Turned Upside Down" to mark what was clearly an event of massive historical significance. The opening verse goes like this:

Listen to me and you shall hear,
news hath not been this thousand year:
Since Herod, Caesar, and many more,
you never heard the like before.
Holy-dayes are despis'd, new fashions are devis'd.
Old Christmas is kickt out of Town.
Yet let's be content, and the times lament,
you see the world turn'd upside down.[1]

Today, as I write this in 2023, the world is once again turning upside down, and once again it is happening in America.

Unless you are very young (and good for you reading this book, if you are!), America is no longer the country you grew up in. It's not the country you expected to live in. In many ways, it's not a country you ever *imagined* you could be living in.

America has had periods of crisis before, periods of stagnation, periods of decline. But not since the days of 1776 has America had a *revolution*. Not since the creation of our Constitution have the values it embodies been more explicitly under siege, or more in danger of being overthrown and replaced.

Sixty years ago, America went through a profound transformation that abolished segregation in restaurants, theaters, transportation, and schools. Laws that prevented black and white Americans from learning together, living together, or even marrying each other were exiled to the ash heap of history. Jim Crow was destroyed forever. America was closer than ever before to being the country it aspired to be in the Declaration of Independence, one where "all men are created equal."

Yet at virtually the exact moment of this triumph, the seeds were planted for a disastrous shift that is now in full bloom. The federal government, only a few years after anti-black segregation went out the door, began building a new system, with new discrimination, only using different words. It turns out that Jim Crow was not nearly as dead as we thought. Instead, it was just dormant, waiting to be revived today under the guise of "social justice."

America's values and norms haven't just evolved. They've been inverted and perverted.

Instead of progressing toward a color-blind society, America has become perhaps the most race-conscious country on Earth, utterly paralyzed by the racial ramifications of literally any discussion on any topic. Whether it's battling crime, growing the economy, educating in schools, or generating pop culture, race wins out before just about any other consideration. In the process, everyone loses except the worst people in society. Criminals win out over police and law-abiding citizens. Parasites are favored over the productive. Merit is thrown out in favor of melanin.

On American campuses, segregation is *coming back*. Schools are opening housing for black students exclusively and are trying to create "black-only spaces."[2] Harvard University holds multiple graduation ceremonies, one for all students, and another just for black students. So do Columbia, Ohio State, and the University of Texas.[3]

As America's values have inverted, its old heroes have simply been toppled. A famous equestrian statue of Theodore Roosevelt, America's greatest conservationist, was removed from the front of New York's Museum of Natural History. A few miles south in New York City Hall, a statue of Thomas Jefferson that stood over city council meetings for 187 years was unceremoniously packed away.[4] In Boston, city leaders removed a statue of Abraham Lincoln with a freed slave, paid for by freedmen and black Union Army veterans, on the absurd grounds that it was racist.[5] The same Puritanical spirit that drove early American religion has been reborn as iconoclasm, the erasure of America's great statues and symbols as nothing but "false gods."

While race stands out the most, race isn't the only area where America seems to have gone a bit, well, nuts. If you can craft an identity group out of it, chances are we've found a way to let it drive us crazy. We're nuts on gender, on sexual orientation, and on immigration.

This neo-Puritan spirit, as everyone reading this book knows, carries the label "wokeness." Its followers are "woke." The revolution they have launched does not just threaten blue cities or blue states. It's a revolution that threatens literally the entire country. Left unchecked, it will devour every state, every town, every isolated corner of the American countryside. It has to, because this revolution's very survival depends on not tolerating any dissent or any difference of opinion.

Don't take my word for it. Let's take a brief tour around the country where wokeness is building.

REPARATIONS

The idea of race-based reparations in America used to be considered a ludicrous non-starter. At best, they were the starting point for a *Chappelle's Show* sketch. Now, in the span of just a few years, everything has changed. In 2018, support for paying out reparations even among *Democrats* was just 32 percent. By 2022, it was up to 60 percent. Democrats dragged independents and Republicans with them, too: incredibly, 18 percent of Republican voters say they support paying out race-based reparations, taking money from one group of Americans to give to another based only on their heritage.[6]

But it's not just that polling has changed. Reparations are no longer theoretical. Reparations are happening right now. Evanston, Illinois has a "Restorative Housing Program" that looks to enrich the descendants of anyone who suffered alleged housing discrimination from 1919 to 1969.

Those who are eligible can get $25,000 from the city to spend on an Evanston home mortgage.

In California, the drive for reparations is far more aggressive and cartoonish. California was never even a slave state, and it abolished school segregation years before *Brown vs. Board of Education.* Yet on the basis of California supposedly being sinful from the moment of its creation, now Black Lives Matter (BLM) activists are demanding they be enthroned as a ruling caste over those of other, inferior skin colors in the state.

In San Francisco, the local reparations panel proposed a one-time payment of $5 million for every black resident of the city. But it didn't stop there. They not only demanded a total jubilee for all debt accumulated by black residents, special exemptions on taxes that others had to pay, a guaranteed annual minimum income on top of the $5 million payout, the right of first refusal for any house put up for sale, anywhere in the city, and for that right to be inherited by one's children, forever. In the words of Revolver News, the San Francisco reparations pitch was "nothing less than a plan to create a new perpetual nobility in San Francisco, with membership determined by belonging to a small, privileged race of supposed victims."[7]

With a starting cost of $175 billion just for the $5 million payouts, San Francisco's reparations scheme clearly isn't going to happen (at least, not without a few decades of Biden-level inflation). But the sheer insanity of that proposal provides cover for the more mundane implementation of new programs in the state that blatantly give away money based on race and nothing more. In 2021, San Francisco created the "Abundant Birth Program," which makes $1,000/month cash payments to pregnant women deemed to be "at-risk," but only if they are black or a Pacific Islander.[8] Making a government program available only to those of two races is flagrantly illegal, of course, but California lawmakers evaded that ban by dressing it up as "academic research." In 2022, lawmakers expanded this "research" statewide. That same year in San Francisco, the city unveiled a new set of direct cash payments, available only to the transgendered, proving that the idea of simply giving favored groups money isn't limited just to race anymore.[9]

Older Americans saw the second half of the 20th century as a steady march toward a color-blind society. But in fact, the rules have been radically re-written, and may be re-written further.

Economist John Kenneth Galbraith once joked that, "Under capital-ism, man exploits man. Under communism, it's just the opposite."[10] It's not a very good joke when it comes to economics, but it applies perfectly to contemporary American race politics: Under Jim Crow, one man could use racial discrimination to oppress another man. And now under woke anti-racism, it's the other way around.

STANDARDS IN FREEFALL

All over America, whatever standards America still possessed in 2020 are fall-ing rapidly. Almost always, it's done in the name of buzzwords like "equity."

Until 2014, New York City required public school teachers to pass a test of professional competency to keep their jobs. Nothing too fancy, a test of 80 multiple-choice questions and one essay covering math, science, humanities, history, communication skills, and a few other subjects. All things you'd probably want a public school teacher to be familiar with, but activists thought otherwise, because the test, like all tests, had racially disparate outcomes. While more than 90 percent of white teachers in New York passed the test, the pass rates for blacks and Latinos were 62 and 55 percent, respectively. Based on that gap, a court ruled that the test violated the Civil Rights Act. Now, after settling a class-action lawsuit, New York has set aside $1.8 billion to pay off people too dumb to make it as public school teachers. Individual plaintiffs have collected as much as $2 million, no actual teaching required.[11]

A standardized test score, either from the SAT or ACT, was once a nearly-universal requirement at America's selective colleges and universities. But in the 2023 admissions cycle, more than 80% of schools treated such scores as optional.[12] At the University of California, once one of the most elite public college systems in the country, the SAT isn't merely optional: Admissions officers are legally *prohibited* from looking at a person's test scores, because doing so would supposedly disadvantage some based on income, disability, or (you know this was coming) race.[13]

Getting rid of standardized tests isn't making the schools more "equal." If anything, it's doing the exact opposite. Critics claim that tests like the

SAT and ACT favor the wealthy who can afford to send their children to test prep courses. Maybe that's a little bit true. But standardized tests are by far the *fairest* way of handling college admissions. Literally anyone can show up one Saturday morning and knock the SAT out of the park. High school grades, on the other hand, reflect four years of studiously dotting i's and crossing t's, and who is more likely to do well on that, rich children whose parents carefully monitor their homework, or poor ones whose parents hardly care, or aren't even present at all? Who is more likely to understand the labyrinthine expectations of "holistic" college admissions, which favor those doing the "right" extracurriculars and covering the "right" topics in their admissions essays? Compared to all that, a single standardized test is much fairer. And yet, hundreds of schools have abandoned tests as an admissions requirement, because the tests don't produce identical results across all races.

The collapse in standards continues the farther up the education ladder one goes.

For the past century, almost all aspiring American lawyers had to pass the bar exam, ensuring they meet a bare minimum of legal knowledge and professional competency. But now that standard is dropping, and just like with the SAT, the justification is "equity."

In 2026, the National Conference of Bar Examiners, which administers the Uniform Bar Examination (used in nearly 80% of U.S. states), is set to roll out a new edition of the test, the "NextGen" exam. In the words of Alabama Supreme Court justice Jay Mitchell, a critic of the new test:

> The proposed NextGen exam will be shorter than the current two-day evaluation, test fewer areas of law, and probe each subject less deeply. Certain topics won't be tested at all. . . . The new exam [appears] far less rigorous and could hamper the ability of states to determine who should be admitted to practice law. The results could be ruinous. States can't maintain functional court systems unless clients and judges can trust the basic competency and integrity of attorneys admitted to the bar.
>
> The proposed exam will also eliminate family law and trusts and estates as tested subjects. Tens of millions of Americans live in rural areas and small towns, where legal needs typically revolve around family law (marriage,

divorce, custody and adoption) and probate matters (estate administration, guardianships and conservatorships). In many rural areas, residents' access to justice depends on the ability of only a handful of practicing attorneys. These residents need to know that new lawyers have the foundational knowledge to serve their needs or at least the threshold understanding necessary to refer them elsewhere.[14]

What justifies such a dramatic downward revision of the bar exam's standards? Anybody who has paid attention in American can guess:

> Two of [NCBE's] stated aims are to "work toward greater equity" by "eliminat[ing] any aspects of our exams that could contribute to performance disparities" and to "promote greater diversity and inclusion in the legal profession." The NCBE reinforces this message by touting its "organization-wide efforts to ensure that diversity, fairness, and inclusion pervade its test products and services."
>
> What does all this mean—and how does it have any relation to the law? Based on the diversity workshop at the NCBE conference, it means putting considerable emphasis on examinees' race, sex, gender identity, national-ity and other identity-based characteristics. The idea seems to be that any differences in group outcomes must be eliminated—even if the only way to achieve this goal is to water down the test.

If NCBE's bar exam update goes as planned, then three years from the writing of this book, America will begin credentialing a wave of lawyers who are, across the board, less prepared and less competent than those who came before. America's attorneys will soon resemble the pathologically incompetent Lionel Hutz from *The Simpsons*, a fictitious lawyer whose legal practice, located in a shopping mall, bears the name "I Can't Believe It's a Law Firm!" Not only will our legal system will be worse off for it, but ordinary Americans, particularly lower-income Americans, will be worse off too.

But that's only the law, you might think. *It's not like we're letting this happen on life-or-death questions.* And that's where you'd be wrong.

Firefighting is an important, dangerous, and high-stakes job. We trust firefighters to save people's lives in dangerous situations where quick action is essential. Being a firefighter doesn't just require brawn, it also requires brains. When a fire truck rolls up to a blazing building, the firefighters need to have a strategy for beating the fire and rescuing any people in danger. That means knowing things like which floors to prioritize, which doors or windows to breach, and where to concentrate resources to contain the fire. All of this requires hard, technical knowledge about how fires behave.

That's why, traditionally, firefighting departments have required competency tests for both new firefighters and those seeking promotions. But in the city of Seattle, recently, firefighters seeking promotion to lieutenant rank were surprised to find the test they were preparing for covered a lot more than just how to stop a blaze:

> The test, which has both written and oral components, is based on a list of texts assigned by the Seattle Department of Human Resources—including, as of this year, *How to Be An Antiracist* by Ibram X. Kendi and *Both Sides of the Fire Lane: Memoirs of a Transgender Firefighter* by Bobbie Scopa. . . . Along with *A Leader's Guide to Unconscious Bias and Fighting Fire*, a memoir by a female firefighter, the books about race and gender span over 800 pages—a large fraction of the total study material.
>
> "This stuff has nothing to do with firefighting," said Wayne Johnson, a retired Seattle firefighter who helped write some of the city's promotional tests. "It has everything to do with social engineering."[15]

Memoirs of a transgender firefighter? What does that have to do with saving lives or putting out fires? Nothing, of course. Why the shift? Take a guess:

> The exam is part of a much larger effort to diversify a department that, as Seattle fire chief Harold Scoggins lamented last year, is "overwhelmingly" white men. Those efforts, critics say, have made the promotion process more about ideology and less about merit, politicizing a public service where competence can mean the difference between life and death.
>
> In fact, in 2021, local officials including Scoggins commissioned a report on diversity in the fire service. One of its recommendations: avoid tests that "rely heavily on knowledge of firefighting."[16]

Every year, America has more than a million fires. Thousands of people's lives depend on the competency of professional firefighters. Yet, instead of picking and promoting them on ability, we are ignoring ability and placing undo importance on buzzwords like "equity" and waging a crusade against the left's favorite bogeyman, "white men."

It's not making Americans safer. In fact, it's doing the opposite. From the 1980s through the early 2000s, fire deaths in America dropped dramatically, from more than 8,000 a year to a low of 2855 in 2012. Then, the next year, the same year Obama was reelected, the same year Trayvon Martin died, the same year that wokeness seemed to emerge as a major force in American life, the trend went into reverse. Every year from 2013 to 2021, except for a COVID hiccup in 2020, the number of fire deaths in America increased.[17] In response, our cities pick firefighters based on meeting diversity quotas and maintaining a knowledge of Ibram X. Kendi's writing.

Even among American doctors, standards are dropping, for the same reason as always.

We have gone from letting the lunatics run the asylum on a metaphorical level, to perhaps a literal level. Worse than putting them in charge of the asylum, they are attempting to take over the oncology section of the hospital.

In May 2023, a new paper appeared in the *Journal of Clinical Oncology*, a top scientific journal for cancer research. The title was "Debunking Sex and Disentangling Gender From Oncology," and it went downhill from there.

> This analytic essay, authored by queer and transgender academic clinicians, researchers, nonacademic community members, and allies, proposes a systems-based approach to degendering oncology, which we define as the conscious and explicit disentangling of gender, anatomy, hormonal milieu, karyotype and other biological factors in oncologic diagnoses, epidemiological analysis, and knowledge production along with eliminating sex from our conceptual framework of bodies and disease . . . [18]

In case you can't digest that unreadable gibberish, the paper is calling for removing biological sex as a factor in treating cancer. That would be very dangerous, because in the real world of actually *treating* cancer, biological sex is one of the most important facts about a person, along with age and medical history, that must be known to guide successful and life-saving treatment. But activists want that flushed, because the existence of "sex" is, of course, most *problematic* for the transgender, the queer, and other members of the alphabet soup community.

My favorite touch is its mention of "nonacademic community members." People who are, in other words, activists. This would all be hilarious in a movie lampooning political correctness on a 90s college campus, but this isn't a movie. The people who want to "degender oncology" might get you killed.

A NEW CASTE SYSTEM

If you read *The New York Times* (and I don't recommend it), you'll eventually notice a tic of the paper's capitalization: When talking about races, the paper capitalizes black ("Black people") but not white ("white people"). To take one example among infinity from one of the *Times'* race-baiting article in 2023:

> Race and housing policy have long been intertwined in the United States. **Black** Americans consistently struggle more than their **white** counterparts to be approved for home loans, and the specter of redlining—a practice that denied mortgages to people of color in certain neighborhoods—continues to drive down home values in Black neighborhoods.
>
> Even in mixed-race and predominantly **white** neighborhoods, **Black** homeowners say, their homes are consistently appraised for less than those of their neighbors, stymying their path toward building equity and further perpetuating income equality in the United States.[19]

It's subtle, but the message is clear: One race is being capitalized, but not the other, because one race is better than the other.

It's not just the *Times*. *The Washington Post* does it, too. So does the *Associated Press*. All of them adopted the practice in 2020, after George Floyd's death. Even in their own explanations for why, the publications said that, in essence, white people were too hateful and evil to be capitalized like their moral betters.

After changing its usage rules last month to capitalize the word "Black" when used in the context of race and culture, The Associated Press on Monday said it would not do the same for "white".

The AP said white people in general have much less shared history and culture, and don't have the experience of being discriminated against because of skin color. . . . "We agree that white people's skin color plays into systemic inequalities and injustices, and we want our journalism to robustly explore these problems," John Daniszewski, the AP's vice president for standards, said in a memo to staff Monday. "But capitalizing the term white, as is done by white supremacists, risks subtly conveying legitimacy to such beliefs."[20]

In other words, AP says, white people have less culture, and while it might be worth capitalizing them just to emphasize their role in perpetrating racism, doing so would empower "white supremacists" (yet capitalizing black, apparently, has nothing to do with black supremacists).

Cut through all of this flimsy reasoning, and the reality is obvious. There is only one explanation for why the capitalization rules were changed and then applied differently for different races. It's a case of reverential capitalization. In the worldview of those who write for the *NYT, WaPo,* and the AP, black = good, and white = bad. Though this is a widely followed practice, surprisingly it's not found in all news outlets. I never thought I'd say something like this, but to credit CNN, they capitalize both white and black when referring to someone's race. Of course, I think capitalizing either white or black needlessly elevates the importance of race, but at least it is a fair and consistent practice. Well done there, CNN!

This wacky capitalization standard pronunciation is textbook wokeness, and not just because it's now literally in the AP's style textbook. Using jargon and facile, half-baked reasoning, left-wing journalists found a way to put the races in a hierarchy, in which a favored race (black) is placed higher, while whites, the designated villain of American society, are placed at the bottom.

Years of propaganda like this has created a disturbing new sense of racial hierarchy in the heads of young Americans, and this hierarchy is emphasized almost everywhere. In the public schools of Portland, Oregon, the following definitions were produced by the state education department to guide high schoolers on how to think about race:

Centering children of color: Applying a racial equity lens to create and design policies and practices that intentionally lift up and protect children of color.

Whiteness: Refers to the way that White people, their customs, culture, and beliefs operate as the standard by which all other groups are compared.

Deconstructing whiteness: Challenging whiteness by understanding how racism functions and our role in it, exploring internalized racism and barriers to internal change, developing a personal vision for racial justice, and building skills to be accountable allies to people of color.

Penetrate the jargon, and definitions make it clear what Portland wants educators to do. They want to tell white students they are bad and privileged, and explicitly favor non-white students. Of course, you might shrug this off saying, "It's Portland, so what can you expect?"

Except it's not *just* Portland. The excerpt you read above was produced by the *North Carolina* Department of Public Instruction. And this kind of propaganda isn't aimed at high schoolers, but at preschoolers![21]

This new social hierarchy has birthed bizarre neologisms. Scarcely a decade ago, the term "BIPOC" didn't exist; now it drenches the pages of *The Washington Post.*[22] The term, an acronym for "Black, Indigenous, and people of color" is a replacement for other general labels like "minorities" or "non-whites," revised to be explicitly more hierarchical:

BIPOC centers "Black" and "Indigenous" to give their names visibility. According to the Sunrise Movement, "By specifically naming Black and Indigenous people we are recognizing that Black and Indigenous people face the worst consequences of systemic white supremacy, classism and settler colonialism." This highlights the unique experiences that Black and Indigenous communities have to whiteness and how other communities of color can perpetuate this relationship.[23]

In other words, black and "Indigenous" (the newest label for Native Americans) are oppressed more (specifically, oppressed more *by whites*, the designated evil race), and so they must be set apart and elevated above other races.

This is toxic and evil when it's just words, but of course, momentous and even life-or-death decisions are being made based on this new caste system, too.

In the winter of 2021–22, the last substantial wave of coronavirus in the U.S., one of the most useful therapies for averting death was infusing a patients' blood with monoclonal antibodies. But these antibodies were not always readily available, meaning that the treatment had to be rationed, reserved for those at the highest risk. But instead of evaluating risk on *actual* risk factors, in multiple states eligibility was substantially dictated by race:

> In New York, racial minorities are automatically eligible for scarce COVID-19 therapeutics, regardless of age or underlying conditions. In Utah, "Latinx ethnicity" counts for more points than "congestive heart failure" in a patient's "COVID-19 risk score"—the state's framework for allocating monoclonal antibodies. And in Minnesota, health officials have devised their own "ethical framework" that prioritizes black 18-year-olds over white 64-year-olds—even though the latter are at much higher risk of severe disease.[24]

In 2021, the Biden administration tried to dole out Covid-19 relief funds first to businesses owned by women and non-whites, purely for identity reasons.[25] Only a time check from the courts stopped them, but with each passing month, the Biden Administration remakes the courts to align more with the values of the Administration.

But even the most conservative U.S. courts haven't dared to halt another sector of America's new caste system.

The U.S. Congress has passed laws demanding that at least five percent of federal contracts go to "disadvantaged" businesses. But today's federal government likes to go above and beyond, so right now about ten percent of federal contracts go to such "disadvantaged" firms. In some departments, it's even higher. Recently, the Small Business Administration told Pete Buttigieg's Transportation Department to get the "disadvantaged" contract figure up to 21 percent.

What counts as disadvantaged? For starters, literally any business owned by anyone who isn't white, even those owned by Indian Americans, the highest-earning ethnic group in the United States![26]

This goes far beyond the federal government, of course. In Chicago, a city in need of cost-effective contracts if there ever was one, 26 percent of contracts must go to minority-owned companies, and there are additional set-asides for women-owned ones. In Maryland, 29 percent of contracts are intended for minority-owned firms; in New York City and state, it's 30 percent.[27]

Some argue that this practice helps even the playing field or gives those systemically oppressed a way out of generational poverty. But awarding contracts based on sex and skin color doesn't make the country better, it just makes government worse. The federal government allows minority companies to be awarded no-bid contracts worth up to $5 million. In New York, no-bid contracts for "diverse" businesses were once capped at $100,000. Now they're at a million, and Eric Adams wants it to be upped to $1.5 million.[28]

Awarding a contract with no bidding process, where the "winning" company doesn't have to be the best option but simply a "diverse" one is a surefire route to corruption and inefficiency. But unfortunately, and perhaps predictably, that's what we get.

In a 2009 study, economist Justin Marion examined contracts on California highway projects before and after state voters banned racial preferences in government programs. Costs on the California projects dropped 5.6 percent relative to federally funded projects in which racial preferences remained in place. Another study, focusing on federal set-aside requirements for disadvantaged firms, found that they increased average expenditure overruns by 35 percent and delays by 6.4 percent, relative to normal government bidding.[29]

All of this favoritism and deliberate discrimination stems from the idea that racism and sexism are rampant in the government and private sector, therefore a heavy hand on the scales is needed to undo the damage. But this is a lie. The only racism in our government, or in business, is the racism our leaders engage in for the sake of "equity."

THE TRANS TERROR

In 2021, in *City Journal*, Abigail Shrier described the legal house of horrors that now existed on America's West Coast.

Ahmed is a Pakistani immigrant, a faithful Muslim, and until recently, a financial consultant to Seattle's high-tech sector. But when he reached me by phone in October 2020, he was just one more frightened father. Days earlier, he and his wife had checked their 16-year-old son into Seattle Children's Hospital for credible threats of suicide. Now, Ahmed was worried that the white coats who had gently admitted his son to their care would refuse to return him.

"They sent an email to us, you know, 'you should take your "daughter" to the gender clinic,'" he told me.

At first, Ahmed (I have changed names in this essay to protect the identities of minor children) assumed there had been a mistake. He had dropped off a son, Syed, to the hospital, in a terrible state of distress. Now, the email he received from the mental health experts used a new name for that son and claimed he was Ahmed's daughter. . . . The age at which minors in the State of Washington can receive mental health and gender-affirming care without parental permission is 13. In other words, the emails Ahmed received from the hospital were effectively a courtesy; the hospital did not require Ahmed's permission to begin his son on a path to medical transition.[30]

Trying to save his son from suicide, Ahmed had instead fed him into a transgenderism industrial complex that threatened to devour him. And only quick thinking on Ahmed's part saved his family.

Ahmed reached out to both a lawyer and a psychiatrist friend he trusted. The psychiatrist gave him advice that he believes saved his son, saying, in Ahmed's words: "You have to be very, very careful, because if you come across as just even a little bit anti-trans or anything, they're going to call the Child Protective Services on you and take custody of your kid." The lawyer told Ahmed the same: "What you want to do is agree with them and take your kid home. When the gender counselors advise you to 'affirm,' go along with it. Just say 'Uh-huh, uh-huh, okay, let's take him home, and we'll go to the gender clinic.'"

Ahmed assured Seattle Children's Hospital that he would take his son to a gender clinic and commence his son's transition. Instead, he collected his son, quit his job, and moved his family of four out of Washington.

Even five years ago, Ahmed's reaction would have sounded deranged to all Americans. Even now, to most people it must seem unbelievable. But it's anything but.

In multiple blue states, right now, the state has grown for itself the power, not just to promote transgenderism, but to step in and take away your children if it decides they are transgender and you, as a parent, are not adequately "affirming" them.

"Taken individually, no single law in any state completely strips parents' rights over the care and mental health treatment of their troubled minor teens," Shrier writes. "But pieced together, laws in California, Oregon, and Washington place troubled minor teens as young as 13 in the driver's seat when it comes to their own mental health care—including 'gender affirming' care—and renders parents powerless to stop them."[31]

With blinding speed, America has raced ahead with one of the most radical science experiments of all time. Even 20 years ago, "transsexuals" (as they were still primarily called then) were comedy fodder, something that was known to exist, but was rare and also profoundly ridiculous. Now, the frequency of "transgenderism" has exploded. Among those over 50, less than one in 300 claims to be trans or "non-binary." Among those 18–29, it's one in twenty.[32] Among those in high school in blue states, it's even higher. In a span of 15 years, America went from zero clinics offering pediatric sex changes, to more than 100.[33]

To accommodate the rapid increase in trans patients, America has embraced radical new treatments with scarcely any debate or any research. The American Academy of Pediatrics endorses the use of puberty blockers on young children who claim to be trans, to prevent them from going through the "wrong" puberty. The drugs required to do this, such as Lubron, have radical life-long effects, from lower bone density to lower IQ as an adult.[34] While advocates claim puberty blockers are fully reversible and a child may go through puberty later in life with no long-term effects, there is zero evidence this is actually true, and foreign health services like Britain's NHS have discontinued their use for that reason.[35]

Children of younger and younger ages are being approved for more and more radical surgeries that mutilate their bodies to "match" their gender identity. The wait for such surgeries, regardless of age, continues to decline. In the summer 2023, a producer with Matt Walsh's show was successfully approved for a testicle removal surgery after a 22-minute telehealth appointment.[36]

As the trans mania has escalated, so has its sacredness. High school and college sports have become a mockery as trans "female" athletes, enjoying the massive performance boost their biologically male bodies give them, demolish the competition with relative ease. The U.S. military, which once banned transgender personnel on the reasonable grounds that they were deeply mentally ill and demanded high-cost medical care, now celebrates trans troops. Virtually every corporation in America participates in Pride Month, which has become a month profoundly linked to transgenderism above all else. Right now, in the vast majority of states, including almost all *red* states, a person can have their birth certificate modified or replaced so that their biological sex is removed, and the sex they "identify" as replaces it.[37] There is no conceit of a person merely *pretending* to be the opposite sex, or even a moment's pause to give space for the idea that the person's gender confusion is a result of a mental health crisis. The official position of the American government and in almost all states, is that a sex change is never to be questioned.

"Never to be questioned" is in fact the central idea of the entire trans moment. In May 2023, the school board in the conservative Los Angeles exurb of Temecula voted against adopting California's newly-crafted "Social Studies Alive" curriculum, due to the curriculum celebrating gay politician Harvey Milk and, more generally, foisting LGBT topics onto children as young as kindergarten.[38] In response, California Governor Gavin Newsom and his attorney general threatened to bring the full fury of America's largest and most dystopian state down on this one dissenting city.

"In the Golden State, our kids have the freedom to learn—and there are consequences for denying that freedom," Newsom said, presumably doing his best to sound like the 80s movie villain he looks like. "California is closely watching the actions of malicious actors seeking to ban books, whitewash history, and demonize the LGBTQ+ community in Temecula and across the state. If the law is violated, there will be repercussions." Submit to Pride, or else.[39]

CRIME

In the upside-down America of 2020, crime is blamed on the police, and America's prosecutors have become self-appointed agents on behalf of America's criminals.

During the 2016 election cycle, while most of America was fixated on the clash between Hillary Clinton and Donald Trump, left-wing mega-donor George Soros pulled off a strategic coup. Like many leftists, Soros was passionate about "criminal justice reform," i.e. punishing criminals less for the sake of "equity." When most people want a law or policy changed, they look to their state legislature, or their governor, or to Washington. But Soros realized that, in practice, prosecutors in major cities could essentially change the law at will, not by rewriting it, but by simply choosing whether or not to enforce it. Not only that, but DA races were far cheaper than most elections, often with low turnout and a reliably left-wing voter base.

And so, in 2016, Soros began a series of interventions in U.S. DA races, repeatedly boosting the most radical candidates he could toward victory. Thus began the reign of the "Soros prosecutors." The basic ideology of a Soros prosecutor is the idea that criminals are victims, and the best way to reduce crime is to *de facto* legalize it.

Across America, the combination of lax DAs fused disastrously with the post-George Floyd attack on police to cause an explosion of crime unseen ever before in American history. Police, realizing that politicians and prosecutors won't support them, have stopped conducting the stops, searches, and arrests that keep crime under control. And even when they do make arrests, a conviction is rare, and a lengthy commensurate jail session even rarer.

Despite lockdowns keeping Americans cooped up at home for several months, in 2020 America's murder rate rose by nearly 30 percent.[40] Instead of stabilizing, it then rose again in 2021.[41]

In St. Louis, Missouri, in the year 2019, city police sought 7,045 felony prosecutions from the office of Circuit Attorney Kim Gardner. Gardner's office prosecuted less than one-fourth of those felonies.[42] Prosecutors left so rapidly that her office had total turnover of more than 100 percent. The approach paid a fitting dividend. In 2020, St. Louis had a homicide rate of 87 per 100,000 residents. If St. Louis had been a country, it wouldn't just have been the most murderous country in[43] the world, it would have *doubled* the murder rate of the next-highest.[44]

Horrifying stories have become routine. In late 2020, Los Angeles man Stefan Sutherland stabbed a construction worker in the neck for making too much noise. Instead of being sent to prison, LA prosecutor George Gascon (whose election was of course backed by George Soros' money) gave him a mental health diversion that quickly left him a free man. In May 2023, Sutherland shot his upstairs neighbor to death, and once again it was over her allegedly making too much noise.[45]

Woke prosecutors are happy to stand down if it means helping criminals, instead happily targeting the innocent Americans they hate. More specifically, they target the Americans who use force to defend themselves and their communities.

On the night of May 30, 2020, Omaha, Nebraska was in the midst of its worst rioting in decades. Just glancing at the date, you know who was rioting, and why. Jake Gardner and his father Dave were caught in the middle, camped out at Jake's bar, The Hive, to protect it from looters. When looters arrived nearby and began smashing windows, the 69-year-old Dave confronted them, and shoved one. After one rioter tackled Dave, Jake came to protect him, soon coming under attack himself. Habitual criminal James Scurlock, fresh off smashing The Hive's windows and looting a nearby architecture firm, tried to put Jake in a chokehold and grab his gun. Protecting himself, his business, and his elderly father, Jake shot Scurlock dead.[46]

The entire incident, captured on video from multiple angles, was a clear case of self-defense, and Douglas County DA Don Kleine declined to press charges for that reason. But then came a relentless, politically driven lynching of Jake Gardner. Local blogger Ryan Wilkins smeared Gardner as a "known white supremacist" with a swastika tattoo who placed hidden Nazi symbolism in The Hive's logo. He used as a source a local sociology professor and second cousin of Gardner, who invented stories of Gardner engaging in racist behavior. Wilkins successfully generated enough political pressure for DA Kleine to appoint a special prosecutor. This special prosecutor indefensibly used Wilkins as a "background witness" for his investigation, and then concocted a ludicrous theory that Gardner, motivated by a Donald Trump tweet, had decided to lie in ambush near his bar to kill a random protester.[47] Operating on this theory, the prosecutor charged Gardner with murder. Having already lost his bar lease in the wake of the shooting, Gardner committed suicide rather than turn himself in. Afterwards, Megan Hunt, a Democratic state senator who had helped spread the lie that Gardner was a white supremacist, celebrated his death.[48] This horror story didn't take place in New York or San Francisco or Portland, Oregon. It took place in Nebraska, a state Donald Trump won by 19 points.

Gardner's case would be an appalling enough tragedy as a one-off, but today any citizen who defends themselves or their community can be at risk. Conservatives closely followed the saga of Kyle Rittenhouse, the teenager who shot three rioters in Kenosha in August 2020, killing two. Rittenhouse was acquitted, but only after a legal saga lasting more than a year. In the meantime, a police officer in Norfolk, Virginia who donated $25 to Rittenhouse's defense fund lost his job.[49] In Utah, a local reporter harassed a paramedic who donated $10 by showing up at his home.[50]

More recently, there is the saga of Daniel Penny, charged with manslaughter for tackling, and then accidentally choking to death Jordan Neely, an insane man menacing passersby on the New York subway. Neely had 42 prior arrests, but rather than locking him away in a prison or mental institution, New York officials were content to let him roam free until he inevitably killed somebody. When Penny prevented that from happening, they finally moved to punish him for the state's negligence.

Daniel Penny was the one to face the consequences, but the truth is it could happen to anyone, anywhere. If you protect yourself, your business, your neighbors, or your community, you're a target in Biden's America.

CONCLUSION

The premise of America, going back to the Declaration of Independence, is that all men are created equal. But the norms that rule woke America are those of George Orwell's novel *Animal Farm*: All men may be equal, but some are more equal than others (also, some of them are women now). Wokeness is devouring all in its path, not just in San Francisco and Seattle, but in West

Virginia and Oklahoma. If you feel that your city or town is safe, then there are only two explanations. Either you're wrong and have simply missed the telltale signs of woke ideology seeping into your community, or the leviathan has simply not had the time to come for your community yet. Nowhere in America is special enough to be immune. The threat to America will spread until it either devours the whole country or is definitively stopped.

CHAPTER TWO

What is Woke?

What has happened to America? In a word, it's *wokeness*. Liberalism has been with us for ages, but *wokeness* is something new, something much more profoundly destructive to everything that came before. Wokeness takes certain trends and impulses that already existed on the left, and sends them into overdrive. If you've ever played the Mario Kart video game series, you might know that there are small yellow arrows that will boost your speed when you drive over them. That's one analogy for wokeness, It's the speed boost pad of liberalism.

Today, you'll mostly hear the word "woke" used by conservatives, but just like "fake news," it actually got its start and was popularized on the left, specifically from the slang term used by black Americans, "stay woke." The phrase first emerged all the way back in the 1930s, but its modern burst of popularity began with Erykah Badu's 2008 song "Master Teacher."

As used in black slang, "woke" described someone "woken up" to important issues, particularly those related to racial justice.[51] As used today by conservatives, it means something different. It's not merely a euphemism or synonym for progressivism, socialism, or even Communism. Today, to call something "woke" captures something different, a dimension to politics that has come almost out of nowhere to dominate first the left and then all of America.

In a single line, *wokeness is a mental illness that believes itself to be the cure.*

THE RUSSIAN NESTING DOLL OF WOKE

A playwright once wrote, "Nothing gives us such a sense of infinity as does stupidity."[52] That's how I feel about wokeness. It is infinite, profound stupidity. But where did this stupidity start? It's hard to find the origin of big concepts like wokeness, as they are often seen as the effect of an earlier event, and those events are the result of an event before that. Behind every story or idea is another story. As the Haitian saying goes, "Beyond mountains there are mountains." In the case of when wokeness as we know it today, it's really a matter of how far back you want to go.

From most people's perspective, wokeness seems to have erupted out of nowhere. They felt they lived in a normal country where things basically made sense, and then almost overnight everything was different: The police were being defunded, their statues were being toppled, their children's schools were filled with transgender ideology, and suddenly they were being told to call Hispanics "Latinx." It was as if the country had been conquered by an alien power.

This isn't simply because people weren't paying attention. Superficial markers of wokeness really did surge dramatically in a very short span of time. Social scientist Zach Goldberg analyzed references to "racists" and "racism" in America's largest newspapers. Starting around 2012, mentions of racism *exploded*. From 2012 to 2019, mentions of racism in *The Washington Post* increased by a factor of six. And it wasn't just because of Donald Trump: Mentions roughly doubled between 2011 and 2014, too.[53]

Another academic, David Rozado, tracked *The New York Times*'s historical use of several dozen words like patriarchy, whiteness, diversity, and so on after another. It showed a jarring, drastic increase in usage during the 2010s.

But why then? Some think wokeness erupted in 2013, with the re-election of Barack Obama. With our man from Honolulu having secured a second term, he didn't need to hold himself back with any of that phony "Hope and Change" rhetoric, so he, or, more likely, his staff, was finally able to let loose with lots of crazy racial policies that would have sunk his 2008 and 2012 campaigns.

Others blame Obama in a different, more indirect way: Barack Obama was supposed to inaugurate a new, permanently liberal, post-racial American utopia. Youthful America went nuts for Obama. They voted for him overwhelmingly and treated him not merely as a promising politician but as a transcendent speaker and visionary of world-historical importance. The press eagerly joined in. If you're a younger reader, just take it from me: You had to be there to understand.

But then, the utopia didn't happen. Politics continued much as before. America's various demographic gaps didn't vanish overnight. Instead of progressing to a permanent liberal majority, America lurched back right in a backlash to Obama's policies, electing a Republican House and turning many state governments a deep red. This disappointment seems to have jolted the narrative of easy progress that young Americans believed in, driving them toward a more vengeful, bitter, and angry version of politics. If Obama had not saved America, it must be that America was far more racist, sexist, homophobic, and all-around evil than anyone had anticipated. Fixing all that evil would take far more aggressive action, and staying woke to that reality, if you will. But others might point to the release of the iPhone, or the founding of Twitter and Facebook, as where woke came from. The rise of social media changed political discourse irrevocably. It gave us the concept of clickbait and rage-farming. The former being an article that made outlandish, attention-grabbing claims in the headline that often didn't deliver (or were outright not mentioned) in the article or video itself. The latter being a news story meant to spark so much rage in the reader or viewer that it not only garnered clicks, but angered people so much that it was widely shared. Social media shrank the world, turning the global public square into something resembling a gigantic high school (and sometimes, a gigantic kindergarten). Smartphone cameras, coupled with the permanence of the Internet itself, created a panopticon where policing a person's every word and action was far easier. And of course, the rise of social media and the online age created more socially maladjusted, mentally unwell people for whom venomous, hate-driven politics is a source of meaning, or at least a way to alleviate boredom.

Others look even earlier and see wokeness as a revival of campus political correctness from the late 1980s and 1990s. The speech climate on campus in the late 1980s was much like it is today, unpleasant, shrill, and often oppressive. Perhaps today's iteration is just the same phenomenon, except the student complainers of 1988 are now professors, able to mold a new generation of exceptionally fragile, easily manipulated millennial and Gen-Z students.

But the only reason that political correctness of the 80s and 90s was taking off was because of the legacy of the decades prior.

Many conservatives like to point toward an infamous clip of former KGB agent and Soviet defector Yuri Bezmenov from the year 1984. In an interview with writer and filmmaker G. Edward Griffin, Bezmenov claimed America was already more than two decades into a long-term psychological project to mentally break its population.

> It's a great brainwashing process which goes very slow and is divided into four basic stages. The first one being demoralization. It takes from fifteen to twenty years to demoralize a nation. Why that many years? Because this is the minimum number of years required to educate a generation of students in the country of your enemy, exposed to the ideology of the enemy. In other words, Marxism, Leninism ideology is being pumped into the soft heads of at least three generations of American students, without being challenged or contra-balanced by the basic values of Americanism, American patriotism.
>
> Most of the activity of the department was to compile huge amounts of information on individuals who were instrumental in creating public opinion. Publishers, editors, journalists, actors, educationalists, professors of political science, members of Parliament, representatives of business circles.[54]

Was wokeness just an ideological virus unleashed by the intelligence apparatus of a dead empire? As tempting as it is to think that, probably not. It's like blaming Russia for the 2016 election result. But the quote does reveal a deeper truth that America was rotting ideologically decades before we started hearing the word "woke."

America's schools and college campuses are horrible now, and they were pretty horrible the year I was born, too, but their embrace of destructive, suicidal, anti-American ideologies dates all the way back to the 1960s when thousands of Marxists and other left-wingers went into academia partly to avoid being drafted into the Vietnam War. Unlike today, there were plenty of jobs available for them, as America was a young country and colleges were growing rapidly.

People who think college administrators are cowardly parasites today would be astonished by what they were like half a century ago. From 1967–69, a group of Black Panthers at San Francisco State College launched a campaign of violence and intimidation at the school, battling police and assaulting students on campus who criticized them. The campaign included no fewer than four *bombings* on the campus, and five more attempted ones, and at one point the violence compelled the school to shut down entirely. Yet incredibly, instead of expelling them, school administrators indulged the radicals, and in 1969 they acquiesced to the creation of a "black studies" department.[55] Within just a couple years, 120 degree-granting black studies departments had sprung up across the country. From the very beginning, the subject was a joke, lacking any academic merit or rigor and existing only for the sake of politics, and so it has remained ever since. Once black studies successfully bombed its way into being an academic subject, women's studies, Latino studies (. . . Latinx studies? Latin@ studies?), and queer studies all followed.[56] It could be argued that wokeness is the natural byproduct of these political, identity-obsessed tumors lurking on campuses.

Of course, one could then point out that the student radicals of the sixties (Students for a Democratic Society, to name the most famous group) were the direct descendants of older, radical college groups such as Intercollegiate Socialist Society (founded by author Jack London in 1905) who were the student wing of Socialist Party of America.[57] Keep going from there, and you get to the big left-wing thinkers of the 19th century.

But even finding wokeness's origins in 19th century political theory has problems. Study the French Revolution closely, and it had many of the hallmarks of wokeness. Hysterical overreactions over something as simple as a person's word choice, purity spirals by true believers, the cynical weaponization of ideology to eradicate personal foes, the creation of a new "year zero" that rejects all the heroes and traditions of the past, and the use of high-flown language about "liberty" and "democracy" to entrench oligarchy and tyranny. The only difference is that back then, getting "canceled" involved a guillotine.

Perhaps wokeness, then, is just a potential embedded within liberalism itself.

But why stop there? Maybe the first woke moment was when Satan convinced Eve to eat the forbidden fruit in the Garden of Eden, telling her it would bring down the Patriarchy with God hoarding all the knowledge of good and evil. Or maybe, just maybe, the first woke moment was when Satan, driven by the sin of pride, rebelled against God.

Ultimately, like a stack of Russian nesting dolls that just gets smaller and smaller without end, you can probably do a near-infinite regression seeking where "wokeness" came from. But in my opinion, this can be a trap. As conservatives, we care about history and tradition. We also care about hierarchy. So, confronted with any force, we ask ourselves "Where did this come from?" and "Who is controlling it?"

But this isn't actually a book about where wokeness came from, or who came up with it. I'm not here to deliver a 50,000-word dissertation on its origins. Plenty of other conservative thinkers, like Christopher Rufo or James Lindsay, have done deep dives into that question.

In *this* book, we are concerned with *defeating* wokeness. And frankly, to defeat wokeness we don't need to know much about where wokeness came from, any more than we needed to know where fascism and the Nazis came from to beat Germany in World War II.

WHAT WOKENESS IS

One reason not to obsess too much about the origins of wokeness is that, in my opinion, the precise origins don't even matter much to the typical believer of wokeness. For most people, *woke* is not a master plan, and it rarely plays out as some kind of grand conspiracy. Instead, wokeness is more of a vibe, a pattern of thought, a social force that plays out in consistent ways over and over again.

Even if knowing where wokeness came from isn't critical, it is very important to know how wokeness *works*.

Eric Hoffer once wrote that, "The inordinately selfish are particularly susceptible to frustration. The more selfish a person, the more poignant his disappointments. It is the inordinately selfish, therefore, who are likely to be the most persuasive champions of selflessness."[58]

Hoffer didn't know the word "woke," but he described it perfectly. Few philosophies are *less* inspiring than wokeness is. While the woke present themselves as caring, progressive, and selfless, the truth is they are the exact opposite. Wokeness is petty, grievance-based and backwards-looking. It's mean-spirited and uncharitable. It is murderously envious, and it cares most about dragging down what is popular, beautiful, functional, and successful, while extolling what is ugly, damaged, and repulsive. There is even something fundamentally psychotic about it.

And yet, this monstrous little ideology has brought America to its knees. And absolutely no one and no*where* is safe. How does wokeness advance so far, even in places where the vast majority of people oppose its agenda?

For the rest of this chapter, I'll explore the various structural facets of wokeness, how it is able to exert such a pull over American life, and in particular how it is *not* in alignment with liberalism as traditionally understood.

Wokeness is obsessed with identity

Human beings are not individuals in the woke cosmology. They are instead a collection of traits and groups that they belong to. Every single person is a representative of their demographic grouping, and those demographic traits are the most important thing about them.

Specifically, the three identities that wokeness is *most* concerned with are race, sex, and sexuality. Being an immigrant or native matters a lot, too. Class, once all-important to the left, matters less and less by the day. Woke liberalism is emphatically *not* the liberalism of Occupy Wall Street. In fact, wokeness is so indifferent to class concerns that some have argued the whole thing was crafted by economic elites as a distraction. But in fact, even before the Occupy movement, alert leftists could see the chasm that was opening. In 2006, left-wing literary critic Walter Benn Michaels wrote:

> Diversity has become the left's way of doing neoliberalism, and antiracism has become the left's contribution to enhancing market efficiency. The old Socialist leader Eugene Debs used to be criticized for being unwilling to

interest himself in any social reform that didn't involve attacking economic inequality. The situation now is almost exactly the opposite; the left today obsessively interests itself in issues that have nothing to do with economic inequality.

And, not content with pretending that our real problem is cultural difference rather than economic difference, we have also started to treat economic difference as if it were cultural difference. So now we're urged to be more respectful of poor people and to stop thinking of them as victims, since to treat them as victims is condescending—it denies them their "agency."[59]

More than a decade and a half later, the situation has only intensified. To the extent the left still wants to redistribute wealth, they are only interested if it's conceived as race-based reparations that take from whites to give to blacks, or taking from men to give to women in the name of fixing the "gender pay gap." And speaking of that . . .

Wokeness uses identity to create a moral hierarchy

In the world of woke, some groups are simply better or worse than others. This hierarchy isn't always perfectly rigid, but anyone paying attention knows the basic outlines. Being male is worse than being female, though being a *trans* female (that is, a biological male wearing a dress) is better than being a biological female. Being straight is strictly inferior to being gay. Being an immigrant is better than being native-born (and being an *illegal* immigrant is best of all). And of course, the races fit squarely into a vicious hierarchy. White is the worst race, black is the best race, and the other races are left to gruesomely fight it out for the middle slots.

Sometimes, the *exact* means of ordering the hierarchy can be tough. Is a Ukrainian refugee woman higher or lower in moral worthiness than a middle-class Haitian man? Like the Coca-Cola recipe, the exact woke moral hierarchy is a closely guarded secret, though unlike Coke's recipe, it can also change without warning.

(By the way, the answer to that is probably the Haitian, *unless* it's post-invasion Ukraine in 2022.)

Wokeness sees disparities as proof of wrongdoing

The world isn't fair, and not all people are the same. That might seem obvious, but to the woke, this simple fact is the source of immense rage. Whenever a disparity exists between two groups, and the disparity favors one *lower* on the wokeness moral hierarchy, the woke take it as proof of systematic discrimination. If white people go to prison less than black people, that must be due to systemic racism by police, by the criminal justice system, or by society as a whole.

The one-way nature of this assumption is critical. On its head, the idea of wanting to allow everyone the same opportunities for success should they choose to take it seems good. However, it is that moral hierarchy that shifts this from merely wanting to help those in need to wokeness. Because once those tables turn and the disparities are shifted, there is no effort to establish an equilibrium between both parties, because the "better" party is now in control. And so, if more men are computer scientists than women, that is because computer science is somehow systemically sexist and exclusionary toward women. But if more women than men graduate from college, that is not taken as evidence that colleges are sexist. As long as the courts imprison black men for robbery, assault, and murder more often than they do white men, the courts will be racist, but if more white men started going to prison than black men, the woke would see nothing untoward.

Seeing social justice arbitration as a means of power for themselves is what mutates what would otherwise be compassion into something more sinister than that. Disputes between rival identities will need a powerful judge to make a ruling in favor of one or the other. There is no prize for guessing who the woke think should be made judge, jury and executioner in all disputes.

Wokeness is selfish and resentful

Conservatives have long known that economic envy drives many calls for socialism. Leftists see other people with more money than them and crave it. Wokeness takes that impulse and generalizes it more widely. The woke are resentful of *any* kind of boon enjoyed by others: attention, beauty, health, wealth (both inherited and self-made), or even basic mental stability. Wokeness treats practically the whole world as zero-sum. If others are happy, the miserable person thinks, it must be that they somehow took something from me.

Wokeness is decentralized and bottom-up

As conservatives, we tend to create and to respect hierarchies. We project this attitude onto our enemies, more than we actually ought to. We like to look for the hidden mastermind behind the troubles we face. And certainly, powerful sinister figures exist, such as George Soros spending millions to install pro-crime DAs in American cities.

But the truth is, wokeness doesn't happen because a few powerful actors decreed it. It happens because millions of people are true believers. Public schools are full of wokeness because countless teachers consider it their moral duty to foist it on their students (and perhaps guide some kids through a ~~castration~~ "gender transition" while they're at it).

Why do you think Elon Musk had to sack roughly 80% of Twitter when he bought it in fall 2022?[60] Partly because he wanted to aggressively cut costs, but another reason was that Twitter's constellation of content moderators and non-technical staff were a huge barrier to creating a non-woke, anti-censorship speech platform. Even then, when Musk wanted to do something as simple as allow the Daily Wire to broadcast *What is a Woman?* on the platform, he had to overcome significant internal resistance within his own company.[61]

The simplest way of seeing this might be to look at the steady creation of bizarre new vocabulary within the world of woke. The collective acronym for America's non-heterosexuals was once "GLB" (gay, lesbian, bisexual). Under the pressure of feminists in the early gay rights movement, that acronym gave way for LGB, for the express purpose of putting women in a stronger position. In the 90s, the "T" was added. But the label has never been stable since. Once "T" was in, every oddball made-up sexual minority wanted a spot. There's been LGBTQ, LGBTQ+, LGBTQIA, 2SLGBTQIA+, and even (I swear I am not making this up) LGBTTQQFAGPBDSM.[62]

No single person ordered this prolonged expansion of what is sometimes now called the Alphabet Soup community. Rather, its expansion is driven by rank and file woke weirdos, who endlessly complain about being left out if their niche self-identified sexuality doesn't get into the gay rights acronym.

Wokeness is psychologically brittle

Wokeness wallows in weaponized weakness (if Elon Musk ever buys *The Washington Post*, have that replace "Democracy Dies in Darkness"). It is the ideology of the wound collector—people who see a "microaggression" in every comment and who see the world as a constant cascade of attacks and injustices weighing them down. It is the worldview for people who diligently collect a list of statements that offended them, so they can present it to a university tribunal, an HR department, or a federal court.

Unsurprisingly, the woke love making videos of themselves having meltdowns—sobbing and screaming at the camera because Hillary Clinton lost the presidency or Ruth Bader Ginsburg died or the Supreme Court repealed *Roe v. Wade*.

Wokeness takes pathetic people and tells them that their weakness and suffering is actually a great moral struggle. It gives them a script to follow, to turn a meltdown into an advantage. It gives them something even better than a real accomplishment: It gives them an excuse. Because an accomplishment may eventually fade, but an excuse for failure can last your entire life.

Normally, the horrible attitude that wokeness promotes would get one nowhere, but at this particular moment in America, it instead confers power.

Wokeness also teaches people to overreact to any provocation, to *always* act like it's the end of the world, because when they act that way, powerful people submit. It makes being a bratty teenager, regardless of your actual age, your whole personality.

Wokeness requires thought control

Relative to prior iterations of American liberalism, wokeness is very concerned with controlling the speech and thoughts of other people.

This is one place where wokeness diverges quite sharply from liberalism as Americans understood it until roughly the past decade. America has some of the world's most robust free-speech laws substantially because of the work of liberals from many decades ago.

But today, that's flipped entirely. More than half of Democrats favor criminal bans on "hate speech" (whatever that is).[63] University speech codes (official or informal) have made a grand comeback. Big tech has built an immense censorship regime to stifle the words of those pushing "disinformation" on gender, race, crime, or foreign policy. Police in blue cities have criminally investigated things like people putting up "It's Okay to Be White" signs.[64]

Why so much censorship?

Part of it is that psychological brittleness mentioned above. Wokeness collects superficial grievances and becomes unhinged by any kind of spoken opposition. But another major factor is simply that the values liberalism promotes have become so *completely* divorced from basic physical reality that only a totalitarian approach can keep people believing in it. The woke assert that a man can take some hormones, put on a dress, amputate his testicles, and pay a surgeon to carve an open wound into his lower abdomen, and thereby be transmuted into a human woman, just as female as the mother who birthed you. This isn't just false; it's ridiculous. Transgender people come off as a parody of the opposite sex. Instead of being a man trapped in a woman's body or vice versa, they've just been a person with a staggering mental illness. Some of them don't even go through with the surgeries I just described, and think they are a woman simply because they had a thought once that they were. It used to seem so obvious something was mentally wrong with these people, and it was easy to spot and identify. That's exactly what the whole world did for decades before the sudden surge of wokeness, and it's what happens in any forum where the woke lose their power of censorship for even a bit.

Other facets of wokeness are at least at war with facts one can see right in front of their face. To believe that the police are systematically racist, one must steadfastly refuse to notice a pattern in who commits crimes in their city, and whose mugshots are showing up on the local news at night. To think that it's sexism that causes boys to work as computer programmers or auto technicians while women become preschool teachers or psychologists, one must fail to notice the vast differences in preferences and behavior that separate men and women.

That is, in the end, what much of wokeness is. It is a war on noticing. And the war must be particularly harsh, precisely because the conclusions are so obvious.

This is also why, while liberals of the past were often quite funny, the woke of today have lost their grasp of comedy entirely. As they say online, "The left can't meme." Late-night shows have become pious recitations of political views. Hosts like Stephen Colbert and Jimmy Kimmel sound so castrated they could pass for being trans. *The Babylon Bee* has become America's top satire website, while *The Onion* is borderline unreadable much of the time.

This is directly linked to the massive censorship that wokeness requires. The whole philosophy of humor, some have said, is noticing the gap between what *is* and what we think *should be*. A man who calls himself a woman, when he's a man, is in some ways the prototypical joke! It's that gap, and the lack of self-awareness that there is a gap, that makes for comedy. Alas, the left is too far gone to appreciate it.

Wokeness is feelings-based

What drives wokeness forward, far more than any particular worldview, is feelings. Woke is, in many ways, more a state of mind than it is an ideology. The specific feelings are a combination of entitlement, bitterness, envy, craving for attention, as well as several other traits.

This is why, even after acknowledging no ideology is perfect, wokeness stands out as particularly incoherent. The woke claim there are no inherent differences between men and women, yet transgender people can know they are "really" the opposite sex because they like wearing women's clothing or enjoyed playing with dolls as a toddler. Transgenderism is so obviously real that questioning it in one's child should be considered child abuse, yet trans-racialism (the belief that you identify as a member of a racial group that you are not genetically a part of) is impossible, and merely claiming it is wildly offensive.

What explains all that? Facts can't, but feelings can. In one moment, the woke are upset and offended to see that men and women have different life outcomes, so they angrily protest that this must be due to malfeasance, because men and women are the same. But then, when some among their number develop a fetish for being a woman, and then the delusion they really are one, they justify it based on just *feeling* in their gut, that it is true. To invert a popular phrase, for the woke, feelings don't care about your facts.

F. Scott Fitzgerald said that "The test of a first-rate intelligence is the ability to hold two opposed ideas in mind at the same time and still retain the ability to function." The woke hold more than two opposing ideas in their mind at all times, but they flunk the "retain the ability to function" part.

Another component of this feelings focus is an obsession with "lived experience." A person's "lived experience," in short, is any claim they make that cannot be proven. The woke *love* lived experience, because it's their way of trampling all opposition based on basic objections like, "Does this make any sense?" "Are the claims you're making even true?" and, "Hey, wait, what are *you* doing in the women's bathroom??"

If a person *claims* to have suffered racism in the form of microaggressions, then to the woke this experience *must* be treated as valid, because their "lived experience" says as much. There is no room to say that a person is unreasonable or simply wrong.

Whenever there's some blow-up on campus, a favorite claim of the woke is that the situation has caused them to, "feel unsafe," and thus their demands must be met. Their feelings are crucial. They can't claim to *be* unsafe, because that claim is ludicrous, namely because the woke themselves are typically the most consistent source of violence on an American campus. But by claiming the supremacy of feelings, they pressure administrators to submit to their will.

Wokeness is predatory

The concept of "cancel culture" is intimately linked with wokeness. But what is "cancellation"? It is, essentially, a predatory act. A cancellation begins by identifying a vulnerability in someone—often a trivial one (errant tweets from a decade ago, an awkward answer in a TV interview, etc.). A crowd is then whipped into a moral frenzy, in which the target's offense is portrayed as utterly unthinkable, unforgivable, and beyond the pale. The person's utter destruction is demanded. An apology is impossible; any admission of fault is only added to the evidence justifying a person's personal destruction. But, crucially, one person's discussion is rarely the only force in play. Woke cancelers always want something. Changes in law, changes in policy, more money for their organizations and more jobs for themselves.

The woke only rarely extract demands by simply mounting a direct assault on a target out of the blue. Instead, they seize on predatory opportunities.

Eric Hoffer said in the *Sixties* that in *America*, "What starts out here as a mass movement ends up as a racket, a cult, or a corporation."[65] Wokeness is revolutionary in that it is all three.

Wokeness is bureaucratic

This pillar is arguably the *most* essential for understanding how wokeness wins, and how to dismantle it. Wokeness does not work through ordinary political mechanisms. The woke don't campaign on wokeness, try to win votes, and then implement their ideas via legislation if they win. Or at least, that's not the secret of their success. Instead, wokeness imposes itself through bureaucratic methods. Rather than change the law to suit their ideology, the specialty of the woke is to nest inside institutions, then reveal that actually, the law *already* mandates their worldview. Very few woke laws are passed. A great many are more or less "discovered."

The 1964 Civil Rights Act, for instance, includes a prohibition on sex-based discrimination in employment. No member of Congress who voted for that bill ever imagined they were also banning discrimination against the transgender, not the least because the word "transgender" was only coined in 1965. Yet in the 2010s, the woke suddenly discovered that the law had banned anti-transgender discrimination all along! After depressingly getting a stamp of approval from the Supreme Court, America suddenly had a new law, and a new woke mandate.

Do you dislike "woke capital" that force business to espouse, practice, and celebrate woke virtues? No worries, everyone does. But woke capital doesn't just exist because companies decided to go nuts. In essence, thousands and thousands of companies have been *ordered* to go woke by a federal bureaucracy that is enormously powerful yet maddeningly vague. A dizzying array of federal laws and regulations threaten them with fines and crippling lawsuits if they violate them, yet often these laws leave it very unclear what is a violation and what isn't. In environments such as that, the woke thrive. They staff the bureaucracies that decide violations, and they staff the HR departments that manage compliance.

Many other facets of wokeness have a bureaucratic character to them. For example, the identity groups that the woke obsess over are frequently bureaucratic creations rather than organic ones. Let's look at racial categories for a moment. While some groups might make intuitive sense (regardless of how frequently the accepted names are changed) like black, white, native, or Hispanic. But consider the racial category of AAPI, or Asian-Americans and Pacific Islanders.

At first glance, you might not take any issue with the term as it's used so much in our cultural vernacular. However, upon closer inspection it becomes clear how arbitrary the grouping of these ethnic groups is. The first issue is the huge and varied populations that come from Asia. The continent includes countries like Japan, Pakistan, the Philippines, Korea, Iraq, and India. Countries in Asia make up more than half of Earth's population, and as such, not all of the countries represented have much in common in the way of shared history, appearance, and apart from the technicality of being on the same continent, aren't even particularly geographically close. But lumping in Pacific Islanders renders the whole category so broad that it loses all meaning. Pacific Islanders are cultures like Samoans, Tongans, native Hawaiians, and Maori people, and their cultures are incredibly different from Asian communities in the way of shared heritage and history, physical appearance, and geographic location. And yet, they are a part of a shared racial grouping for no other reason than a bureaucratic one.

The racial and ethnic categories America obsesses so much over are the essentially arbitrary creations of federal bureaucrats decades ago.[66] Yet now, these arbitrary creations shape every facet of American society. It shows up in the workplace in hiring practices and daily operations, as big businesses are forced to comply with the expectations of America's federal bureaucracy, thereby running on a strong dose of woke ideology.

What Does It All Mean?

All of the above points toward important takeaways for how to *overcome* wokeness.

1. Wokeness will be beaten with *masculine* energy.

Did you notice a pattern to many of the above traits? You should have. One of the biggest ways wokeness differs from the liberalism of the past is in how *feminine* it is. Women are more likely to be woke, and wokeness appeals more to women overall.

The natural way to undermine this, then, is by countering it with what is, broadly, masculine energy. That doesn't mean literally relying only on men. Women are perfectly capable of using masculine tactics, just like there are plenty of psychologically effeminate woke men. What it means is deploying traits like resilience, rigidity, and strength. It means recognizing manipulative or attention-seeking behavior, and not indulging it. It means not giving in to the temptation to conform, when you are told that something simply must be a certain way. It means exercising discipline.

A great many of the traits listed above could be grouped together to say that, in essence, "wokeness succeeds by throwing tantrums." How do you teach your small child not to throw tantrums in public? By refusing to reward them.

Wokeness is the ideology of grievance collectors, whose lives revolve around reciting the ways they are victims and memorizing all the wrongs done to them. A huge amount of woke overreach is prevented simply by recognizing the manipulative whining that lies at the heart of so many woke demands, and simply refusing to acquiesce to them. This takes toughness. But it's what works.

The woke are, fundamentally, physical cowards, the kind of people who try to win fights with a sucker punch. They win their greatest victories when nobody even shows up to oppose them. They wilt in the face of actual courage, be it physical or moral.

2. Wokeness can be beaten by caring less.

Look, I understand that there may be legal reasons why you have to care, or pretend to care, when an employee or associate does something that triggered a pearl clutch, but this is maybe the most basic of defenses against wokeness. You have to shrug it off.

Someone said something "racist" to someone?

"I'm sorry to hear that. That was rude."

That's about all you owe the situation, if even that. But you can't give in to theater. You can't join a fake victim in pretending that some stray word caused "trauma" or emotional distress and is bigger than it was.

The only way we take our conversation back is by controlling the tone. And the tone, when people bring up something offensive that they're acting like is the end of the world, is to be low-key about it or shrug it off. Or best of all, laugh it off.

3. Wokeness can be resisted by making ourselves better.

As the list makes clear, the woke are generally an ugly bunch. Wokeness ropes in the bitter, the angry, the defective, the miserable.

How can we avoid being swayed too much by it? In part, by strengthening ourselves, so that we aren't vulnerable to the lies that wokeness promotes. Raising healthier families will produce better children, who won't be entranced by woke lies. Making ourselves stronger also will drive home the repulsiveness of the woke to onlookers who ultimately would rather join a strong, attractive movement than a disgusting one.

4. Wokeness can be beaten by defanging bureaucracies.

The inherently bureaucratic aspects of wokeness mean that it will carry the advantage whenever rules are made off-screen and out of sight, then enforced selectively. Clear-cut standards and up-or-down votes are the bane of the woke, who prefer vague laws and vague norms subject to endless manipulation and redefinition. Conservatives should be perpetually on the lookout for bureaucratic entities propping up woke morals and when they find them, instead of complaining, they should destroy them.

5. Assume bad faith on the part of the woke.

Wokeness is manipulative and very much *not* about what is good for everyone. So don't assume that it is. When the woke make demands of you, don't look for compromises or ways to satisfy their complaining, because those demands aren't coming from a good place. Instead, reject them outright.

Of course, it's all very easy to simply make lists. Actually translating the list above into action is going to take a major change of attitude on the right. That will be the subject of Part 2 of this book.

PART TWO

CHANGING YOUR ATTITUDE

CHAPTER THREE

Ignore The Left's Skinsuits (OR: It's All Such a Drag)

1. Identify a respected institution.
2. Kill it.
3. Gut it.
4. Wear its carcass as a skin suit,
while demanding respect.
#lefties
—David Burge[67]

Sometimes, one just has to pause and think: *Why drag shows?*

Sure, LGBT rights have become vastly more mainstream and then dominant over America's past 40 years. We've legalized (mostly through judicial fiat) gay marriage, gay adoption, sex changes, and "non-binary" identities. Pride Month might as well be America's Ramadan. But why, specifically, are there so many drag shows? Why is "drag queen story hour" a ritual in countless library systems across America? Why are drag queens brought in to read to kindergartners in public school? Okay, sure, it's not hard to guess why the drag queens like doing it: Some of them want to molest kids, or at the very least pervert them, and all of them get off on the dissociative fetish of pretending to be women and compelling others to treat them like one. But why does *all of society* push this so hard?

But really, when you think about it, it makes sense. The idea of the "wrong body wearing the right clothes" is everywhere in America. America is a country of impersonators, a country of fakes. America, as a country, has become a drag show.

Think about what a drag show actually is. Drag is a perverted impersonation. It is when someone fools around by wearing the outfit of someone or something they are not, typically in an exaggerated, cartoon form. (Perhaps leftists wouldn't have loved drag if someone had called it "gender appropriation" early on.)

Historically, drag shows were comedic. The entire joke was the ludicrous idea of a man pretending to be a woman. Today, while queens are still garish parodies of women, for the many trans drag queens out there, onlookers are expected to affirm that they are *really* women.

This is now what the Left does *in every sense*, to *every* institution. The Left takes an imposter, for example, someone who hates an institution or class, puts that person in charge of it, dressing them up like they are a member of it, and asks us to pay them our respect. Far too often, they get away with it.

And nowhere is this more obvious than in the U.S. military.

In the spring of 2021, Fox host Tucker Carlson was confused. Why on earth, he wondered, was the U.S. military gloating about rolling out flight suits specially fitted so *pregnant women* could wear them?

"Pregnant women are going to fight our wars," Tucker said. "It's a mockery of the U.S. military."[68] Tucker, with his special talent for pointing out obvious things that others won't say, noted the rank absurdity of a global fighting force having to care about having clothes for expectant mothers in its toolkit alongside ships and shells and bombs.

"[While] China's military becomes more masculine," Tucker said, "our military needs to become, as Joe Biden says, more feminine."

But if Americans like Tucker were surprised by maternity flight suits, what came next was more jarring. When Tucker complained about the priorities of the military, the military sniped back, on Twitter, no less.

"Women lead our most lethal units with character. They will dominate ANY future battlefield we're called to fight on," Sgt. Maj. of the Army Michael Grinston tweeted in response to Carlson.[69] Army Gen. Paul Funk, head of Training and Doctrine Command, tweeted that servicewomen, presumably including the pregnant ones, were "beacons of freedom."[70] Master Gunnery Sergeant Scott H. Stalker, Command Senior Enlisted Leader at U.S. Space Command, used his official Twitter account to trash Tucker, calling his show "drama TV" and bashing him for not having military experience (Tucker might have replied that he and Stalker have been involved in the same number of victorious wars).

The most bizarre response of all came from the II Marine Expeditionary Force, an active-duty military unit, which used its Twitter account to blast out an image of a female soldier doing a fireman's carry.

"What it looks like in today's armed forces @TuckerCarlson. Get right before you get left, boomer." When one Twitter user begged the Marines to worry about China instead of a Fox TV host, the account replied, "Come back when you've served and been pregnant."[71]

Seeing active-duty military officers, and even entire units, publicly feud with a television host was extremely strange behavior, to say the least.

Traditionally, the U.S. military is an apolitical entity. It has to be, because a politicized military is death to a free country. From Argentina to Turkey to Thailand, countries less fortunate than America have been plagued by politically motivated coup d'états from the armed forces. For two and a half centuries, America has enjoyed a military squarely under civilian control, one which doesn't wade deeply into partisan or ideological arguments. But look at the military of today, and that's changed.

Take a glance at him, and you'd think that Mark Milley was sent to the Pentagon straight from central casting. With his impeccable uniform and severely rectangular head, he looks every inch the kind of man who would be Chairman of the Joint Chiefs of Staff.

Unfortunately, like a drag queen who looks the part of a woman but whose deep voice betrays him, Milley's own fraud was obvious the second he opened his mouth.

"I want to understand white rage," Milley told the House Armed Services Committee in 2021.[72] "What is it that caused thousands of people to assault [the Capitol] and try to overturn the Constitution of the United States of America? What caused that?" Milley asked. The crowd that intruded into the U.S. Capitol was a multiracial one, upset over an election outcome. What they did had absolutely nothing to do with "white rage" (whatever that is), but with his testimony Milley lent the military's endorsement to a press-invented narrative in which "systemic racism" and evil white people are the chief threats to American well-being.

Over the past three years, the whole military has steadily followed Milley's lead. Shortly after January 6, the military created a "Countering Extremism Working Group" to root out supposed political thoughtcrime within the ranks. The man put at the head of this working group was Bishop Garrison, the Defense Department's Senior Advisor on Human Capital and Diversity, Equity, and Inclusion (a job I am fairly sure did not exist during World War II).[73] Before becoming the Pentagon's top diversity man, Garrison had a lively Twitter career in which he said all Trump supporters were racist, misogynist extremists.

"Support for [Trump], a racist, is support for ALL his beliefs," Garrison tweeted in 2019. "He's dragging a lot of bad actors (misogynist, extremists, other racists) out into the light, normalizing their actions. If you support the President, you support that. There is no room for nuance with this."[74] This was the DoD's point man on defining what "extremism" was and deciding how to "counter" it.

There is no room for nuance, indeed.

Reader, make no mistake: they now view <u>you</u> as America's enemy.

In spring 2021, the military issued an announcement that henceforth, it would (for free) provide transgender soldiers with all of the expensive sex-change treatments they required to fulfill their delusions, provided they were "medically necessary."[75] Of course, it is literally never medically necessary to lop off a man's otherwise healthy penis and testicles, or to construct a fake penis by removing thigh tissue and pinning it on a confused woman, or to pump a person full of opposite-sex hormones. Besides not being necessary, such treatments typically make a person far less physically fit to serve in the armed forces or participate in combat. But no matter. Our military now exists not to win battles but to provide expensive elective surgeries for delusional soldiers. I'll let you draw your own conclusions about the symbolism of America encouraging its own army to self-castrate, a practice that used to signify that an army had been conquered and was subsequently being slaughtered by the conquering group.

In the fall of 2021, the U.S. military imposed a service-wide mandate to take the Covid-19 vaccines, on pain of being forcibly separated from the service.[76] This wasn't a matter of protecting soldiers' health. The vast majority of military personnel are under 35, and are in excellent shape (at least the ones who don't castrate themselves). Soldiers, sailors, and airmen are at statistically near-zero danger from any variant of Covid. Imposing the vaccine wasn't a matter of health. It was an ideological imposition, and acted as an ideological filter, letting the military push out thousands who felt strongly enough against the shot to refuse it.

The military, once fiercely meritocratic, has now politicized its promotion methods. The U.S. Army has an "Equity and Inclusion Agency," sporting the motto "Diversity is the Force, Equity is the Goal, Inclusion is the Way."[77] In early 2021, the Defense Department announced plans to "remove aptitude test barriers that adversely impact diversity"—that is, they would lower standards to ensure more people of the right race or sex could be promoted.[78] In summer 2021, a naval admiral gave a jarring recommendation for how the process could be accelerated:

> Earlier this month the Navy's chief of personnel made a revealing remark that received little public attention. "I think we should consider reinstating photos in selection boards," Vice Adm. John Nowell Jr. said at a conference. Officers up for promotion used to submit a photo as part of the review. A couple of years ago the services eliminated the photo requirement, aiming to remove any bias.
>
> Adm. Nowell suggested the result wasn't what the Navy hoped for. "We look at, for instance, the one-star board over the last five years, and we can show you where, as you look at diversity, it went down with photos removed." In case that wasn't clear, he continued: "We're very clear with our language to boards that we want them to consider diversity across all areas. . . . I think having a clear picture just makes it easier."[79]

In other words, promotion boards should start discriminating against white people, ASAP. That same year, the Air Force announced a brand new strategy, not for winning wars or securing the border, but for lowering the number of pesky white males who fly America's fighter jets.

"Diversity is a warfighting imperative," an Air Force lieutenant colonel said when the policy was announced.[80]

Even elite combat units aren't immune. When the Obama Administration opened up Ranger school to women, commanders were pressured to lower standards and allow women many opportunities to pass tests that male candidates only got to attempt once. 'A woman *will* graduate Ranger school,' they were told.[81]

The attempt to turn the U.S. military into a sort of jobs program is pathetic. That our leaders think it should be a jobs program running on DEI quotas, like this is any old business we can afford to sabotage in the name of "representation," even more so.

The rot isn't some new product of the Biden years, nor is it exclusive to Democratic administrations. Even in 2019, West Point offered a class on "The Politics of Race, Gender, and Sexuality."[82] The class's four assigned textbooks were[83]

- *Critical Race Theory: An Introduction*
- *Race, Gender, Sexuality, and Social Class: Dimensions of Inequality and Identity*
- *Queer Theory Now: From Foundations to Futures*
- *Feminist Thought: A More Comprehensive Introduction*

"The class will serve as an introduction to the theoretical concepts of post-modernism," the course overview says. "This will include a focus on feminist theory, critical race theory, and queer theory. . . . Throughout the class, cadets will be expected to apply these theoretical frameworks to problems of American public policy and demonstrate this through their written work."[84] The academy that once trained Ulysses S. Grant, Dwight Eisenhower, and Douglas MacArthur now trains future Kimberlé Crenshaws.

This flood of wokeness might all be defensible if the U.S. were acquitting itself well in its missions, but it's not. With twenty years and nearly unlimited money, the U.S. military achieved essentially nothing in its war against the Taliban. With 20 years of preparation to train and prepare an Afghan military, our leaders managed only to craft a Potemkin army that folded the moment U.S. troops weren't immediately on hand to back them up.

Everywhere you look, the decay is evident. Research in 2023 found that a quarter of Army troops were obese.[85] Deadly accidents are increasing and are such a crisis that after two fatal helicopter crashes in spring 2023 the Army temporarily ordered all non-essential flights grounded for safety reasons.[86] But the greatest sign of decay of all is this: Americans have stopped wanting to serve. Despite generous benefits, a shaky overall economy, and no foreign wars being fought, the U.S. Army missed its recruitment goal for 2022 by a whopping 25%.[87] The Americans who once filled the ranks of America's all-volunteer force aren't showing up anymore.

Our military no longer serves as a strong, admirable moral bastion of our country. It no longer seems to stand for excellence in actions, physicality, combat, and character. No longer does being a soldier mean you are the best of the best. Instead, it has taken on the guise of something that is ever-changing based on the current political climate, the vigorous nature of many of the branches has been removed or lessened significantly, meaning that the pride that came with wearing the uniform of one of our nation's armed forces has also fallen by the wayside.

In a lot of ways, that's what the United States military of today has become—an institution full of people who hate America's values, hate its history, and hate its heroes. They reject everything, competence, meritocracy, accountability, that made the military such a successful and, ultimately, beloved institution. But despite all those changes, it still *looks* the part, most of the time. It still has the spiffy uniforms and fancy equipment of the military that won America two world wars, so that members can act out a performance imitating the behavior of the people who once defended your country. In two words, it's a drag show.

Can you even imagine General Milley being in charge during one of the world wars? If General Milley was in charge during World War II, he would have taken one look at our roster of white male generals, and sacked Dwight Eisenhower in favor of whichever American woman looked most like Rosie the Riveter. (All the better if she was pregnant.)

Why am I rattling all this off? It's not just to complain about what has happened, but to make an important point. The U.S. military simply *is not* the institution it once was. It is no longer the entity famed for courage and competence that made it so beloved by American conservatives, even when other facets of America's government were going into decline. It's not the institution we defended so fiercely from the left's attacks back in the 60s and 70s. That institution has fallen. Today, the left is giving us the U.S. military in drag show form.

The most scandalous part of this sad decline isn't any part of the above. No, the most scandalous part is that the GOP basically pretends it isn't happening.

During the 2023 debt ceiling showdown, Republicans had an excellent chance to extract substantial cuts to America's out-of-control federal spending. But instead, a large cadre of Republicans insisted that *all* spending cuts needed to be taken from domestic items. Military spending, they insisted, needed to increase. Senator Lindsey Graham wanted an increase of ten percent! In the end, Republicans ended up making concessions to the Biden Administration, making *fewer* cuts to domestic spending so that Biden would also agree to a 3% hike for the military budget. Almost immediately after the deal passed, Republicans began hunting for ways to get around the defense spending cap.[88]

This has important ramifications. The U.S. military, like every other branch of our vast government, is a bureaucracy. Above all, it wishes to protect its funding. As long as Republicans remain fanatical about increasing defense spending, they are implicitly endorsing the military's behavior. Institutions, like people, respond to incentives, and our woke military has no incentive to change.

Conservatives still love their military. But in 2023, we need to seriously ask ourselves *why* we do. And if there isn't a satisfying answer, we have to rethink that unconditional love.

Repeat this exercise for every institution in America. Your eyes might see a man wearing clerical vestments, standing at an altar or at the head of a congregation. Your brain interprets these signs to say "This is a man who loves God and knows the Bible." But then the man opens his mouth and says that Jesus was a socialist refugee who would support open borders, or that God is pro-choice and non-binary, or that marriage can be between two men or two women or even three men and one woman. Surprise, this isn't a Christian leader at all. You're watching a drag show!

The J. Edgar Hoover Building in Washington and the George Bush Center in Langley are both filled with an army of serious-looking, seriously-dressed people who talk about "national security," but the FBI and CIA are, of course, both drag shows as well.

In 2013, President Obama made John Brennan, the man who admitted voting for Communist Gus Hall in the 1976 presidential election, the head of the CIA. A Communist in charge of American intelligence? Drag! Yet still, the GOP kept deferring to the ideas of a hopelessly compromised CIA. When the CIA lent its support to the Russia hoax, Republicans took it seriously, at least, seriously enough that they wasted their two-year window of unified Congressional control on pointless Russia hearings.

One of the agency's biggest intelligence concerns of the past six years was a frenzied quest to figure out how Russia was afflicting its agents and American diplomats with "Havana Syndrome," only for the definitive investigation to determine that CIA agents were simply hallucinating the illness out of paranoia. That "Havana Syndrome" sounded like the name of a forgotten 80s band or a 90s political thriller, and not, you know, a real condition, should've been the first tip that something was off.

The FBI, meanwhile, has pivoted from hunting foreign terrorists to inventing domestic ones. According to former agent-turned-whistleblower Steve Friend, FBI overseers have set "quotas" for agents to reach in terms of finding and prosecuting "domestic extremism," which is the real reason that alleged cases of domestic extremism have risen four-fold in the past decade.[89]

One can go on, and on, and on. Remember the Boy Scouts? It's hard to think of a more wholesome activity, historically, for American young men. For a hundred years, the Scouts promoted good citizenship, religious piety, upright morals, conservation, and useful skills. I myself achieved Eagle Scout rank in high school.

But the Boy Scouts of your childhood are no more. In fact, they aren't even boys. The Boy Scouts of America are now "Scouts BSA" with girls, transgender "males," and gay leaders. Do I think it's bad for girls to learn outdoorsmanship and self-reliance? Not at all. But all-male environments have a special character when it comes to raising and training young men. Now, in acquiescence to political pressure and a craving for more membership, the Scouts got rid of that.

As recently as 2014, the Scouts forbade boys and leaders from participating in gay pride events while wearing their uniforms, due to Scouting's traditional ban on affiliating the Scouts with particular political causes.[90] Now, that ban is long-forgotten, and Scouting groups like the Order of the Arrow publicly celebrate Pride Month.

After George Floyd, the Scouts publicly declared allegiance to Black Lives Matter. A year later, it introduced a new "Citizenship in Society" merit badge and made it mandatory for anyone who wants to become an Eagle Scout.

"The focus of the Citizenship in Society merit badge is to provide you with information on diversity, equity, inclusion, and ethical leadership," the badge's summary says.[91]

The Boy Scouts, too, are now a drag show (maybe *that* will be a merit badge within a few years!)

The drag show dynamic even applies to the major non-profits of the American left itself. The ACLU was once an organization centered on defending a strict interpretation of the Bill of Rights. Even conservatives who despised the ACLU for its work purging prayer from public schools often still respected the organization for its strict, absolutist position on freedom of speech. When neo-Nazis wanted to parade through suburbs that not only had a large population of Jewish residents but a large population of Holocaust survivors, ACLU lawyers (often Jewish themselves) stepped up to defend that right.

But that ACLU is gone, replaced with an ACLU obsessed with transgenderism and Black Lives Matter. In the first three years of Donald Trump's presidency, the ACLU's annual reports didn't mention free speech or the First Amendment even once.[92] When Abigail Shrier's book *Irreversible Damage* came out in 2020, exposing the dramatic harm to children by the transgenderism fad, a transgender ACLU attorney, Chase Strangio,[93] said that "stopping the circulation of this book and these ideas is 100% a hill I will die on."

Similarly, the Sierra Club, although environmentalist, was at least a group focused on *the environment*. The group even favored restrictive immigration policies on the grounds that immigrants would damage the environment and gradually develop America's wilderness. But by 2020, the Sierra Club was responding to George Floyd's death with statements denouncing the "racism" of its long-dead founder, John Muir. In 2022, the group put out a statement condemning the reversal of *Roe v. Wade*, something of no relevance to the environment whatsoever.

What happened to the Sierra Club and ACLU? Simple! They're in drag too, with obedient wokeists parading around as though they still represent those groups' long-forgotten traditional priorities.

How about Joe Biden? What is that shambling, incoherent mess, barely aware of his surroundings as he mumbles through the State of the Union, if not a drag president?

And needless to say, many parts of the U.S. Republican Party are like a drag show. Whenever you see an article that offers "the conservative case for gay marriage,"[94] "the conservative case for reparations"[95] or, someday soon, "The conservative case for sex-change operations for kids," you're looking at conservatism in drag.

Conservatives notice these changes, and even complain about them, yet our substantive response has often been glacially slow. We might *say* the military is now woke, that the FBI and CIA have discredited themselves, and so on, but if it doesn't change our actions and our behaviors, what good is it?

It took *decades* for conservatives to finally notice that Hollywood had gone from all-American to anti-American, that the era of stars being men such as John Wayne was long past. Similarly, conservatives are only now waking up to see how many other American institutions hate their country, their history, and their historic people.

The left's slow-motion takeovers work so well because us conservatives, by disposition, are primed to respect hierarchy and institutions. We admire tradition and old, time-tested things. We understand that leaders and authorities are needed to keep society out of anarchy. We recognize that institutions, their norms, and their traditions are reservoirs of wisdom and expertise that keep civilization going. These traits are, most of the time, deeply admirable. It's why conservative communities, absent left-wing infiltration, remain stable, functional, and happy.

Leftism has always been hostile to those same traditions. Historically, they have sought to topple hierarchies and destroy institutions. The French Revolutionaries beheaded the king. Anarchists threw bombs at government officials and one of them even murdered President William McKinley.

But ironically, as leftism has grown in power, and evolved into wokeism, its approach toward overthrowing conservative institutions and hierarchies has changed. The left has realized it does not need to obliterate an institution, only control what it does.

• • •

The Italian communist Antonio Gramsci argued that the left could win by taking control of cultural institutions, and then from there dictating the prevailing ideology of society. The man who, decades ago, translated many of Gramsci's works into English was one Joseph Buttigieg, father of, yes, you guessed it, Democratic presidential candidate, Transportation secretary, and boy wonder Pete Buttigieg.[96] Pete himself is a good example of this "subtle takeover" strategy in practice. Buttigieg used political connections to land a cushy, extremely safe paper-pushing job in Afghanistan for five months, skipping past basic training, weapons training, and basically anything else that involved having to exert oneself in the slightest.[97] Then, on the campaign trail, he presented himself as a heroic veteran of America's foreign wars. Despite zero experience in the relevant industries, Pete became Transportation secretary, and promptly oversaw some of the worst transportation-related meltdowns in U.S. history, from a cataclysmic backlog at the port of Long Beach, to the FAA's first mass-grounding of flights since 9/11 (with no terrorist attack to blame), to the disastrous train derailment in East Palestine, Ohio. And on top of that, Buttigieg, married to a man and proudly pro-abortion, is presented as one of the staunchest Christians in the U.S. government. Drag, all of it!

The Left figured out long ago that the best way to destroy the things they hate was not to openly call for their destruction. No, that was too obvious and would set off the alarm bells that the body was being attacked. Instead, the Left, through the lessons learned from their communist forefathers, mastered the art of subtle infiltration. They take over the institutions they wish to destroy by joining them and undermining them from the inside. Once they put their impersonators in charge of an institution, they demanded continued and unquestioned loyalty to it. You'll notice that the Left, finally in charge of America's highest offices, no longer repeats the Bush-era slogan "Dissent is the highest form of patriotism."

This kind of organizational takeover preys on the conservatives' loyalty towards established institutions and traditions. It also preys on our emotions, both our emotional attachment to an institution as it once was, and our hopes that it could, somehow, be restored. But in many cases, once an organization has reached the "drag show" phase of its decline, there's no turning things around.

So, should conservatives stop believing in institutions? No! But it's crucial to wise up and recognize that a name is just a name. An institution can be dead long before its name actually vanishes. Fifty years ago, being conservative might have meant conserving institutions and, protecting them, but today it is more important to conserve the *ideas* those institutions embodied, which requires refounding, reforming, or even abolishing institutions far more than it involves keeping the lights on in a specific branch or organization.

• • •

Monitor the causes that you give money to. Does this charity, this school, or this organization still actually reflect the values or accomplishments that made you love it in the first place? If it doesn't, don't complain to your friends. Complain to the organization, and then stop sending them money until they shape up. And if shaping up isn't in the cards, look for new causes to support.

Do you give money to your alma mater? If so, why? For the vast majority of college graduates reading this book, your alma mater now hates you, your values, your children, and your God. Giving them money isn't preserving anything. It's making you a sucker.

Reader, Jesus told us to love our enemies, *but not like this*. Loving your enemy is different from subsidizing them. Turning the other cheek is different from financing your enemy's UFC training to better strike you.

Speaking of which, if there are warning signs in your church, by all means, act quickly to try and protect it. But if an honest assessment makes it clear that your church has already lost its way entirely with red flags like the pastor preaching pro-BLM sermons and LGBT+ affirming virtues are being extolled with impunity from the pulpit, then your church isn't in danger, it's in drag. The best thing you can do is leave, but make sure you also then complete the critical next step and *start* attending another one. Be it a church, a charity, or any other group meant to serve the community and effect change, never use an institution's ruin as an excuse to check out and do nothing. Use it as an opportunity to act to change things for the better.

In short, conservatives should be far less afraid of breaking things in the name of fixing them. Don't let the left use military funding as blackmail to prevent real spending reform. Realize that claims from the CIA or FBI, devoid of actual hard proof, are barely more valid than press releases put out by the DNC. Recognize that some schools and churches, like rabid animals, are better off being put down than kept alive as a diseased, hostile relic of what they once were.

There's another form of "organizational drag show" that conservatives should watch out for, and that's phony pandering to conservative sensibilities. A spectacular recent example was Black Rifle Coffee Company. Black Rifle took advantage of conservative hostility to the stereotypically-liberal company, Starbucks, by adopting an overtly right-wing aesthetic. Starting with the name (it's a *gun*, very conservative, right?), the company bombarded customers with imagery intended to signal it was very *not liberal.*

> When Starbucks promised to hire refugees, BRCC pledged to hire veterans. The company ran a promotion donating free bags of coffee to police officers. Its products are adorned in pro-military, pro-police kitsch. Black Rifle was supposed to be the rare company willing to openly market to the majority of America that doesn't enjoy riots, protesting the flag, 13-year-olds getting castrations or double mastectomies, and every other piece of the ideological package that has become America's de facto ruling ideology.[98]

However, the warning signs were there that this company wasn't the beacon of conservative values in the midst of a market largely dominated by woke and liberal companies. The more time passed, it became clearer that Black Rifle's ads were less "conservative" and more like a relentless parody of masculinity, with ads that featured bikini-clad women, machine guns, flamethrowers, and lots of gratuitous swearing.

And sure enough, it was all an act. When Kyle Rittenhouse was photographed wearing a Black Rifle t-shirt, the company lost no time in denouncing him. Then, in 2021, the company cooperated with *The New York Times* for a lengthy profile. In the interview, the company's CEO Eric Hafer not only explained that a coffee bag with St. Michael the Archangel on it (the patron saint of military personnel) was being scrapped for good, saying the image of the Archangel was now an image used by white supremacists, but he also said many of the company's fans were "racists" he wished he could pay to get rid of.

Black Rifle turned out to be another kind of drag show.

For the woke, performance is reality. Superficial deception is metaphysical truth. A man in a dress with the right pronouns *is* a woman. A pastor who teaches lies is still a Christian. It's all a game of dress up. For the woke, nothing is intrinsically real or true, and they're after the uniform that commands your respect.

Don't fall for it.

CHAPTER FOUR

Escape the Frame!

Think about all the great inventions of American history. This is the country of the airplane, the atom bomb, the microprocessor, and the Internet. No country did more to build the modern industrial, digital world than the United States. But America's innovations aren't just in science, technology, and mass production. America is also a great cultural innovator. American culture rules the world, for better and for worse. Our exports, from rap music to Batman to The Simpsons, dominate global headspace.

And another of America's great cultural exports, and great innovations, is advertising. As the great champions of free-market capitalism, Americans are phenomenal salesmen, and we love a good sales pitch. Sometimes, we love the pitch more than the product. Only about one in seven Americans has Geico car insurance, but most of us can remember half a dozen Geico ads. Tens of millions of people watch the Super Bowl only for the ads that show between the actual plays. Millions of people will race to YouTube to watch the trailer for an upcoming film, and a trailer is nothing but a slickly done ad, a promise of what the movie *could be* as opposed to the reality of what it actually is.

Americans are, in short, the most successful people in the world at marketing and advertising. In other words, Americans are experts at a type of friendly-looking deception because the heart of advertising is *framing*. In advertising, framing is about shaping a person's perception of their own needs. "You have a problem, and this product will fix it." "You should associate this drink with having a fun time." "You will be missing out if you don't see this movie on the big screen."

You can guess where I'm going with this. The political battle in America isn't just a battle over policy. It's an *advertising* battle. And that means it's a battle between two sides over whose framing is better.

Framing is one of the biggest reasons Donald Trump had so much political success from the moment he launched his 2016 campaign. Donald Trump has been selling his persona on TV for decades. He causes other people to think about and react to him constantly, and he's almost always the one deciding what the topic of the day is. When Ted Cruz announced his presidential run-in spring 2015, he made only a single reference to President Obama's disastrous handling of the border, late in his announcement speech.[99] The border was simply one of many issues in 2016, and not a particularly dominant one. Then, Trump came along, said rapists and drug dealers were flooding over the Rio Grande, and he would build a wall and make Mexico pay for it. Bam. Immigration was framed as a *dominant* issue in the race, and for months it was practically all anyone could talk about. Trump had a special talent for cutting through fake nuance. The D.C. uniparty would characterize the border as *difficult* and *complex* and *so very hard* to get right because that feigned nuance was a ruse to never fix things. Trump called out the B.S in the most emphatic way possible.

Trump's framing power worked defensively, too. After his upset win over Hillary Clinton, the press began blaming the outcome on an outbreak of "fake news." Rather than weakly complain, "Nooooo, that's so *unfair,* stop saying that!," Trump stole the frame. Trump became the world's biggest fan of talking about fake news except he made it clear that only his foes and critics were ever guilty of it. Soon, fake news was a favorite of the MAGA movement, and almost completely abandoned by the establishment journalists who first adopted the term. Within just a few months, CNN's Chris Cuomo was complaining that calling a journalist "fake news" was like calling them the n-word![100] Nine times out of ten, adopting your opponent's preferred lingo is a terrible strategy, but Trump deduced an exception to that rule, which is the sign of a master pitchman.

But Trump aside, one has to be honest. The left is usually better, *much* better at the framing fight. So strong in fact, that they don't just convince swing voters. On many issues, even conservatives operate entirely within a frame constructed by our enemies, specifically to keep us politically hobbled.

Consider how something like gay marriage went from totally unheard of and politically toxic to a central part of the national ideology in the span of just 20 years. This required a whole host of framing shifts. The clinical word "homosexual" was replaced with a new one, "gay"—a word which previously meant being happy and carefree. Homosexuality went from an act ("sodomy") to a type of person (almost a nationality!), and from a choice (or something which one might be predisposed towards) to something innate to one's being from birth. Gay people were recast as virtually identical to straight people, and the serious and sometimes dangerous differences in lifestyle were brushed away. Marriage was recast from the bedrock social institution to primarily being a means of romantic fulfillment and self-actualization, and if that's all it is, why not conclude that "love is love"? Not only that, but eventually even the terms "gay marriage" or "same-sex marriage" were shunned in favor of "marriage equality." After all, who doesn't like equality? The gay rights movement rolled out a new term, "homophobia," to describe their opponents. This had a double-whammy impact of making disagreement sound quasi-medical (and therefore pathological), while also providing a handy way to make opposition sound like nothing more than an angry mob of ignorant, hateful bigots. The whole thing was a masterclass in frame-shifting and propaganda. And so, within 15 years, California went from banning gay marriage via a democratic vote to passing a law declaring it child abuse to not "affirm" a grade schooler's transsexualism.

But the most devastating aspect of this shift isn't simply that the left won a political victory. It's that they morally conquered a large share of conservatives. When you have conservatives arguing that Democrats are "the real homophobes" because they favor immigration from Muslim countries with anti-gay laws, it's a sign that the woke framing is 100% dominant.

The left's successes go far beyond just gay marriage, of course. Consider the issue of "homelessness." Society has long had words to describe the addicted, anti-social types who often drift from place to place with no permanent abode. A century ago, they were "bums," or "vagrants," or "tramps." In 1877, the dean of Yale Law School wrote "As we utter the word tramp there arises straightway before us the spectacle of a lazy, shiftless, sauntering or swaggering, ill-conditioned, irreclaimable, incorrigible, cowardly, utterly depraved savage" (Academia used to be good for something!).[101]

Social reformers concerned with fixing the bum problem focused on getting bums to work jobs, or on improving them morally by depriving them of alcohol or other causes of addiction. And for the hundreds of thousands who couldn't be fixed another way, there were state-run mental hospitals.

But in the last twenty years of the 20th century, a new euphemism took hold, "homelessness." Prior to 1980 the term scarcely existed, but then almost overnight it was used everywhere. The bums, hobos, and mentally ill in America were rebranded as "the homeless."

The "homeless" label strips away all the realities that make the "homeless" such a blight, as it doesn't focus on the public drug use, the anti-social behavior, the routine crime, and so on. Instead, it shifts the focus to the so-called problem is a lack of housing, typically "affordable housing." This is a lie. The great social ill in San Francisco isn't that the local bums can't afford housing. It's that, most of the time, they are absolutely intolerable even when *given* housing.

Rather than clarifying the problem, the word "homelessness" obscures it. It lumps those who have merely fallen on hard times in with violent junkies and rebels who wanted to drop out of society. The vast majority of people who "experience homelessness" do so only briefly, for a handful of days, before finding a new job or finding a place to stay with friends or relatives. None of them are what we mean when we discuss the problem of "homelessness."

Yet even that euphemism shift has worn out its welcome for the woke, who today promote new euphemisms such as "the unhoused" to retreat even further away from reality.

One doesn't even have to focus on specific issues to see the woke's power at moral framing come into play over and over again. Consider, for instance, how the woke have steadily manipulated the word "violence" toward their own ends for years.

In mid–2021, Democrat Rep. Alexandria Ocasio-Cortez demanded that the Biden Administration extend a moratorium on evictions, because "eviction is violence."[102] In late 2021, Democrat Rep. Ayanna Pressley described student loans as "policy violence."[103] When I made a speaking appearance at UC-Davis in early 2023, the school's chancellor suggested *I* might be arrested for "inciting violence," when all the violence that day came exclusively from Antifa and other far-left goons.[104] Yet I certainly can't *not* speak either, because as all of us know well by now, "white silence is violence."

Yet as it labels every word and every policy it doesn't like as "violence," the woke deny the violent character of *actual* physical force.

"Destroying property, which can be replaced, is not violence," 1619 Project creator Nikole-Hannah Jones said on CBS News during the Floyd Riots. Two months later, CNN famously described riots in Kenosha as "fiery but mostly peaceful."

Revolver News described the ramifications of this, and more importantly, how to stop it:

> The left is able to constantly move the line on what is considered "violence" because they have steadily succeeded in blurring the lines between actual, real violence and everything else. Cowardly politicians have tolerated actual riots, looting, and assaults, thereby making it easier to pretend that "words that wound" actually wound. Paradoxically, when American cities like Chicago or Washington D.C. become violent "sh*tholes" (to use a former president's terminology), it normalizes violence, and thereby makes it easier to pretend other normal things are "violent" too.
>
> The way to blunt the left's "violence" rhetoric is to stop being controlled by it. Conservatives must refuse to concede any similarity between the violent, society-destroying behavior of the west and the just functioning of an orderly society. That means sharply punishing real crimes and adhering to the laws that really matter. There is a very real connection between throwing rioters in prison and halting the left's effort to rewrite the dictionary.[105]

So, how do we turn back wokeness? It starts by refusing to give a single inch on framing. This has to happen on two levels. First, don't let the woke set the frame tactically by deciding what words are used. But second, and even more importantly, police your own thinking to make sure you aren't letting them set the *moral* framework of debate. We should be confident that our worldview is correct. Even if we aren't fully certain what is right in a given situation, we can *definitely* be certain that the left is wrong. So quite simply, *stop giving them a pass.* Chase a clear-cut, black-and-white, Luke Skywalker vs. Darth Vader attitude toward every issue possible.

Here's how to refight the framing battle on several key issues.

DIVERSITY, EQUITY, AND INCLUSION

As much as possible, we ought to abolish the word "diversity" from our vocabulary. Why is "diversity" a value at all? That might sound like an odd question to ask. Isn't diversity clearly a good thing?

No, not really. Diversity is sometimes good, and sometimes bad, depending on the situation. That's obvious, but all of us have gotten used to mindless diversity worship simply because of a Supreme Court ruling, 1978's *Regents of the University of California v. Bakke.* In that case, the first major Supreme Court ruling on affirmative action, the court decided that explicit racial quotas were unconstitutional, but a school might "consider" race as a means of achieving greater "diversity."[106] Ever since then, American institutions have mindlessly praised diversity, as the official court-sanctioned method of engaging in explicit racial favoritism.

So, you know what? It's time we reject that frame. Modern DEI (Diversity, Equity, Inclusion) programs don't promote "diversity," or even "inclusion" for that matter. They certainly don't promote "equity." They are quota systems, built to reflect woke hierarchies. They exist to impose discrimination against whites, men, heterosexuals, and Americans. "Diversity" parades as a term that celebrates people from different walks of life coming together for a common goal, but in actuality it is a codeword for the same types of people who all think the same way, installing their people in positions of power. Henry Ford once said of his famous Model-T cars, "Any customer can have a car painted any color that he wants so long as it is black." Similarly, the woke say, "You can be as diverse as you want, as long as you're woke." They are not promoting "diverse voices," righting a past wrong, or anything else other than racial discrimination.

Instead of dancing around this and carefully selecting our words, conservatives should say these things, explicitly. We oppose discrimination based on race, skin color, and sex. And no, we shouldn't engage in the stunt of arguing that affirmative action and quota systems hurt the groups that benefit from them. Sure, it's true that affirmative action creates mismatch, causing minority students (in particular black students) to attend schools they aren't qualified for and take classes they aren't prepared for. But this kind of argument is a classic case of caving to the woke worldview. Simply making the argument at all is conceding that we should treat black interests as superior, when in reality we should treat *all* races equally, and not favor or disfavor any of them.

HATE SPEECH

Here's the truth: "Hate speech" isn't real. The very term only dates to the late 1980s. Before the term existed, society *already* had phrases for impermissible, speech-related behavior like "incitement to violence," "fraud," and "threats."

Yet conservatives routinely allow themselves to be dragged into debates about whether the First Amendment protects "hate speech," or whether particular words or phrases "counts" as hate speech. The left, arguing that "hate speech" is outside the First Amendment's purview, has spent decades trying to then classify all speech it dislikes as falling into this "hate" category. Conservatives sometimes fall into the trap of complaining that the left bans hate speech against Muslims, or blacks, or immigrants, yet routinely tolerates far uglier words targeting America's designated white male villains.

It's time to stop putting up with this and stop playing into the losing fight of discussing hate speech. It is a label ginned up by the left and mainstreamed by them, and so they will always control its definition to their advantage. By using the term "hate speech," we are buying into the Left's framing that sufficiently "hateful" needs to be against the law, or at least subject to social punishments comparable to being illegal. But it's literally never necessary. Speech that calls for violence against a group is simply called "incitement to violence," and it can be criminalized on those grounds. The vast majority of other speech is either actual political advocacy, or disruptive trolling by the mentally unstable. Neither practice needs the "hate speech" label to describe it, so it's time we get rid of the label. Not only does the term not protect anyone more effectively, it legitimizes ruining lives because a woke person or group decides someone has engaged in it.

AFFIRMATIVE ACTION

One of the saddest signs of conservative capitulation to a woke frame is affirmative action. Rather than call it out for what it is, a flagrant discrimination against people for being white or Asian or male, conservatives frequently play footsie with the issue. Often, they prefer to argue that affirmative action is bad because it hurts the *beneficiaries* most of all.

"How Affirmative Action at Colleges Hurts Minority Students" argued a headline from The Heritage Foundation in 2015.[107] That same year, a National Review piece argued that affirmative action was bad because it "reinforces the negative stereotypes many white students hold, further increasing tensions on campus."[108] In other words, the problem with openly discriminating against white people isn't that it wrongly denies them opportunity based on skin color, but that it might make their racism even worse!

It's hard to imagine a weaker framing. It's like arguing that slavery was bad because it made slaveowners lazy. It's an argument practically made in a lab to be unconvincing. Actual recipients of affirmative action *know* it's helpful to them. It gives them college spots, scholarships, jobs, salaries, and status they wouldn't have otherwise. They won't be swayed by arguments that *actually* it's bad to get handed nice things for free. Meanwhile, this argument format concedes *every* important assumption to the left:

- That racism is a huge problem in need of fixing.
- That affirmative action's problem is only one of effectiveness, rather than the morality of discriminating based on race.
- That the beneficiaries of affirmative action, and what happens to them, matter more than the invisible people harmed by racial discrimination.

With the Supreme Court's 2023 ruling in *Students for Fair Admissions v. Harvard*, sharply restricting the use of racial preferences in college admissions, affirmative action is back in the spotlight. And with that, it's a good time to fix our framing. For one, we should retire the phrase "affirmative action" as much as possible. The phrase is a *classic* euphemism, a neologism coined by a Democrat president (JFK) to mask a reality. Affirmative action *is* racial discrimination. It's discriminating against whites and Asians, based on their appearance. It's time we say as much and demand that this anti-American, unconstitutional discrimination be abolished. Don't concede the good intentions of supporters, and focus on the ugliest aspects of this regime. For instance, the way Asians are systematically labeled as having deficient personalities to justify denying them a university seat, a practice as warped as any Jim Crow literacy test.[109]

TRANS

One of the places where conservatives have already made great progress is on the trans issue. We've learned to stop talking about "gender-affirming care," the woke nomenclature, and instead learned to talk about "child mutilation," the grisly reality. In my opinion, we could go even further, though.

"Gender-affirming care," for boys, means being put on chemical castration hormones that eradicate sexual function. Then, after a few months, it means being put on estrogen. It means undergoing a surgery where the patient undergoes an irreversible surgery in which a doctor amputates one's penis and testicles. When that's done, the doctor doesn't replace them with a vagina, because that's impossible. Instead, he carves out an open wound before using plastic surgery techniques to give the same superficial appearance as female genitalia. Then you have to shove a foreign object (a "dildo") in for hours every day, or it will close up like the wound that it actually is. It bleeds, and it gets full of bacteria. It stinks and gets infected. It may burst its stitches and then they need to be sewn back up. In the highly plausible event of complications, it will need numerous follow-up surgeries, but even if there are no complications, this new "vagina" will never be remotely like a real one. The owner will have no womb, no ovaries, no ability to have children. If he went on puberty blockers early enough and for long enough, he will never be able to orgasm.

For girls, "gender-affirming care" is the same thing in reverse. It means cutting off the supply of estrogen, then replacing it with testosterone. It means crudely amputating breasts as early as possible, leaving jagged scars. Sometimes, the blood flow to the nipples will be messed up, causing them to rot and fall off. All of this work from hormones and surgery still only leaves the typical recipient as a short, woman-shouldered "boy" with a weak teenage boy mustache, so some of them go further. They have all the skin and muscle hacked out of one of their forearms, creating a grisly wound that will take months or even years to heal, if it ever does. This skin and muscle are used to construct a crude tube that is attached atop the hole that once contained their now-amputated uterus.[110] This "neopenis" (the technical term!) can only become erect by installing a pump system inside the body that can be turned on and off to fill this fleshy tube with a saline solution (often, the pump is activated by hitting a switch inside a fake scrotum). None of this will make it actually feel like a real penis. Instead, it will largely feel numb, assuming it doesn't simply rot and fall off, as it sometimes does.[111]

Are you disgusted? Good. That is what "gender-affirming care" is. It treats "gender dysphoria" as helpfully as a lobotomy treats anxiety.

Want to stop submitting to the woke worldview? Stop pretending that *any* of the above is normal, defensible, or understandable. Stop pretending that the people who perform the above procedures have good intentions. They don't. They are profiteers and mad scientists, modern-day Mengeles, and they deserve long prison sentences. We should say as much. Never, *ever* call it "gender-affirming care." Call it bodily mutilation. Call it delusion-enabling surgery. Call it a crime, and never treat it as anything but. Mention the word *castration* a lot.

The reason being, when we treat these practices as normal, people begin to believe it is. So never, ever treat it as normal or tolerable. There are no "queer kids," only children being groomed and sexualized by adults. There is no such thing as a "trans child," only a child transvestite. And there is no such thing as "affirming" a gender, only child abuse.

The way the tide has turned on transgenderism offers some general lessons for conservatives. Notice the pattern to left-wing tactics. They need to constantly change the name of something to conceal what is really going on. This only works for so long before people catch on. Eventually, a brand is ruined and it's time for a Hollywood-style "reboot," with a new label.

The best way to fight the Woke's love of euphemism and their skill at framing is to call things by their real name. Sometimes, that just means using the *original* name, but sometimes we need to get creative and call things by what they really are, even if that means deploying a new name ourselves.

Of course, simply saying people should reject woke frames is easy enough. What helps is having an example.

Besides Trump, one of the great heroes of framing on the Right in recent years is my friend, journalist Chris Rufo. Rufo's great accomplishment wasn't that he discovered something previously hidden. Rather, he gave a rhetorical framework to describe what people could already see.

Millions of parents could see that something was disturbing about their children's schools, especially as 2020 wore on. Teachers were forcing children to fill out "privilege checklists" that singled them out for being white or Christian. Schools taught children that America is built on "stolen" land, that it is systemically racist, and that white people hold unconscious biases that manifest in racist behaviors and so-called "microaggressions."[112]

Rufo's brilliance was to take this battery of practices and slap a label on it. The flagrant anti-white content parents saw in their children's schools was "Critical Race Theory," he said. It was a direct offshoot from radical Marxist theory, meant to push radical left assumptions into the brains of impressionable young people. And it wasn't a minor threat, he said, it was everywhere.

"Critical race theory has become, in essence, the default ideology of the federal bureaucracy and is now being weaponized against the American people," Rufo said during an appearance on "Tucker Carlson Tonight" in September 2020.

The impact of Rufo's appearance on the show was enormous, because President Trump happened to be watching the segment. Trump demanded action from his administration, and within a few days an executive order had appeared abolishing the mandatory diversity trainings and other racist lectures that Rufo successfully branded as "CRT." The fact that Biden later revoked that executive order is beside the point. Rufo had taken an issue where conservatives knew they were under attack, but didn't know what to say, and gave them the vocabulary to fight back. Parents could take aim at specific lessons in their local schools. State legislatures could start tailoring laws to control what was pushed in the classroom, restricting or banning outright the anti-white lessons that instructors had been sneaking into their lessons plans for years.

In an early 2021 Twitter thread, Rufo described his victory explicitly in framing terms.

"We have successfully frozen their brand, critical race theory, into the public conversation and are steadily driving up negative perceptions," he said. "We will eventually turn it toxic, as we put all of the various cultural insanities under that brand category. The goal is to have the public read something crazy in the newspaper and immediately think 'critical race theory.' We have decodified the term and will recodify it to annex the entire range of cultural constructions that are unpopular with Americans.[113]

Just as important as what Rufo said is what he *didn't* say. He didn't concede that woke teachers have their hearts in the right place when they berate and belittle white students about their privilege. He didn't moan that schools were being *unfair*. Instead, he marked woke teachers and administrators explicitly for what they really were, sinister, hateful, wicked people laundering a racial grievance in the guise of social justice.

Rufo has also avoided one of the most common pitfalls of conservatives. He hasn't bothered himself with constantly calling out left-wing hypocrisy.

As a general rule, in fact the right should *always* be careful about accusing the woke of hypocrisy. It's not that the left aren't hypocrites. They are. In fact, their love of hypocrisy is so intense it might eventually join their list of sexual orientations (LGBT...H?).

But accusing a person of hypocrisy too much is a risky game. Such accusations implicitly concede that the opponent's framing of the issue is the right one, and they're simply not following it with enough vigor. The best use of pointing out hypocrisy isn't to win an argument with the enemy. Instead, its best purpose is to keep one's own allies on-side. Train conservative fellow travelers to spot woke hypocrisy so that they realize that woke moral arguments are shams, always made with an eye toward maximizing power, rather than any moral consistency.

The next time you find yourself in an argument with a wokeist, ask yourself a few key questions:

- Am I constantly trying to prove that I'm *not* something like sexist or racist? If you're constantly trying to defend your basic character, that's a good sign you're trapped in a moral framework set by a wokeist.
- Am I using clear language, or a bunch of euphemisms picked by the woke?
- Am I actually making the case for my own values, or just accusing my opponent of not following his own?

Reclaim your frames, reclaim the argument, and then reclaim the country.

CHAPTER FIVE

Being Called Racist
Isn't The End of the World

In Maoist China, at the height of the Cultural Revolution, the worst thing one could be accused of was being a class enemy, finding yourself in one of the so-called "Five Black Categories," landlords, rich farmers, counter-revolutionaries, bad elements, and right-wingers. People accused of being one of these were forced to endure "struggle sessions" in which their "friends," family and even their spouse who were terrified that the alleged crime would mean guilt-by-association for them, and would join a mob in publicly humiliating the accused as a counter-revolutionary traitor. It was a warning to the masses. Should you find yourself similarly accused, and you will discover yourself hounded by a frothing mob and left to feel utterly alone. No one in society will want to be associated with you.

Importantly, the struggle sessions succeeded by being profoundly aggressive and fanatically unreasonable. Defense from an accusation was essentially impossible. Attempting to rebut allegations only made things worse. Often, the only tactic available to the accused was to desperately apologize, hoping (often in vain) that it would save their lives.

Maoist China was not a good place to be. But fortunately, we Americans are above such travesties. Or are we?

Howard Cosell is one of the most legendary sports broadcasters in American history. For the first fourteen years of its existence, Cosell was the star of ABC's *Monday Night Football,* the most popular sports show (often the most popular show, period) in America. He gave us "He could…go…all…the…way!" He notified the world of John Lennon's murder, and popularized "nachos" as an iconic American sports food.

But Cosell's time with *Monday Night Football* ended suddenly and stupidly on September 5, 1983, when Cosell quipped about black Washington Redskins wide receiver Alvin Garrett, "That little monkey gets loose, doesn't he?"

Cosell said that, far from referencing Garrett's race, he was referring to his small stature (Garrett was only 5'7", quite short for an NFL player). Though the term "monkey" has been used in pejorative ways towards black people, for Cosell, "little monkey" was a term he used for anyone with a shorter stature, regardless of race. He'd even referred to a similarly diminutive white player as a "little monkey" on a broadcast that aired some eight years before. But it mattered little. The Rev. Joseph Lowery of the Southern Christian Leadership Conference denounced Cosell, and burdened by the controversy, he left *Monday Night Football* at the end of the season.

There's nothing particularly special about Cosell's story. In pro sports alone, for decades random, stray comments have wrecked careers and ruined reputations. Four years after Cosell's tribulation, legendary L.A. Dodgers general manager Al Campanis was fired after two decades of success because, during a *Nightline* tribute to Jackie Robinson, when asked why more black men had not become baseball managers, Campanis suggested that, on average, they "may not have some of the necessities" for the job. Campanis had been teammates and a close friend of Jackie Robinson's even before Robinson shattered the MLB color barrier, and had vocally supported civil rights, but it didn't matter; the Dodgers fired him within 48 hours.[114] Worse than that, Campanis wasn't merely unemployed, but disgraced.

As you can see, 2016 and 2020 were nothing new. People have been getting "canceled" on bogus or exaggerated racism allegations for decades. The only difference is that the left has more power today, and is eager to use it, and with the rise of the Internet, there are more potential targets than ever before. In the past, celebrities might fear having their careers tarnished when a live mic caught an awkward turn of phrase. But today, thanks to the deadly combo of smartphones and social media, literally everyone is at risk of being America's racist of the week.

In 2016, high school freshman Mimi Groves received her learner's permit to drive. She celebrated by sending her friend a three-second Snapchat video, in which she said "I can drive, n****r." Why did she pick that word? Who knows. Maybe she was imitating America's hip-hop artists, who are considered "cool" and use the word constantly with impunity. Maybe she wanted to be transgressive, as so many teenagers do.

Sadly, Mimi's friend wasn't much of a friend. Instead of letting the video vanish, as Snapchats automatically do, the friend passed it around. One of Mimi's classmates, Jimmy Galligan, saw it and in a calculated manner decided to save it, waiting to release it at the most opportune moment.

That moment came a whole four years later, as Mimi finished high school and prepared to enroll at the University of Tennessee. The year was 2020. I don't need to tell you what the country was like then. Having waited until Groves had chosen a college, Galligan published the four-year-old clip on social media for the entire world to see. The result was swift and devastating. Groves was preemptively kicked off UT's cheerleading team, and then withdrew from the school altogether under intense pressure from school officials.

"They're angry, and they want to see some action," an admission official told Groves and her parents.[115]

This story may not sound remarkable to you. Maybe you even think Groves got what she deserved. But pause and think for a moment about the actual moral forces in play. Groves used a bad word in a private video made for a friend when she was *fifteen*. She used it to brag about getting a driver's license, not to attack anyone. The number of people hurt by what she did was exactly *zero*.

Yet Groves had her entire life derailed over it. She was vilified nationwide. Government officials, in the form of UT's cheer squad and admissions department, took a direct role in punishing her for what was, quite literally, a victimless crime. In an instant, the years of hard work Groves put in were, "vaporized," as her mother put it. She ended up enrolling in online classes at a community college rather than attending her dream school.

Now imagine if, instead of using one word in a video at 15, Groves had been caught shoplifting, or cheating on her boyfriend, or committing an assault. All three cases would be vastly more immoral, and more harmful to actual people, yet Groves would never have been notorious for any of them, and other than some slap on the wrist from the criminal justice system, her life would be nearly unaffected.

Meanwhile, it is clearly Galligan, Groves' doxxer, who comes off as the more malicious, destructive individual, engaging in a calculated act of elaborate cruelty. In return, *The New York Times* rewarded him with a profile treating him like some kind of folk hero.

> For his role, Mr. Galligan said he had no regrets. "If I never posted that video, nothing would have ever happened," he said. And because the internet never forgets, the clip will always be available to watch.
>
> "I'm going to remind myself, you started something," he said with satisfaction. "You taught someone a lesson."[116]

There are cases of national outrage even less justified than Groves. In 2021, Army sergeant Jonathan Pentland was captured on video berating and shoving a black man, telling him he was in "the wrong neighborhood" and needed to leave.

"You either walk away or I'm going to carry your ass out of here," Pentland said.

Clear-cut racism? Not at all. The man was a local nuisance. In one incident just days before he had stuck his hand down a woman's shorts. In another he repeatedly picked up a woman's baby and tried to walk away with it (a practice once prosecuted as "attempted kidnapping").[117] Yet police had done nothing to stop him, and when the man began harassing yet another woman, it fell to Pentland to stop him. And while woke mobs online interpreted Pentland's quip about the "wrong neighborhood" as some defense of a segregated community, Pentland's neighborhood was thoroughly mixed-race.

All those nuances were irrelevant to the Biden Administration, which soon announced that the *Department of Justice* was investigating what was, at worst, a minor neighborhood scuffle.[118] Meanwhile, police let a massive mob gather around Pentland's home and vandalize it. In the end, a court convicted Pentland of misdemeanor assault. To his credit, he said he had no regrets.

The above stories, as flimsy as they are, at least had the benefit of actually happening. Plenty of instances of alleged racism are entirely made up.

The most notorious, at least in recent years, is almost certainly the fully fabricated hate crimes performed against actor Jussie Smollett. People were rightly horrified when the actor claimed he had not only been accosted on the street and attacked for being a black man, but that his attackers had put a noose around his neck, either with the intention to use it to hang him right then, or to simply threaten him with the dark history of lynching that would frighten anyone, but especially a black person. The thing was, the entire attack was staged. Smollett hired men he knew to feign an attack on him, and everything from the physical violence to the ominous noose around his neck was nothing more than a spectacle. The next logical question is, of course, why would Jussie Smollett fake a hate crime against himself? [119] Because accusing others of racism, and claiming victimhood for oneself, is a source of power.

Realizing we can win, wanting to win, and demanding that Republicans help us win are important attitude shifts to defeating woke in the long term. But if you're going to make just one mental shift that will drastically improve your ability to resist wokeness, and not allow it to overwhelm or outmaneuver you, it's this one shedding your existential terror of being called racist. Stop letting malicious allegations of the same against others control your behavior.

• • •

Before we go any further, let me be clear that none of this is about racism being a good thing. It's not. It's evil. I'm simply referring to be calling a racist when your actions are anything but. You see, contrary to the left's claims, real racism in the real world today is, happily, quite rare. Historically, people frequently *did* treat people unfairly as mere representatives of their racial group, meriting unequal treatment on that basis alone. Southern plantation owners argued that Africans were racially suited best for chattel slavery. Some distorted the Bible, arguing that black people were the descendants of Noah's son Ham and cursed to be slaves. After the Civil War, the Ku Klux Klan used mob violence and terror to prevent blacks, as a group, from voting or exercising civil rights. Then, for a century, Jim Crow systematically enshrined whites as a superior race, and blacks as an inferior one, across large swathes of America.

That was racism. And today, that breed of racism is essentially extinct. Membership in the Ku Klux Klan or similar avowedly racist groups is virtually non-existent. How many of you have ever seen a Klan rally, even once in your life? With the largest Klan groups struggling to muster a hundred members, it would be hard to even *hold* a Klan rally.[120] Honestly, you know as many Illuminati and Stonecutters members as you do Klan members. Possibly more.

Restaurants and hotels that cater only to white customers are illegal, but even if they weren't the number of "whites-only" restaurants in America would likely number in the single digits. Private clubs and private schools are still allowed to be officially whites-only, yet none of any importance are. Excluding someone from anything simply by virtue of being black isn't just considered wrong, but also trashy and pathetic, as it should be.

Yet as anti-black racism in America has faded into non-existence, politically motivated shrieks of "racism" are more popular than ever, perhaps the single most overused and hysterical accusation in American politics. The hysteria is so profound, and so animating, that it's not even people and organizations that get accused of racism anymore. In 2021 a large, geologically noteworthy boulder was removed from the University of Wisconsin campus because, 100 years ago, a news article had called the boulder a "n****rhead," a now-obsolete term for such large boulders. This century-old slur was too much to bear, and so away the racist rock went, dumped (at the cost of more than $50,000) on some university-owned land in the Wisconsin wilderness.[121]

But while the accusation may be hysterical, the left's use of it is not. This attack gets used so much because it *works.* Calling someone a racist helps the left achieve its political goals while silencing and neutering its enemies.

When confronted with accusations of racism, many conservatives believe that their way out is to argue back, and somehow "prove" that they aren't a racist. However well-intentioned, trying to prove you aren't a racist is a setup you are designed to lose, for all kinds of reasons. First, it's difficult if not impossible to prove a negative. You might as well be a landlord in Maoist China, trying to prove to a kangaroo court that you're not a class enemy. Good luck.

This ties into the second point, trying to prove you're not a racist implicitly puts you on defense. The person running around trying to put out fires, or explain away some evidence against them, looks weak and vulnerable. Psychologically, it invites onlookers to assume there must be *some* kind of truth to the accusations. The left has so thoroughly poisoned the well, rhetorically, that even *trying* to mount a defense against allegations is immediately spun as a stale "white person claims they're not racist using dumb reasons" cliché.

One of the most common defenses you'll see when someone is accused of racism is when he or she says, "But I have a black friend!" The tactic is so common that it's regularly ridiculed in the press. In 2019, *The New York Times'* John Eligon did a whole article mocking "The 'Some of My Best Friends Are Black' Defense."[122]

"It's a myth that proximity to blackness immunizes white people from doing racist things," Eligon wrote. The Associated Press has its own article bashing the argument.[123] So does *Psychology Today* ("Why Every Racist Mentions Their Black Friend").[124]

The argument is ridiculed so often that it's simply assumed to be incredibly flimsy. But is it? Given that everybody is free to pick their own friends and close associates, choosing to have one of another race actually *is* a solid defense against viewing that race as innately inferior. But because the left holds so much institutional and rhetorical power, it has simply labeled this argument as pathetic and laughable, and thus made it so.

But most importantly, trying to fend off accusations of racism is difficult because the woke left has given itself a monopoly on defining the word itself, and is perpetually rewriting its meaning. In fact, a person who claimed that all people should be judged exclusively by their personal traits, while ignoring their race, would be labeled an idealist in the 1940s, a liberal in the 1960s, a conservative in the 1990s, and a "racist" today.

One of the strongest signs of the woke left's power to unilaterally redefine racism is when activists make insane claims like "black people can't be racist." Georgetown professor Michael Eric Dyson has said as much.[125] A 2007 indoctrination session at the University of Delaware taught that *all* whites are racist, but that it is impossible for *any* non-whites to be racist.[126] The half-baked argument in favor of this is that racism is "prejudice plus power," only white people have power, ergo only whites are racist. This definition is nonsensical. When blacks can be elected president, how do they lack power? What power does the KKK have? It's also totally different from the definition of racism used by the wider public, or by the left when they are trying to cancel someone for supposed racism. But all of that doesn't matter. What the woke are really doing is simply flexing their power to redefine words at will to its benefit.

• • •

The left even changes the supposed definition of "racism" from moment to moment.

In one popular Medium article, "6 Reasons White People Give To Say They Aren't Racist" the author, a black woman, states, "Trying to make the distinction between Black and white people is also in itself inherently racist."[127] It is the top highlighted comment in the whole article.

Yet we see the opposite as well. If one does *not* try to make any distinction at all between black and white people, that *also* is considered racist. Heather McGhee, a black author who has run a liberal think tank, even penned an article for TED called "Why saying 'I don't see race at all' just makes racism worse."[128] One sentence, put in bold, says "Color blindness has become a powerful weapon against progress for people of color, but as a denial mindset, it doesn't do white people any favors, either."

So, seeing race and distinguishing black and white people (to say nothing of Hispanic and Asian people, whom you'll notice are selectively left out of many liberal articles concerning race in America) is racist, but, also, *not seeing* race and *not distinguishing* between blacks and whites is also racist.

If you just said to yourself, "Wow, Charlie, it seems like everything white people do is racist according to the woke," then you've figured it out. Congratulations. Put down this book for a second, go to the kitchen, and grab yourself a treat.

Another classic example of the slippery definition of racism can be found in the world of real estate, and who moves into it what homes and neighborhoods. According to the woke, when white people fled crime and urban blight during the 1960s and 70s, depopulating large neighborhoods just as black Americans moved into them and crashing property values, that was "white flight." It was, of course, racist.

But in the 1990s and 2000s, when crime fell, the children of suburbanites began moving back into cities and into historically or even entirely black neighborhoods. Supply and demand being what it is, this raised property values and by extension prices. So, is this a good thing, the undoing of racist "white flight?" Not at all. Now, whites are engaged in "gentrification," and this is somehow even *more* racist than white flight was! But if whites don't move into those neighborhoods, but instead keep to themselves? Oof, you know what that is. That's racist, too.

Almost any given choice a white person makes in moving, whether from neighborhood to neighborhood or from country to country, will be called racist. If you're drawing the same conclusion again, that almost anything a white does the woke will call racist, go grab yourself another treat. Actually, wait, don't. I have another chapter on losing weight later in this book.

The definition of "racism" isn't just a moving target, but also a constantly expanding one. A TikTok video that went viral in summer 2023 summed up the left's perspective quite effectively.

"If you use any of these terms or phrases in reference to black people, you are just as racist as [a] person that actually uses the n-word," said the video's narrator, "anti-racism educator" Ashani Mfuko. "Here are the words: Thug, ghetto, welfare queen, lazy, race-baiter, race grifter, threatening, angry, dangerous. Or you say that we're 'playing the victim,' or we are a 'diversity hire.' What you actually mean to say is the n word."[129]

Of course, literally none of the above statements are racist. Those comments don't demean a person for who they are or things like the color of their skin. Rather, those comments serve to criticize *behaviors* (thuggishness, laziness) or to call out unfair, unequal treatment doled out based on skin color. The real purpose of labeling all the above as "equal to the n-word" isn't to halt the virus-like spread of racism. It's to insulate certain people from *all* forms of criticism, by taking advantage of the public's fear of being labeled racist.

To state the obvious, if *everything* in America is racist, then nothing is. And that's the deep truth behind the moving target of claims of racism. They are so inconsistent, so all over the place, because America is practically devoid of real racism. Time travel to 1910s Georgia and finding real racism would be easy. Blacks couldn't vote, couldn't attend the same schools as whites, couldn't marry whites, couldn't work or play sports or eat or live alongside whites. Through a mixture of laws and social norms, blacks were second-class citizens, and this system was backed up with a very real threat of mob violence. All of that is gone today.

The lack of actual racism to complain about is precisely why the left has had to cultivate the ridiculous concept of "microaggressions," minor verbal or even unconscious actions that supposedly expose a sinister racist heart lurking within. Examples of evil microaggressions include:

- Showing interest in someone's background ("Where are you from?")
- Trying to compliment someone ("You're so articulate!")
- Believing in meritocracy ("I believe the most qualified person should get the job.")
- Saying you prefer to ignore race ("There is one race, the human race.")
- Asking someone to quiet down *or* speak more loudly (yes, both).

I didn't make any of these up, all of the above are taken directly from a "Racial Microaggression" chart published online by the University of Minnesota.[130]

Pause and think for a moment about how ridiculous this is. No, *really* think about it. When we indulge in humoring "microaggressions," we aren't just going on a silly hunt for racism where it doesn't exist. We are letting society be controlled by the most manipulative and shrill among us.

The concept of microaggressions is not new, though the name is of recent coinage. Like so much of wokeism, we find precedents for it in the history of communism.

Dorothy Healey was the "Red Queen," a Communist Party leader in Los Angeles in the middle of the 20th century. In her memoirs, published in 1990, Healey describes how the concept of racist microaggressions, then called merely "white chauvinism," crowded out meetings between black and white communist members in 1950s Los Angeles:

"The great irony of the McCarthy period is that we did almost as much damage to ourselves, in the name of purifying our ranks, as Joe McCarthy and J. Edgar Hoover and all the other witch-hunters combined were able to do.... [W]ith the white chauvinism campaign of 1949–1953, what had been a legitimate concern turned into an obsession, a ritual act of self-purification that did nothing to strengthen the Party in its fight against racism and was manipulated by some Communist leaders for ends which had nothing to do with the ostensible purpose of the whole campaign. Once an accusation of white chauvinism was thrown against a white Communist, there was no defense. Debate was over. By the very act of denying the validity of the charge, you only proved your own guilt. Thousands of people were caught up in this campaign—not only in the Party itself, but within the Progressive Party and some of the Left unions as well. In Los Angeles alone we must have expelled two hundred people on charges of white chauvinism, usually on the most trivial of pretexts. People would be expelled for serving coffee in a chipped coffee cup to a Black or serving watermelon at the end of dinner.

... Those day-long meetings, which went on day after day, were just terrible. At one of them I said something to the effect that Taylor's failure to carry out his responsibilities had enhanced whatever problems of chauvinism existed in the Party. Betty screamed at me that my use of the word "enhance" was in itself a chauvinist remark, because it was putting the blame on the victim rather than on the oppressor. Whites were the oppressor, and nothing Blacks could do could "enhance" the atmosphere of racism.... One of the great ironies of the white chauvinism campaign is that we lost a large number of Black members because of it. They were just contemptuous of the whole thing because it had so little to do with fighting racism in the real world outside the Party's ranks. And the FBI later made effective use of the "white chauvinism" issue as part of its own repertoire of dirty tricks." [131]

Sound familiar? The entire passage could easily be describing Oberlin College today. Why is it so incredibly similar despite a gap of more than seventy years? Simple, because the actual practices of the extreme left have changed very little. Whether you call it "white chauvinism" or "racism," using minor verbal or subconscious tics as proof of vast ideological thoughtcrime is a tool of control by the left.

This, of course, is why another popular trope of American conservatism is doomed to failure. Many conservatives have noticed the inconsistencies of the left like how shallow their commitment to racial equality is, how quickly they heap abuse on blacks who don't go with the program have tried to argue that, "Democrats are the real racists." I've been guilty of making this argument myself. But it's a losing argument. Why? Because it's competing on a playing field set by the woke and entirely controlled by them. They're the faction that literally defines what racism is. Why would they ever allow the definition to work in your favor? The answer, of course, is that they won't. Instead, racism will *always* conveniently mutate so that it always produces the same result: The woke can be as hateful and as inconsistent as they want, and always be paragons of virtue, while you can never say anything at all without being smeared as a racist.

And yet, despite this, conservatives are routinely tricked into yielding to the left, making concessions or surrendering outright, in an effort to prove they aren't racists. A classic example was the creation of the Juneteenth federal holiday in 2020.

Prior to 2020, Juneteenth was an extremely regional holiday, mostly observed in Texas. In 2002, only eight U.S. states observed the holiday in *any* form, however superficial. In spring 2021, a whole year *after* making Juneteenth a federal holiday, sixty-two percent of Americans told Gallup they knew little or nothing about it.[132] Joe Biden never once mentioned Juneteenth on his Twitter account until 2019, despite many years in which he tweeted on that very day.[133] In a six-year period from 2012 to 2017, CNN and MSNBC mentioned the holiday a combined ten times.[134]

The sudden push to make Juneteenth into a national holiday wasn't part of an organic desire to commemorate the end of slavery. Instead, it was bound tightly to a sustained attack on America's history, institutions, and values. It was linked tightly to the 1619 Project, a historically dubious, politically motivated effort to redefine 1619 (the year the first African slaves arrived in colonial America) as America's "true" founding, and declare slavery and its aftermath as the central historical fact of America's existence. Nikole Hannah-Jones, the creator of the 1619 Project, showed her intent by having on her Twitter banner an image of "July 4th, 1776" crossed out, replaced by the new date of "August 20, 1619."[135]

The truth of this is shown in the official name of the Juneteenth federal holiday: "Juneteenth National Independence Day." Placed two weeks before America's actual Independence Day, Juneteenth is an effort to create a "separate but equal" holiday, turning our unifying holiday of July 4th into a source of division instead. The move made political sense. Just the act of celebrating July 4th as children makes young people more conservative and patriotic when they grow up.[136]

All of this could be seen at the time. In the weeks after George Floyd, when Democrats demanded creating this new federal holiday, virtually every elected Republican folded. In the House, only 14 Republicans voted against the new holiday, and in the Senate not a single Republican dissented.

• • •

What was their reward? Were they praised for proving they were not racist? Not at all! When Senator Ron Johnson showed up at a Juneteenth celebration in Milwaukee the following year, he was "drowned out by a chorus of boos," with the crowd chanting "we don't want you here."[137]

In the years since, the new Juneteenth holiday hasn't been used to celebrate unity or confirm that America has moved past racism. Instead, it has become a useful bastion for the left to *further* denounce America, and demand new, radically divisive and destructive race-driven policies.

"It's Juneteenth AND reparations," Rep. Cori Bush tweeted for Juneteenth 2023. "It's Juneteenth AND end police violence + the War on Drugs. It's Juneteenth AND end housing + education apartheid. It's Juneteenth AND teach the truth about white supremacy in our country. Black liberation must be prioritized." Don't you feel more unified already?

Republican support for Juneteenth didn't prove to the left they weren't racist. It did the exact opposite. The holiday's creation has simply become *more* proof that the country, and particularly conservatives, are racist. Surrendering to malicious screams of "racist!" only emboldened the left. As always, appeasement failed.

This was all bad enough with the largely symbolic matter of Juneteenth. Now think of all the serious, substantive policies where conservatives are cowed by their fear of being called racist. Cries of racism happen most of all when trying to make any kind of serious political change that threatens the domination of wokeness. Screaming "racism" is an all-purpose cudgel, essential for the woke to both gain power and to keep it.

This comes up most often when it comes to crime. It isn't racist to notice that America has racial inequalities when it comes to crime—it's the natural product of having a brain endowed by God with pattern recognition. America's black neighborhoods have the most crime, and the most criminals, and it's not close. To pick one example, in George Floyd's home of Minneapolis, about 19 percent of the population is black.[138] But in 2021, about 83 percent of shooting victims, and 89 percent of shooting perpetrators (when a description was known), were black.[139] That year, there was one black shooting victim for every 150 black residents, and almost all of them were shot by another black person.

Every decent person wants this problem to be fixed. But any honest fix is going to require honesty, not lies. It's going to mean putting police in black neighborhoods, where the criminals are. It's going to mean punishing black wrongdoers, to protect their neighbors and communities. It's going to mean that police stops, arrests, police shootings, and prison sentences all show a racial skew.

• • •

Given that the woke are overwhelmingly the ones responsible for crime in Minneapolis exploding in from 2020 onwards, they have exactly zero right to try to dictate how crime is solved. Yet they try to do so anyway, using exactly one tool in their arsenal: Pointing and screaming "that's racist!"

It's pathetic, but the far more pathetic thing is that *this works*. Before, during, and after the George Floyd riots of 2020, Republicans have repeatedly wilted in the face of claims that policing, criminal justice, or any kind of law and order in America are racist, because black Americans are arrested, charged, and convicted of crimes more often than other groups. Repeatedly, the left tells the lie that police are systematically racist—even though big-city police departments are among the *most* racially integrated institutions in American life (far more diverse than Silicon Valley, Wall Street, or the Ivy League). And repeatedly, the right has indulged this lie, by trying to collaborate with the left on "police reform" or "criminal justice reform" whose only real purpose is lowering standards of law and order. These concessions never produce a political gain. Republicans never prove they aren't racist, because proving such a thing was never possible in the first place.

The winning move against all this rhetorical sleight-of-hand? *Recognize* what it is, and more importantly, *refuse to be manipulated.* Instead, do the opposite. Show confidence and moral firmness. If you want to beat the left, *stop giving them the power they crave.*

Will this get you called racist by activists, politicians, and perhaps by major newspapers? Yes. But guess what? They were going to call you racist anyway, so you might as well stand up for yourself.

This isn't just about your own personal response, either. Remember those Maoists I mentioned at the start? Once they accused someone of being a counter-revolutionary, they drove their friends and family to turn against them as well, often from sheer self-preservation. The woke use allegations of racism the same way, as a tool to split conservatives and get us to abandon or turn against our own allies. Remember Jake Gardner, the Omaha bar owner whose railroading and subsequent suicide I recounted in Chapter 1? Liars smeared him not merely as a racist, but as a full-blown white supremacist with a swastika tattoo. As a result, in the lead-up to his suicide Gardner was practically without allies. Reporter and author Joe Sexton described the sad situation which still prevailed after Gardner's death:

> Marines who had fought with Mr. Gardner did not want their friendship made public, and worried that their families would be harmed. A close family friend of the Scurlocks said she was fired from her job at a nursing home after other staffers said the memorial pin she wore would upset patients.
>
> It was a Black former Marine who captured that tragedy of Omaha most powerfully. He had served with Mr. Gardner, gone to his bar, appeared on a news segment with him to talk about their service. Mr. Gardner, he said, had treated him like a brother throughout. . . . Yet the Marine told me he would not be named. He said he might lose his job if he were. He told me he was sorry but felt he was without a choice.[140]

The woke lie, and they lie about nothing more than so-called racism. They fabricate hate crimes with depressing regularity. As such, it's our duty to not fall for crocodile tears, and not to be emotionally manipulated. If more people stood up for Jake Gardner, he might still be alive today. And more generally, if more people refused to take the left's politically motivated shrieking at face value, then "cancel culture" would cease to exist.

When even an ex-Communist like Dorothy Healy can admit that complaints about racism are mostly bogus distractions that eat away at group cohesion, surely we can believe it.

Read these next sentences a few times. Repeat them to yourself, and then remember them every time in the future you find claims of racism in the wild: *Complaints about racism are 95% of the time a cry for attention, a distraction, or a power play. I will not lose my mind and freak out, especially by the fear of guilt-by-association, when I see a finger pointed at someone calling them a racist. I will fear God more than I fear anyone in HR.*

While I've focused on accusations of racism in this chapter, this is a general principle for all the labels the left lobs at its enemies, be it racist, sexist, ableist, bigot, homophobe, or transphobe. All of these words function, essentially, as magic spells, meant to fill the target with fear and paralyze them with inaction. If conservatives live in fear of mean words that the left will call them, then they will always be in a position of servile inferiority to them. Every day will just be one of waiting for an inevitably approaching doom.

But when you reject the left's attacks and stand firm, anything is possible. Five years ago, conservatives were terrified of taking any serious legislative action against the rising tide of transgenderism, and if you looked closely, they mostly seemed to be motivated by the fear that they'd be called mean names and have their reputations damaged. The wave of new laws blocking child mutilation and protecting girls' sports that passed in 2022 and 2023 was presaged by a mental revolution inside conservative heads. We realized that, actually, protecting children is more important than avoiding getting labeled a "transphobe." And once we did that, passing legislation was easy. When the left screamed "transphobe," we ignored them.

The same can be done on *any* policy issue. We have the power to secure the border and say that America should put our own citizens ahead of the "citizens of the world." We have the power to pass voter ID laws, and to restrict mail-in ballots. We have the power to promote Western civilization, American history, and the English language in our schools. We have the power to be tough on crime and put criminals in prison rather than immediately back on the street. We have the power to abolish affirmative action and other identity-based quota systems, and to impose merit-based systems for hiring and promotions in government jobs. All of these things will get us called racist and bigoted.

Let it happen. We know that our ideology rejects racism. We are the side that rejects quotas, discrimination, and favoritism. We are the ones who believe in objective merit, objective standards, and objective truth. We should act fearlessly against allegations of racism because we *know* they are false.

CHAPTER SIX

Curing Red State Laziness

If you're a grown-up conservative, there's a conversation you've probably heard, or even engaged in yourself, many times. It goes more or less like this:

Person A: Did you hear about what those students at Woke U are doing? They just had a sit-in at the school president's office demanding the creation of an Indigenous Underwater Basket Weaving Studies Department! And they just destroyed a statue of Abraham Lincoln on the grounds that he was racist!

Person B: Haha, well, those college students will get a hard dose of reality when they enter the *real world.*

As I hope most people realize by now, this is a *very* unhelpful attitude to have. While the woke left was steadily taking ground on school campuses, we simply consoled ourselves that the "real world" would sort them out. Instead, those woke activists turned the colleges into wokeness factories. Those factories then supplied the academic gobbledygook justifications that justified wokeness everywhere else. The activists themselves, meanwhile, took jobs in media, tech, government, the HR departments of basically every other industry, which they used to spread their ideas into the entire world. They didn't get a dose of the "real world." They remade the world in their image. While we sat smugly, doing nothing, the left remade the whole world into a college campus.

The state of Oklahoma has four million people, split up across 77 different counties. In both 2016 and 2020, every single one of those 77 counties voted Donald Trump for president. A Democrat has not won a statewide race in Oklahoma since 2006 (and needless to say, it was a different breed of Democrats winning races then). In the state's 101-member House, as of this writing, 81 members are Republicans and just 20 are Democrats. The Senate is just as extreme: Out of 48 members, just eight are Democrats. Even the state's largest city and capital, Oklahoma City, hasn't so much as elected a Democratic mayor since the 1980s. As states go, Oklahoma is as blood-red as it gets.

Within this deeply conservative state sits the University of Oklahoma, home to nearly 30,000 students and seven NCAA football titles. Each year, to sustain the university's operations, the Oklahoma legislature allots some $120 million in taxpayer funds, about one-fifth of OU's budget.[141] The school is governed by a seven-member board of regents, appointed by the governor, and they are in turn overseen by the nine-member state board of regents for higher education, *also* appointed by the governor.

A state-funded school, in a deep red state, governed in its entirety by the regents picked by Republican governors, with funding allotted by an overwhelmingly Republican legislature. Everything is in place for the University of Oklahoma to be a profoundly conservative institution.

So *why*, then, is it instead home to this?

The Gender + Equality Center will be hosting its first drag workshop on September 25, and local drag performers Nikita and Allen will be leading the workshop.

This workshop will help participants learn how to create a drag persona, performance tips and networking as a drag performer. Nikita and Allen will also lead participants into a deeper discussion of the history of drag and useful materials to continue exploring drag.

Nikita and Allen are local drag performers and have performed at Crimson & Queens, the annual drag show hosted by the GEC. This event will also help newcomers who are interested in performing in Crimson & Queens in the future.

Quan Phan, the LGBTQ+ programs coordinator for the GEC, hopes the workshop can help participants who are interested in drag performance.

"We want to give students earlier opportunities to explore and practice drag as an art form in a safe and supportive environment," Phan said in an email.[142]

Where to begin? Why does OU have an official, school-supported "Gender + Equality Center"? Why is that center recruiting local drag queens to perform at an official, state-backed "annual drag show"? Why is the center hosting workshops to train people to become drag queens themselves? Why does the center have an official "LGBTQ+ programs coordinator" working as a state employee?

There's more. Why does the University of Oklahoma have a Department of "Latinx Studies"?[143] Why does it have a Center for Social Justice? And why does that Center for Social Justice literally have a paid staff position for a dedicated "activist in residence"?

> The WGS Center for Social Justice's Activist-in-Residence Program brings social justice activists to campus to interact directly with students. . . . Once on campus, activists hold workshops, lead discussion groups, teach classes, screen films, assist in planning projects and campaigns, and are available to students for informal conversations. The WGS Center for Social Justice believes the personal contact and hands-on approach of the Activist-in-Residence Program truly benefits students and works toward **our mission of inspiring students to become involved in social justice activism.** The residency program covers the AIR's travel expenses and includes an honorarium.[144]

$120 million in support every year from the overwhelmingly conservative citizens of Oklahoma, and in response OU gives them professional left-wing activists.

How about Oklahoma's other major state-funded school, Oklahoma State University? A quick glance at their website brings us this: "Since 2008, OSU undergraduates have been required to enroll in a diversity designated course. In Fall 2019, there were approximately 100 diversity courses and 121 sections offered, according to the Office of the Registrar."[145]

Uh oh! OSU boasts that it has more than 70 diversity-related student, faculty, and staff organizations. It has a "Diversity, Equity, and Inclusion

Task Force" which is crafting "our system-wide strategic plan to align with the goals of the DEI strategic plan." And yes, you read that right. They are indeed making a strategic plan for executing their strategic plan.[146] They boast about planning an annual diversity summit, and all the work done by their "senior inclusion officers."

We all know enough at this point to say what this is. Call it diversity, call it inclusion, call it whatever you want, what it actually is left-wing politics backed and funded by the state government.

Why does Oklahoma have it? It's not that Oklahoma's many Republicans are "fake conservatives" who are really liberals at heart. I know enough of them to know that's not the case.

Instead, what's going on, bluntly, is that Oklahoma Republicans didn't stop it from happening. The British historian Robert Conquest once remarked that "Any organization not explicitly right-wing sooner or later becomes left-wing," and Oklahoma is proving that maxim true every day. Oklahoma conservatives might enjoy mocking and attacking left-wing colleges, but they were actually hands-off in controlling how those colleges behave. And so, they got exactly what could be expected. Like a kudzu weed, anywhere it is left to its own devices, wokeism will spread everywhere.

But I feel bad and don't want to just beat up on Oklahoma here, so let's take another example from another state. In 2022, the University of Tennessee attracted attention when journalists noticed the university was requiring every one of its sub-school and administrative units to generate a "Diversity Action Plan." In response, UT's engineering, architecture, and communications schools all added mandatory diversity statements. The provost's committee's plan included adding "diversity champions" to every hiring committee.

As Revolver News noted at the time, nothing about this woke eruption at UT was a surprise. Immediately after George Floyd's death in 2020, school chancellor Donde Plowman had encouraged the entire school to read Ibram X. Kendi. Two months later, Plowman promised the school and the entire world that UT would be implementing "diversity action plans." Plowman pledged that those plans would involve more race-based hiring and promotions (for "equity"). She also promised that the school would work with something called the "Critical Race Collective," hiring a fellow from the collective to "work with the Division of Diversity and Engagement to coordinate antiracist teach-ins, conferences, and other programming."[147]

. . .

All of that was open and public in 2020, yet it took two years for UT's slowly developing diversity action plans to generate so much as a mildly viral Twitter thread in response. Revolver couldn't hide its exasperation.

> Plowman's position as chancellor at UT-Knoxville isn't a command from heaven. Plowman is an appointee of University of Tennessee president Randy Boyd. Boyd, in turn, is an appointee of the UT Board of Trustees (which also confirms chancellor appointments). And who chose them? The Board of Trustees has eleven voting members, and every single one of them is appointed by the governor of Tennessee. Ten of the commissioners also require confirmation by both houses of the state legislature.
>
> **In other words, every aspect of this development has happened under the supervision of the Tennessee state government, and by extension, of the Republican Party.**
>
> In Tennessee, Republicans control almost ¾ of the state house, and they have held at least 70 out of 99 seats since 2012. In the state Senate, they outnumber Democrats more than four to one and have for a decade. The last time a Democrat won a statewide election in Tennessee, Saddam Hussein was still alive.
>
> The point is, if any state can take action against an out-of-control public university without too much political danger, it's Tennessee. But instead, Tennessee Republicans have mostly sat helplessly as their institutions are hijacked for other ends.[148]

"Sat helpless" is the understatement of the decade.

It's not only universities where the cancer of wokeness flourishes at red state taxpayer expense. To take one state at random (seriously, this was the first one I checked), the Kansas Department of Administration, which oversees the operations of the Kansas state government, has a "State Executive Branch Workforce Diversity, Equity & Inclusion Initiative." Their mission? According to their website it is, "To emphasize the importance of diversity, equity and inclusivity throughout all aspects of State of Kansas employment policies and practices in order to provide for a workforce that is representative of the diversity of the State's population and a workplace that is comfortable for all employees."[149]

Despite attempting to hide in the midst of that bland, sterile phrasing, the truth of the matter can't hide, and it's chilling. If reading that sentence and its attempts to bore you out of seeing the truth didn't set off all of your internal alarm bells, then with all due respect you have not been paying attention for the past decade.

Dig into the materials put out by this department, and you'll quickly find all kinds of poisons. The Department of Administration's recruitment guide recommends maximizing "diversity" in the state government by making "experience with diverse groups" a mandatory qualification for government jobs.[150] The department's page links directly to materials produced by ComPsych, such as "Transgender Persons in the Workplace" guide which instructs people to accommodate transgender employees by using new pronouns, not using their birth names (you may have heard birth names called "dead names"), and letting them use the bathrooms and locker rooms of their choice.[151] ComPsych's materials, in turn, encourage people to go to left-wing activist groups like the Human Rights Campaign or GLAAD for more information.

It's all boring to read, which is, of course by design. However, despite trying to get people to stop reading by boring you with dense phrasing and overly corporate and political language, the basic idea they are trying to get across is clear-cut: The Kansas Department of Administration is nudging the government in a woke direction. Why is that happening, when Kansas voted for Donald Trump by 15 points in 2020? Sure, the state does have a Democrat governor, but it also has a Republican supermajority in the legislature, capable of overriding that governor's vetoes. So why is that legislature funding a single woke thing in the state government?

Over and over, the pattern recurs. Wokeness is routinely endemic at major institutions in red states that could have easily stopped the growth before it got too bad, but instead ignored the problem and did nothing to keep their communities headed on the right path. Rest assured that, no matter what red state you live in, your government is sponsoring similar follies, most often at its state-backed universities. In late 2021, the American Enterprise Institute found that Ohio State employed 132 "diversicrats" at a total payroll cost of $13.4 million, money that could have supplied full-tuition scholarships for more than a thousand students.[152] At Kentucky's University of Louisville, the school has one DEI-related employee for every 20 faculty members.[153] In 2022, the University of South Carolina's business school was caught offering a program for high school students that explicitly barred whites from even applying.[154]

It's also important to notice that the reverse isn't happening in blue states. You'll find that New York is not inadvertently dumping millions into a university apparatus that promotes Constitutional originalism, gun rights, or Christianity. California's legislature is not casually shipping government dollars to pro-life pregnancy centers. Nor is there an obscure corner of the Massachusetts state bureaucracy publishing guides that call transgenderism a mental delusion.

The rapid and upsetting growth of these woke ideas and agendas is even more frustrating when you realize stopping these poisons would be trivially easy, as developments over the past year have shown. In February 2023, a piece in *The American Mind* profiled how woke sentiments steadily increased at Texas A&M, considered by reputation one of America's only remotely conservative state universities.

> By 2017, STRIDE training, aimed at revealing the systemic and implicit biases of such fraught categories as "best candidate" and "merit," was mandatory for faculty assigned to search committees. Similar programs were adopted for tenure and promotion committees. Accountability, Climate, Equity, and Scholarship Faculty Fellows Program (ACES) fellowships sought to recruit minority candidates with "diversity skills" to A&M. Hate reporting systems were adopted to help transform the campus climate.
>
> . . . A&M soon had more DEI administrators than University of Texas at Austin. Its DEI personnel spread to colleges, where more plans, more intense equity training, and more programming was "incentivized."
>
> Well over 60% of all A&M departments now require DEI statements for job applicants. DEI statements are judged using the Berkeley Rubric, which scores candidates low if they seek to "treat everyone the same," while

giving extra points to candidates willing to set different standards for different races and sexes. Search committees are encouraged to set a minimum score on the Berkeley Rubric for candidates to make the cut.

. . . DEI commitments have weakened A&M's old curriculum. No physical fitness or foreign language requirements remain. History and political science requirements have been "broadened" from surveys in American history to narrow DEI classes like "Blacks in the United States, 1607–1877." Science requirements now include "life science" classes informed with global warming dogmatism. A&M now has two required general education courses infused with DEI ideology: an "International Cultural Diversity" requirement and a "Cultural Discourse" requirement. This is not your father's A&M. A&M leadership continues to obscure its intentions. As one wag put it, the job of red state university presidents is to lie to red state legislators. [155]

Two weeks after the publication of Yenor's piece, amidst a howl from Texas's "red state legislators" and an angry command from Gov. Greg Abbott, A&M announced it would no longer require diversity statements of new hires.[156] That's all it took to undo years of poison, angry sounds from the state government.

As great as the recent red state push against critical race theory, DEI, ESG, and other threats has been over the past year, there is once source of constant frustration that constantly lurks in the back of my head. And that is, *Why did it take until now to do anything?*

Why are red states so prone to letting poisons fester? One reason, frankly, is that red state Republicans are often smug, when they should be alert. I've traveled all over the United States for Turning Point USA, and it's an attitude I see far too often. People enjoy reading about the latest insanity out of Portland, or Berkeley, or New York City, then bless their stars that they live in a *red state* where that would never fly, and then they think no more about it. They read about woke radicals on a blue state campus, and don't even pause to wonder if the same radicals might exist, or even hold jobs, at their state's own flagship. Among those who do realize the truth, even fewer make the leap to thinking about how to *stop* it.

This is indefensible. For one, many of these same conservatives will *gloat* about people fleeing failing blue states to come to more economically viable, pro-growth, pro-family red states. Yet they rarely think about the imminent threat this poses to the values that made their state successful.

The left doesn't think this way. Rest assured, they are *very* aware of opportunities that come their way due to America's internal migration.

"Reverse Migration Might Turn Georgia Blue," bragged *The Atlantic* in 2018, two years before reverse migration turned Georgia blue for Biden.[157] "Is the California Exodus Turning Arizona Blue?" wrote Bloomberg, days before Arizona shocked the country by voting Democrat for only the second time since 1948.[158] Conservatives need to start realizing that just because they find themselves in a red state today, there is no promise that their state will remain red tomorrow. This reality paired with a wave of smugness and complacency means that a shift can happen quickly, so it's vital to remain alert and vigilant to protect your family and your community.

However, smugness isn't the only problem causing conservatives to lose vital ground. The other reality is that often conservatives are just too nice. Another British writer, Horace Walpole, once observed that "No country was ever saved by good men, because good men will not go to the length that may be necessary."[159] If wokeness is creeping up on a campus or in a bureaucracy, stopping it requires a degree of sharpness. It might mean passing legislation that explicitly lays people off, possibly dozens or hundreds of people. It means picking a fight, one that might not reap immediate rewards at the ballot box. It means possibly inviting an angry lawsuit. It means starting a bureaucracy war with professional bureaucrats. It means inviting angry protests by college students who cry and scream and throw stink bombs and chain themselves to desks and collude with the press for favorable coverage. It means possibly upsetting a friend, a family member, or even your own son or daughter whom you haven't protected from buying into all the tenets of wokeness she hears at her high school.

Yet another source of red state inaction, I think, is a flawed moral premise that tolerance is always a virtue. And sure, much of the time, it is. Tolerance can be beautiful when it is coupled with compassion. Understood properly, tolerance is a kind of patience. It's also a *modus vivendi*, a way to "live and let live" in a world where people and groups have wildly different values.

But letting people who despise you and your way of life take your money to promote ideas that are socially corrosive or outright evil is not tolerance. It's just being stupid. While "live and let live" isn't strictly wrong, it's been rendered out of date by events. "Live and let live" was sensible when America had robust free speech and when America's schools taught math and patriotism.

Another reason for conservative inaction, frankly, is political laziness. As conservatives, we're often happy to simply let events take their course, unless some kind of crisis grabs our attention and moves us to action. We are, by disposition, people who are happy with what we have. On average, we're older than liberals. We're more likely to have families that take most of our attention. For the most part, we don't like bossing other people around. Unlike the woke, we don't dream up new grievances against people that only drastic government intervention will solve. Most of the time, this is a virtue. But in times of crisis, a preference for inaction is a dereliction of duty.

But perhaps the most unfortunate and indefensible reason for conservatives to sit around instead of acting is one of the core tenets of the Christian beliefs that so many of us share. While many people dread and fear the end of the world, those who follow Christ are not only not afraid of it, but some actively look forward to it. Because our faith means that the end of all things on this world means that Christ will finally return and win a final victory over death and all evil. It's an amazing promise of hope, the power of God, and the world to come. However, I routinely meet Christians who believe the end of the world is so imminent, that fighting too hard on political topics is "pointless" since Christ will simply return to resolve things on our behalf.

To that I could say many things. First off, Christians have been predicting the end of the world during their lifetimes since the days of the apostles. Martin Luther thought the end of the world was so imminent that he worried it would arrive before he could finish translating the Bible into German.[160] We are nothing special in seeing the end times, so shirking our duties to care for our families and our communities because we're certain Christ's return is near isn't a solid plan because the entire human race has been historically bad at predicting the end of the world.

However, even if the end times are near, that should only make us fight *harder* against evil. Are we looking forward to standing at the Last Judgment and explaining to God why we sat on our butts doing nothing against evil, because we figured He would take care of it? If we're here, on this planet, still breathing, it means that God still has work for us to do. I, for one, don't want to have to answer to why I decided to ignore that call for my own comfort and laziness.

And so, even if you are convinced and convicted that Christ is coming back tomorrow, I still would strongly encourage you to do everything you can today to make a difference in this world. Because there is a lot that needs doing, and we need everyone to do their part. Turning the tables on wokeness will mean reclaiming our sense of agency, not just over our own lives, but particularly over our states. Conservatives routinely complain that we have lost almost every institution in the country, from universities to non-profits, corporate America, the military, the FBI, and so on. It's all true. The single great exception to this trend is our states. Red states are where we can elect powerful, durable majorities in government. Red states are where we have total control overpaying the bills. Red states are where we can take confident action knowing we'll likely enjoy multiple election cycles to see an effort through. Red states, in short, are where our change in attitude must become a change in action. But we have to put in the work to keep in that way.

For too long, we've seen our red states as places of refuge and a place where we could relax and let our guard down. They are no longer that. They are homes that are being burglarized, wells that are being poisoned, cities that are under siege. Red states are a power base for fighting a political war. We have to treat them accordingly.

CHAPTER SEVEN

Reject the Cult of Defeat

In the very first edition of the magazine *National Review*, founder and conservative intellectual William F. Buckley said that his magazine's purpose was to "stand athwart history, yelling Stop, at a time when no one is inclined to do so."[161]

To rephrase that, Buckley might have written "Nobody is on our side, and our big idea is just that we should stop doing the current thing."

Not exactly a rallying cry that gets the home crowd cheering, is it? The sense of gloom overflows throughout Buckley's essay, now nearly 70 years old.

> *National Review* is out of place, in the sense that the United Nations and the League of Women Voters and the New York Times and Henry Steele Commager are in place. It is out of place because, in its maturity, literate America rejected conservatism in favor of radical social experimentation.
>
> . . . Radical conservatives in this country have an interesting time of it, for when they are not being suppressed or mutilated by the Liberals, they are being ignored or humiliated by a great many of those of the well-fed Right, whose ignorance and amorality have never been exaggerated for the same reason that one cannot exaggerate infinity.[162]

You could reproduce the exact same paragraphs today, and the only necessary change would be that Buckley would rename the well-fed Right to "grifters."

There is a psychological pattern on the right that might be called the "culture of defeat." People on the right are predisposed to believe that we have been losing for a long time, are losing right now, and will continue to lose in the future. "Conservatives always lose" is a refrain that has been repeated almost as long as "conservative" has existed as a label people affix to themselves.

"Much of conservative doctrine is, if not quite bankrupt, more and more obviously obsolescent," wrote *National Review* contributor James Burnham in 1972.[163]

In 1994, Sam Francis published an entire book titled *Beautiful Losers: Essays on the Failure of American Conservatism*, writing in the title essay that "American conservatism . . . is a failure, and all the think tanks, magazines, direct mail barons, inaugural balls, and campaign buttons cannot disguise or alter that. Virtually every cause to which conservatives have attached themselves for the past three generations has been lost, and the tide of political and cultural battle is not likely to turn anytime soon."[164]

In fact, the idea that conservatism "always loses" is so pervasive that some conservatives want to stop even applying that label to themselves, convinced the word itself bears some kind of cursed juju that dooms any cause that touches it to defeat. In October 2022, *The Federalist's* John Daniel Davidson wrote a piece titled "We Need To Stop Calling Ourselves Conservatives."

"The conservative project has failed, and conservatives need to forge a new political identity that reflects our revolutionary moment," he wrote.[165]

It would be easy for me to find examples to make the case that all of these conservatives were completely correct: That American conservatism was losing 70 years ago, and has never stopped losing, no matter how actual elections went.

But it wouldn't be a fair or accurate argument. Because, as it happens, conservatism *doesn't* always lose. There isn't some culture of defeat in conservatism but is definitely *can* be a self-fulfilling prophecy. The defeatist mindset hobbles conservatives and convinces them to mope around at home and online, which is easy, rather than doing the work to win, which is hard. After all, it's a lot easier to not try and tell yourself you were doomed to fail from the start rather make a plan, put in the blood, sweat, and tears, and risk failure. But if conservatives can shake that defeatist mindset, we can do great things. To quote the slogan from a former presidential candidate whose name escapes me at the moment, "Yes We Can." And not only *can* we do great things, but *we already have.*

A SHORT HISTORY OF CONSERVATIVE TRIUMPH

Go back to the time of Buckley's founding essay for *National Review,* and there would be ample ways to argue that conservatism has simply been losing for decades, no matter how many essays Buckley and Co. put out yelling Stop. Abortion became legal. Marriage got redefined. America's border opened and stayed open.

But consider the changes that didn't happen. Buckley lamented that in 1955, Communism was ascendent everywhere. Today, the USSR has collapsed entirely and its Communist empire has collapsed with it. Buckley bemoaned that trade unions pushing socially left-wing agendas were strangling the freedom of American workers. Today, trade unions are the weakest they've been in decades.

After World War II, the top marginal tax rate in the U.S. was above 90 percent. When Ronald Reagan became president, the top tax rate was still 69 percent. During his time in office, the top rate fell all the way below forty percent, and it's remained at or below that threshold ever since.

Of course, cultural conservatives might say "Taxes, trade unions, and Communism? Who cares! Conservatives might win on economic and regulatory issues that appeal to big business, but we always lose the culture war!"

But even that isn't actually always true! Granted, the long-term drift of American society over the past century hasn't been in a direction that I or most of you care for. But at the same time, there are several examples of cultural, or culture-adjacent, issues where the long-term drift has helped conservatives and our values.

Consider homeschooling. Of course, learning at home, under a tutor, at a church, or otherwise outside government control was the norm in America until the late 1800s. That changed with the push for universal public schooling in the second half of the century. By the early 1900s, public schooling was practically universal, aside from some Catholic schools and a handful of elite private academies for the sons of the rich and powerful. Learning at home dwindled to the point of near non-existence. In 1973, just 13 thousand children were being homeschooled.[166]

Not only that, but even if a parent wanted to educate at home, the law in most states was profoundly hostile. As recently as 1983, halfway through Ronald Reagan's first term, homeschooling was illegal in eleven states. Several more only allowed homeschooling if a parent was a certified teacher. Others imposed burdensome requirements to obtain government permission or present an approved curriculum.[167]

But as public schools became more ideologically liberal, more danger-ous, and lower quality, so too began a homeschooling revival for the ages. A few pioneering activists led the way, first by winning in court, and then by winning in state legislatures. In 1967, parents Barbara and Frank Massa, representing themselves *pro se*, argued before the New Jersey Superior Court that they had the right to school their children at home—and they won.[168] In 1972, three Amish parents challenged Wisconsin's law compelling school attendance. The case went to the Supreme Court, and the Amish won with the Supreme Court ruling that Amish religious freedom under the 1st Amendment overrode Wisconsin's compulsory education laws. In 1978, when Peter and Susan Perchemlides refused to send their son Richard to Amherst, Massachusetts public schools, the city put out a warrant for their arrest. Their successful legal challenge, in liberal Massachusetts, no less, af-firmed the right to homeschool in the state.

Emboldened by those legal victories, parents began pushing for laws guaranteeing their rights. In the 1980s and early 90s, dozens of states passed legislation explicitly legalizing homeschooling and loosening requirements to practice it. Ever since, homeschooling has exploded in popularity. By 1998 850,000 children were homeschooled. Just 18 years later, in 2016, the number was at 1.7 million.[169] Since the Covid lockdowns, hundreds of thousands if not millions more children have had a taste of homeschool-ing, and while many of those children have since returned to conventional schools, many others have stayed home permanently.

America is a huge global outlier in the First World on this topic. In Japan, Germany, and many other countries, homeschooling is illegal with no exceptions. In most other countries it is at least far harder to do than here. Just like on free speech and gun rights, America is indisputably the global leader in liberty when it comes to letting parents control their children's education.

Speaking of gun rights, that is another realm where conservatives have won epic victories over the past few decades. Half a century ago, despite the clear text of the 2nd Amendment, America was *not* the clear-cut global leader in the right to bear arms. Instead, that status is a modern creation, forged through conservative activism. The media and the Biden Administration's constant desire to crack down on guns creates a sense that gun rights are under siege, but the "siege" is more of a rout . . . for the anti-gun faction. In 1986—not even forty years ago!—sixteen U.S. states had no right to carry a concealed firearm. Some of those anti-gun states included Tennessee, Arkansas, Kentucky, Ohio, Oklahoma, Arizona, and Texas. Most other states were "may-issue" states for concealed carry licenses, allowing people to obtain them but allowing government officials to deny them for often-capricious reasons. Only eight states were "shall-issue" states where a license was easy to get, and just one state, Vermont, had constitutional carry, where citizens could carry a handgun on their person with no permit at all.[170]

Over the course of the 90s and 2000s, a gun rights revolution took place. By 2010, the number of "shall issue" permit states had more than quadrupled from eight to 36, and Arizona and Alaska had joined Vermont as constitutional carry states. From 2010 to the present, a second revolution in gun rights has occurred, as "shall-issue" states became constitutional carry ones. Today, 27 states have fully unrestricted constitutional carry. A law-abiding American can drive from Arizona, up to Idaho, then down to Florida without ever passing through a state where he needs a permit to carry a gun.

The revolution happened at the federal level, too. In 1994, Congress voted to ban so-called "assault weapons" (in reality, this mostly just banned guns with features that made them look scary on television). But the bill was passed with a ten-year sunset provision, and when those ten years were up, Congress didn't renew the bill. In the 20 years since, it still hasn't.

But perhaps homeschooling and guns aren't enough to fully convince you. After all, if there's one area where conservatives are especially convinced they always lose, it's "culture war" issues. There is no culture war issue more salient than the abortion issue. So, how has that gone? Well, certainly, we're far more left-wing than we were 60 years ago, entirely thanks to the Supreme Court's ludicrous *Roe v. Wade* ruling imposing abortion-on-demand in all 50 states. But *Roe* turned out to be abortion's high-water mark in America. Instead of giving up, in the wake of *Roe* American Christians launched the global pro-life movement to resist the onslaught of abortion. Ever since, a relentless legal and regulatory campaign by the pro-life movement has steadily rolled back abortion in America. Activists built the annual March for Life in Washington up from a minor event into the single largest conservative gathering of the year.

Along the way, there were many, many defeats and disappointments. From the beginning, pro-life activists treated Supreme Court nominations as a high priority, pushing for the appointment of justices who would overturn *Roe*. But in 1992's *Planned Parenthood v. Casey* decision, no fewer than three post-*Roe* Republican appointees (Anthony Kennedy, Sandra Day O'Connor, and David Souter) defected to keep *Roe* in force. In 2000, the Court even struck down a Nebraska ban on partial-birth abortion. That same year, in *Hill vs. Colorado*, the Court upheld a Colorado law meant to restrict pro-life activists from providing sidewalk counseling outside of clinics—a right that had already been curtailed by the federal Freedom of Access to Clinic Entrances Act, which treated pro-lifers like a terrorist group three decades prior to January 6, 2021.

Mastering the judicial nominations game to stack the federal bench with judges who would tolerate tougher abortion restrictions and eventually overturn *Roe* itself took decades. It was hard, often unrewarding work. But it paid off in 2022, with the *Dobbs v. Jackson Women's Health Organization* decision. In the year and a half since the *Dobbs* decision, Republicans in more than a dozen states passed laws dramatically increasing abortion restrictions, or banning the procedure outright. The battle over abortion is far from over, but it is beyond doubt that many thousands of babies' lives have been saved by the victories, small and large, of the past 50 years.

I share these examples to make sure you understand that conservatism is *not* just an effort to slow down a preordained defeat. And as the fight against abortion shows, when conservatives are focused, determined, stay the course, and are prepared for longer fights, we can do great things.

SUCCESS IS A MINDSET

In psychology and economics, there is a cognitive bias known as "loss aversion." In short, as humans we are wired to fear losses more than we desire gains. Losing a thousand dollars we already have will cause us more unhappiness than getting a thousand dollars unexpectedly will cause us joy.

I can't prove it, but I suspect a greater vulnerability to this cognitive bias explains much of the conservative cult of defeat. As conservatives, we are extremely sensitive to the many things we care about that are vanishing or in decline like our communities, our religious faith, and our freedom of speech. But on the flip side, we tend to not give nearly as much attention to the areas that are actively improving. The fact that we can opt our children out of public schools, and educate them however we want is at least as important as the fact that our public schools are flooded with transgender propaganda, yet we are enraged by the latter without properly appreciating the former.

I don't have the power to remake human psychology all by myself; I can't even master my own psychology. I'm just like most conservatives, more likely to get angry about defeats and betrayals than I am to get happy about wins.

But ultimately, I *do* want to win. That means recognizing that victory is possible, and then it means finding out how that victory happens.

There is a vocabulary word that is much in vogue among activists of the left. The word is "praxis." In ancient Greek, it literally means "doing." Praxis, in short, means the practice of something, as distinct from the mere theory about it. Historically, Marxists have been very concerned with praxis. Old Karl exhorted philosophers not only to understand the world but to change it. From Lenin to Mao to the Frankfurt School to the critical race theorists ruining your local college, Marxists have put out a nearly uncountable number of pages on what praxis, precisely, will bring the reality they dream of into being. All of that effort is one reason Marxists have been able to implement their agenda so often, despite a pristine track record of every Marxist regime, without fail, being a total calamity.

So why have conservatives picked up sustained victories on guns, homeschooling, and the right to life, but not on other issues? It's not simply a matter of these conservative positions being more popular than others. Polls have shown America to be sharply divided on guns; on abortion, plenty of polls suggest that pro-abortion views are more popular than pro-life ones.[171, 172]

No, it's not popularity. What has allowed conservatives to win on guns, homeschooling, and on the unborn's right to life is *better praxis,* in the form of superior *effort, strategy, and organization.* To borrow a phrase from Nietzsche, on all of those issues, conservatives have a Will to Power. This means we have the agency, desire, and determination to reshape the world into what we want. These are all issues where advocates are powerfully committed, and where they put in the time to organize, march, protest, lobby, and write bills. That last part in particular is crucial: Pro-lifers, gun rights advocates, and homeschoolers almost always know *exactly* what kind of laws they want. They don't vaguely beg lawmakers to "do something." Instead, they decide what their goals are, and then pressure lawmakers to make that goal reality. When Republicans win elections at the state level, new pro-life and pro-gun legislation is on the docket immediately, because activists are diligent about demanding it. If the lawmakers don't oblige, they look to unseat them in favor of someone who will, or they run for office themselves to make it happen.

In summer 2022, first-term Republican Congressman Chris Jacobs, representing suburban Buffalo, came out in support of an "assault weapons" ban after a shooting at a supermarket. The result was instantaneous: Every gun rights group that had endorsed Jacobs immediately withdrew its backing, as did many elected Republicans. An effort to recruit a primary challenger began immediately. The backlash was so immediate and so total that just one week after announcing his change of heart on guns, Jacobs announced his retirement from Congress.[173] Now, ask yourself: How many other issues are there where even the slightest defection can instantly end a Republican's political career? If we want higher-quality Republican lawmakers, then our goal should be to expand that list of issues.

Besides being energetic and demanding, the pro-gun and pro-life movements are also vigilant, always watching for subtle attacks by the other side. For half a century, the federal Hyde Amendment has barred the federal government from directing federal funds toward paying for abortions. The Amendment has never been a permanent part of federal law; every year it must be renewed. There are several other pro-life amendments that operate in a similar manner:

- The Weldon Amendment, which bars the federal government from discriminating against anti-abortion health care providers.
- The Smith Amendment, which blocks federal health plans from covering abortion
- The Helms Amendment, which blocks foreign aid funds from going toward any use of abortion as a family planning method.

On most issues, laws that tenuous would easily be shoved aside in a flurry of budget negotiations. Left-wing Democrats have repeatedly demanded it, loudly. Yet that has never happened to the Hyde Amendment, or most of its sister amendments. Even during the first two years of Joe Biden's presidency, with unified Democrat control of Washington, they all survived, because pro-life groups made it abundantly clear to Republicans that their continued existence was non-negotiable. And so, when it came time for Senate Republicans to make a deal to avoid a budget filibuster, the amendments stuck.

Finally, it goes without saying that all of these movements are fearless, fully confident in their own moral superiority over their enemies. None of them are ever remotely trapped in a frame set by their enemies. The pro-life movement never worries one iota about the opinion of Planned Parenthood or NARAL.

So, I've heard enough about conservatives "always losing." We can win fights for election integrity, against pro-trans legislation, ESG, or woke mandates from the federal government. We just have to organize. We have to demonstrate to often-distracted lawmakers that we care about those issues just like we care about others, and crucially, we have to be ready with *specific policy demands.*

For decades we haven't cared enough about the rising tide of wokeness, and instead of being alert, we've often been smug. We whine to our family and friends about what we *see* on the news on social media or to family and friends but do perilously little to *change* the news. We complain about new laws invented by the left, but far too often we don't propose an alternative law of our own, and lobby Republicans to pass it. We get invested in elections, but then winning that election, too often, is its own reward, with little payoff expected after the fact. And when we lose that election, far too often, it feels easier to wallow in self-pity and that defeatist attitude, moaning, "We always lose!" instead of getting back up, dusting off, and riding back into battle.

But all of that can be changed, and it can be changed quickly. There are already a lot of promising signs on many issues. Consider the rampant anti-white and anti-Asian discrimination in American life that goes by the anodyne, deceptive label of "affirmative action." It's been around for decades at this point, and in many places is more widespread than ever, so under the cult of defeat hypothesis, conservatives could easily decide fighting back is pointless because we "always lose." Fortunately, not everyone agrees. In California, left-wing activists in 2020 tried to amend the state's constitution to reverse a 90s ban on affirmative action and explicitly legalize racial discrimination. The campaign received enormous financial backing from corporate America and was endorsed by almost every institution in the state. It would have been easy to not bother opposing it at all. But conservatives did step up to oppose it, and in 2020, while California voted for Joe Biden by more than 30 points, they rejected affirmative action by 15.

Three years later, in summer 2023, the Supreme Court struck a blow against racial discrimination when it ruled that Harvard and University of North Carolina's affirmative action policies were unconstitutional. That ruling didn't fall out of the sky. Just like the *Dobbs* ruling against abortion, it was the product of a multi-year legal effort by activists, who kept fighting even though prior Supreme Courts had delivered disappointing rulings in affirmative action cases. That ruling is important, but the follow-up will be even more so. And fortunately, the readiness to follow up is there. America First Legal, founded by Trump Administration veteran Stephen Miller, sent a letter to the deans of 200 law schools warning of lawsuits if they tried to evade or ignore the Court's decision.[174] As I write this, other lawsuits are being prepared to target racial discrimination in government hiring and contracts. If conservatives want even more momentum, they should look to pass laws banning discrimination at the state level.

Believe it or not, that's all you need to do to win politically. Believe you can win and put in the effort. It's that simple.

CHAPTER EIGHT

Hate the Game, but Play by its Rules

The 2022 election was a very tough one for me. I was deeply invested in the many excellent candidates we fielded that year, especially in my own state of Arizona. Kari Lake would have been an excellent governor, Blake Masters an excellent senator, and Aba Hamadeh an excellent attorney general. I expected all of them to win, and for Republicans to dominate all over the country. I was confident . . . too confident. Even when election night arrived and the vote totals started to come in, and showed our candidates trailing, I assured listeners on my show that Kari Lake was going to be governor, guaranteed. I stayed upbeat even into the following days, as the gap stubbornly refused to close.

In the end, it never did. All of the candidates I'd fought so hard for in Arizona lost. So did other promising candidates around the country. Worst of all, in Pennsylvania Dr. Mehmet Oz lost to John Fetterman, an embarrassing vegetable of a man with zero accomplishments who couldn't even talk (thanks to a stroke caused entirely by his abominable health habits) and who'd sponged off his parents for his entire life.[175]

I didn't just feel upset; I felt humiliated. It wasn't just because I'd been so confident going into election night. It was because I knew, deep down, that this wasn't just a failure of messaging. It was a failure of tactics. For no reason at all, we conservatives had taken an inferior tactical approach, and that left us with fewer votes on election night, despite running against a president with an approval rating of under 40 percent. We took a winning position, and we squandered it.

PLAYING TO WIN

I grew up in Chicago in the wake of Michael Jordan's dominant Bulls teams, but truthfully I'm not much of a basketball fan today. It's not just that the NBA has become by far the most woke professional sports league, with a year-round deluge of both Pride and BLM content. It's also about issues with the game of basketball itself. To be blunt, basketball games have crummy endings. The team that is losing tries to slow the game down by fouling their opponents and turning the game into a free-throw contest. It's not very fun to watch and drags out the end of the game for ages, but every team does it while trailing because, objectively, it's the right strategic move. Until the league changes its rules, it's likely here to stay.

I'm sure you've heard the idiom, "Don't hate the player, hate the game," and the game of basketball is a perfect example of this. It's also something to keep in mind when trying to weave your way through the American political system.

As conservatives battling to save America, we must be in this fight to *win*. Throughout Part 2 of this book, I have made the case for changing our attitude in a whole host of ways by resisting woke emotional manipulation, by being more energetic, and by realizing that we not only can win, we morally deserve to win.

But one last attitude shift is needed. We need to be willing to pursue the *tactics* that will help us win.

So, let's talk about political tactics. There are plenty of electoral and political strategies that I think are distasteful, or unclean, or not particularly democratic or classy. In an ideal America, they wouldn't exist. But, mostly due to the actions of our foes, they have become a part of our politics. In the past few years, Democrats have become experts in techniques like mail-in voting, ballot harvesting, and early voting. They've recognized that American politics is not just a battle of ideas, but a literal game where power is handed to the team that scores more points. During the 2020 campaign, conservatives endlessly ridiculed Joe Biden for his anemic campaigning, his empty rallies, the total lack of genuine love he inspired compared to the passionate enthusiasm and intensity of the MAGA movement. But on January 20, Biden was the one taking the oath of office, because his team was the one that scored more points in the election game.

The left is also more experienced in other political tactics. They know how to organize a boycott and terrorize apolitical and even conservative companies into submitting to their will. And unlike most red state lawmakers, when the left wins power, they know there are a lot of things they can do with it that aren't just passing legislation.

When we watch sports, all of us understand when a team does everything it is allowed under the rules to win. It's time we applied that attitude to saving our country as well. After all, it's how you win.

OVERCOMING THE SCARS OF 2020

Tens of millions of American conservatives carry deep scars from the election night of 2020. After being told by the press all fall that Donald Trump was doomed, when November 3 rolled around, the president once again dramatically outperformed the polls. He dominated in Ohio and Iowa, which were supposed to be close. In Florida, where polls supposedly had him losing narrowly, he won by more than three points. And in the upper Midwest states that had flipped from Obama to Trump in 2016, it looked like Trump had once again defied every expert prediction. Just after midnight on Nov. 4, Trump had big leads in all three of the former "blue wall states." In Pennsylvania, with 75% of votes counted, he was up a whopping 11 percentage points.[176]

You remember what happened then. All of us do. The harvested ballots pouring in. The mail-in votes, some arriving after Election Day itself. The non-existent signature verification. The failed legal challenges.

2020 left all of us shell-shocked. But the harm of that election wasn't limited to the presidential race. It also caused us to self-destruct in 2022.

Back in 2012, Republicans were more likely to vote absentee than Democrats (and consequently, *The New York Times* at the time was happy to note that fraud is "vastly more prevalent" in mail votes than in-person ones).[177] In 2020, with the incredibly rushed rollout of mass mail-in and drop-box voting using Covid as an excuse, we'd all become suspicious of early voting methods. By 2022, we were all deeply hostile. Rejecting mail-in voting, and casting ballots on Election Day instead, became a cultural marker for conservatives. It became a way of symbolically affirming our suspicions about 2020, and our opposition to letting it happen again. Polling before the 2022 vote showed a *49-point swing* in the results between people voting early (who leaned Democrat) and those voting on Election Day (who leaned Republican).[178]

I played my own role in this, sadly. I spent the fall of 2022 strongly encouraging overwhelming turnout on Election Day. While I did say I was fine with voting early in-person at polling places, I didn't push it aggressively. I bashed other methods of early voting, like voting by mail. I didn't trust it. I still don't.

But in the end, this backfired disastrously.

Here in Arizona, more than sixty percent of the entire state lives in Maricopa County, which contains almost the entire Phoenix metropolitan area. The rest of the state is split between Pima County and the Indian reservations, which are ultra-blue, and the rest of the state, which is ultra-red, so Maricopa County decides Arizona's election.

And on Election Day in Maricopa, the voting machines didn't work. At more than a quarter of Maricopa's polling places, vote counting machines had errors that prevented them from reading ballots.[179] All throughout Election Day, I watched in horror as my friends throughout Phoenix sent me text messages about long lines at polling places and wait times lasting an hour or more. My friends stuck it out and voted anyway. But how many people decided that their one vote wasn't going to matter, and simply left without casting a ballot? How many people saw tweets about the problem, and simply didn't turn out at all?

Did the voting machines truly just have surprise errors, or was the whole thing planned? The answer is that *it doesn't matter*. We made the decision to push election-day voting above all else, leaving ourselves vulnerable.

Even without any election machine malfunctions, there are plenty of other reasons that emphasizing election-day voting over all else is damaging to our cause. For one, it strains the resources of campaigns. Both sides of the political spectrum spend a large amount of time and effort nagging people they know lean their way to get out and vote. Once a person has actually voted, they can stop. So, if you're a reliable Republican voter, by voting earlier you aren't just adding another vote to the tally for the right side, you're also saving our candidates time and money, because they don't need to expend effort pestering you to vote. When Election Day rolls around, Republican campaigns are still scrambling to make sure almost all their voters get to the polls, while Democrats are only chasing down the last few lazy holdouts they haven't picked up ballots from yet. Expanding the window of voting also lets resources be used more efficiently. Consider driving voters to the polls. If Republicans all vote on election day, then we need a lot of cars to ferry people around. If Democrats are voting across a three-week period, they can get a lot more mileage (literally) out of a single car, and a single driver.

And then there's all the marginal impacts that are hard to measure, but surely exist. If a Democrat plans to vote early, but forgets, they can still show up on Election Day, no harm done. But if a Republican plans to vote only on Election Day, but then gets sick, or has a family emergency, or has a crisis at work, or simply forgets, that's it. The clock can't be rewound. If they don't vote, they don't vote, and it's a missed vote for Republicans.

In 2020, 1,661,000 people voted for Donald Trump in Arizona. In 2022, only 1,288,000 voted to make Katie Hobbs governor. If Republicans had the same turnout as in 2020, we wouldn't have just kept the governor's seat. We'd have swept every race in Arizona by a decisive margin. Instead, we lost. The Democrat strategy for keeping their turnout high—vote early, vote by mail, and harvest ballots everywhere possible—beat our strategy of flooding the zone on election day. It was the superior strategy.

And so, I've changed my mind on early voting and on ballot harvesting. It's not that all of us need to vote early or vote absentee or vote via drop box. But Republicans should adopt the same mentality as Democrats. That means every piece of paper in the box is one point. We are trying to score as many points as possible. We should pursue *any* tactic that gets pieces of paper into the ballot box.

In states with loose ballot harvesting laws like California, that will mean leaning in hard on ballot harvesting. In California, virtually *anyone* can return the ballot of someone else, so long as it is approved—even paid campaign staffers and party operatives. Democrats, naturally, have harvesters traveling about collecting "votes" from the homeless, or going door to door in mega-blue areas like the slums of Oakland. The least Republicans can do is field our own harvesters, in places with red-leaning demographics such as gun shows, country concerts, and above all, church gatherings. One of my close friends, Pastor Rob McCoy, realized the importance of ballot harvesting before I did, and carried out major harvesting efforts among his congregation. The efforts of McCoy and his fellow pastors in California may be the reason we have a Republican House of Representatives, because California is a state where Republicans most overperformed in 2022.

This isn't just talk. In summer 2023 I had Turning Point Action put $5 million toward developing ballot-chasing operations in Wisconsin, which I believe will be one of the decisive states in the 2024 election.[180] Hopefully by the time you read this we'll have been able to allocate even more money to other crucial battlegrounds.

At the risk of sounding like Barack Obama for a moment, let me be clear: In an ideal world, I would have American elections take place on a single day. There would be no ballot harvesting. Absentee voting would only be for rare cases, like the seriously ill or military service members on deployment. Ballots would all be counted on election night, with no tallying of votes that arrive by mail days or even weeks afterward. I believe this system is the one that would best prevent fraud and generate the most trust among members of the general public.

But that's an ideal. In the world we live in, right now, different rules prevail. We must play by them to even have a chance of changing them.

So instead of being sour about voting early, it's time to get enthusiastic about it. Become familiar with the laws that currently exist in your state. If you live in a red state with sharply curtailed absentee and early voting, congratulations, that's great. But if your state has rampant early voting, or legalized ballot harvesting, accept that, and figure out how to make the most of it. Get in contact with local campaigns or party organizations and figure out what events *you* could try to collect ballots at.

And don't be afraid to get creative in your own personal life as well. Host a dinner party or barbecue a few weeks before an election, where your friends can only attend if they join you in voting early beforehand. Turn in the ballots of your family members, to make sure they aren't "too busy" when Election Day comes. Republicans are more sociable than Democrats. We have more robust family lives, more close friends, more churches and more non-political community organizations. Take advantage of that!

Above all else, don't allow yourself or the people you know to become so demoralized they don't vote at all. The left is in a psychological war against you where they want you to give up and tune out. Instead, make *them* regret the day they made early voting the norm.

HOW I LEARNED TO STOP WORRYING AND LOVE THE BOYCOTT

There is another tactic Republicans should embrace more than they have in the past—the boycott.

Boycotts have always been a more potent weapon for the left than for the right. The reasons why are varied. One of the biggest reasons is simply that, overall, the woke have simply cared more about politics. With no families to focus on, no God above and no Hell other than the one they make for themselves, the woke have few things to care about besides advancing their agenda at all times.

But as of 2023, there are promising signs of that changing. In 2023, after a clueless Anheuser-Busch employee set up a marketing partnership between Bud Light and mentally imbalanced transgender influencer Dylan Mulvaney, Americans launched an impromptu but massive boycott of the Bud Light brand. Sales plunged by about a quarter, costing the company hundreds of millions of dollars.

Why was the boycott of Bud Light so successful when so many other conservative boycotts have failed? There are a few reasons that stand out:

- Beer is an extremely fungible product. There are more than a dozen major beer brands and literally hundreds of minor ones. Beer is a cheap, consumable, easy-to-find product, so swapping out one type for another is extremely easy.
- It was easy to have a quick impact. Beer is a high-turnover product, so people could easily join in by changing their subsequent purchases. Even if people didn't want to throw out their existing beer stockpiles, they could easily join in as soon as those were used up.
- While beer has many brands, actual brand loyalties are fairly weak.

People might be die-hard fans of Apple products, or Disney, or the NFL. But few people are fanatical about specific beer brands, so if that brand annoys them, they can quit it easily.

- The overall environment is friendlier to conservative boycotts. Elon Musk's Twitter purchase made social media drastically more pro-free speech, making it easier for conservative boycotts to gain momentum online.
- It went viral. Once news of the boycott's success became the story, it fueled even more boycotts and the momentum kept building.
- Beer is a social product: Beer is drunk at parties, sporting events, and other gatherings. Among friends, it's easy to see if someone is observing the boycott or not—and tease them if they're not.

That last part is perhaps the most important reason that the Bud Light boycott was such a success. The turn against Bud Light was not an *angry* boycott. It was an almost comedic one. Thanks to a single misfired ad initiative, Bud Light gained a reputation as "the gay beer." Nobody wants to be seen drinking the gay beer.

Bud Light wasn't the only company to have a bad 2023 thanks to conservatives. Another major boycott hit Target, which was targeted (heh) for prominently displaying disgusting Pride-themed clothing near the front of its stores. The clothing included things like "tuck-friendly," "women's" swimsuits (designed to mask male genitalia) and pro-trans clothing sized for preschoolers. Reacting with disgust, conservatives began publicly encouraging each other to shop elsewhere. Target stock fell nearly fifteen percent in a matter of days, costing the company more than $10 billion market cap.[181]

Target was a tougher brand to boycott than Bud Light. As a big-box retailer, the appeal of Target is that you can buy almost *anything* there, cheaply. Replacing that is harder than replacing a cheap beer because you not only need to be fully dedicated to the cause, you also have to put some forethought and extra work into sticking to your convictions. Instead of a quick Target run to the store down the street, boycotting the retailer could require driving further away from home, or shopping at multiple stores rather than just one. And it's easier to hide your patronage, should you decide to not follow the boycott. Nobody can tell you're shopping at Target unless they're also shopping there with you, and once you bring the goods home nobody will know where you bought them.

Despite the organizational challenges and the struggles of keeping conservatives true to the cause, the boycott had a real impact. By early June, analysts were downgrading the outlook of Target's stock.

From those markers, we can infer a few rules for future conservative boycotts:

- Pick products that are easy to replace. A boycott should be easy to join.
- Pick brands with physical products, or physical retail outlets. The Bud Light boycott was powered up by clips of people destroying old stockpiles of the beer, or photos of dozens of unbought cases sitting on shelves. The Target boycott drew energy from clips where people complained to store staff about the "tuck-friendly" Pridewear, or stunts where people loaded up carts with huge amounts of Pride product, but then "forgot their wallet" and had left it unpurchased. Viral videos and incidents give boycotts energy. They make them fun to participate in.
- Pick brands that *aren't* infamous for being liberal. This might be counterintuitive, but it's crucial. A famously liberal brand knows what it is. It's pandering to the left, and it knows most of its customers won't care about angry conservatives. Big-tent brands, or even "conservative" ones that misstep and pander to liberals, have far more to fear from becoming a political target. They will be more sensitive to a boycott, and any damage they sustain will send a stronger message to other companies.
- Pick just one or a handful of targets at once. One of the most surefire ways to rob a boycott of energy is to ignite one angry campaign after another. Regular people can't keep track of everything they're supposed to be angry at, and will forget or tune out completely. A very successful boycott of one company will achieve more than a hundred that go nowhere.

Conservatives should remember that a boycott doesn't have to bankrupt a whole company to be valuable. Even if Bud Light ultimately recovers as a brand, they suffered a huge scare and lost hundreds of millions of dollars in sales. Not only that, but the marketing VP responsible for Bud Light's Mulvaney partnership, Alissa Heinerscheid, went on a "leave of absence" that insiders described as a soft firing. The man who hired her, Daniel Blake, got the axe as well. Even if there is literally no other long-term impact, that makes the boycott valuable, because for every true believing woke foot soldier in corporate America, there is another person who is simply an ambitious corporate climber, happy to use wokeness to get ahead while it appears invincible and triumphant. If those people see that aggressive wokeness can derail a career, they'll back off from it, and that alone is a win, even if their moral compass doesn't budge an inch.

There are other benefits as well. Boycotts can spark division within the other side. As the Target boycott escalated, the company tried to tone down the backlash by muting its participation in Pride Month. Soon, the company's caution got it denounced by the very LGBT+ mafiosos it had been trying to pander to. By the end of May, a coalition of gay groups issued a demand that Target "release a public statement in the next 24 hours reaffirming their commitment to the LGBTQ+ community." Target didn't respond.[182] By late June, Target received a threatening letter signed by the attorneys general of New York and 14 other blue states, telling them to put Pride clothing back on public display.[183]

Looking ahead, there are ways we could make boycotts even better. America doesn't have many conservative institutions left, yet at the same time, it does at least have quite a few institutions that might respond to conservative pressure. For instance, one in seven hospital beds in America is at a Catholic hospital.[184] These hospitals employ plenty of non-Catholic staff, but they still adhere to Catholic religious doctrines set by the United States Conference of Catholic Bishops. They don't provide treatments that Catholics consider immoral, which obviously includes abortion, but also procedures like vasectomies or tubal ligations for the purpose of birth control.

Well, suppose America's faithful Catholics started pressuring Catholic hospitals to use their business heft more. Planned Parenthood's total revenue in 2022 was about $1.9 billion.[185] CommonSpirit Health, just one of *many* Catholic hospital systems in America, had 2022 revenues of more than $34 billion.[186]

The economic heft of Catholic hospitals dwarfs that of the abortion industry. Imagine if rather than just avoiding abortion, they took a more active role in delegitimizing the child butchering industry. Suppose Catholics pressured their bishops, and then bishops ordered the hospitals to *boycott* medical companies that work with Planned Parenthood or other leaders in the U.S. abortion industry.

Just like with ballot harvesting, in an ideal world we wouldn't have boycotts. I generally believe in a "live and let live" society. I'd be happy to shop at stores owned by liberals who disagree with me, while they shop at stores owned by conservatives. There is more to life than politics.

But sadly, the left has shown they don't agree. The left made the destruction of Christian cakemaker Jack Phillips in Colorado into a *national* cause, repeatedly bringing lawsuits and civil rights cases against him to try and ruin him for not making a gay wedding cake. President Obama used a White House Correspondents' Dinner to bully the small-town Indiana pizzeria Memories Pizza, which went out of business a few years later. Ultra-left Oberlin College in Ohio defamed tiny Gibson's Bakery because it dared to call the police on thieving students, then tried to bankrupt it through the court system after it sued.

The left even gets its government bodies into the boycott game. California's state government boycotts nearly half the United States for not loving LGBT enough, sanctioning us like we're selling uranium to North Korea.

When the enemy wants to destroy, refusing to fight back isn't noble. It's stupid.

WHAT NOT TO DO

Not every woke tactic is ripe for imitation, though.

One of the left's most toxic powers is its ability to stoke incredibly violent, criminal behavior and then memory-hole it as never happening.

"Black Lives Matter protesters were overwhelmingly peaceful, our research finds." So said a headline at *The Washington Post* in Fall 2020.[187] It's a lie—if not literally, then a lie by omission and distortion. You know it's a lie. You remember the looting and the curfews. You remember Antifa burning down a Minneapolis police station, and Chicago having a record 18 murders in a single day.[188] Thousands of business owners, thousands of police, and millions of Americans who lived in terror during summer 2020 all know it's a lie, too. And the *Post* simply told it anyway, knowing they could get tens of millions of mindless followers to repeat it. Harvard, *Time,* and CNN all pushed the same lie.[189, 190, 191]

Urban left-wing prosecutors made the lie into reality by deliberately undercharging and under-punishing the monsters of summer 2020. In New York City, a majority of looters and rioters were never even arrested. Among those who were, most of the arrested looters had charges dropped, while others had their offenses downgraded to mere trespassing.[192]

The left has an apparatus for getting what it wants through committing crimes. They've done it for decades. Many of today's most parasitical woke institutions, like black studies departments at universities, were created in the 60s and 70s to appease race rioters and other criminals.

There are some conservatives who see that and get the lesson that *we* should be more violent and aggressive to get what we want. This is a mistake, and not just because wanton violence is wrong. It's also a mistake because it's stupid. To be conservative is to be the force favoring order, decency, tradition. The left thrives on entropy, decay, and rot. Such rot is their natural habitat. For as long as the left-right division in politics has existed, criminals have leaned left and the left has leaned criminal.

The systematic manhunt for January 6th participants should illustrate this perfectly. Whether they were provoked by federal agents or not, the J6 rioters achieved nothing, other than hurting their own lives and damaging their movement. "But the Left gets away with it!" is a rallying cry that gets you and your friends thrown in prison.

ARE WE AT WAR OR NOT?

But I'm not telling us to pull back on aggression. Far from it. It's just that anarchy and chaos is always to the left's benefit, and never ours. Want to adopt new, more aggressive tactics against the left? Look first at what you can do in government.

There's a movie from about fifty years ago called *The Candidate*, which starred Robert Redford. It was written by a former Democratic speechwriter for Eugene McCarthy, and it's about a campaign for a Senate seat. (Ironically, the movie, which again is *half a century* old, takes place in the same year Joe Biden was first elected to the Senate. Now that's old!)

The titular "Candidate" runs an unlikely campaign that he is expected to lose, but this being Hollywood, he pulls off a surprising victory. At the end of the film, depicting the aftermath of election night, there is a famous scene where the candidate looks at his campaign manager, with a mob of journalists swarming about to swarm him, and he says to him, "What do we do now?"

Redford's candidate had thought campaigning through but had given no real thought to what would happen, and more importantly what he'd do, if he actually *won* and wielded power. That scene remains a microcosm for far too much of the Republican Party today. In the Trump era, we know what we want to hate, and we know what we want to complain about, but most of us (even, or especially, our politicians) don't know what we want to do with our gains.

In 2016, conservatives talked a lot of trash about Hillary Clinton's email scandal. The chant was "lock her up," which, of course, never got any real traction apart from frequently being shouted at conservative rallies. Maybe that was a worthwhile show of good faith, but if so, it ought to be our last one. Because ever since 2016, the left has made it plain they take "lock them up" as a far more serious commandment. From Robert Mueller and Jack Smith at the DOJ, to Crossfire Hurricane, prosecutors in Fulton County and at the New York DA's office, the left has spent more than half a decade systematically hunting for excuses to put Donald Trump and his associates behind bars.

By the time of this book's release, the former President might in fact have gone to jail, or narrowly avoided it, for something that Hillary Clinton pretty much did as well with no consequences whatsoever.

In New York, federal prosecutors tracked down pro-Trump Twitter poster Doug Mackey and charged him with violating the Ku Klux Klan act from the 1800s because he posted a meme ridiculing Hillary Clinton voters.[193] At the state level, Attorney General Letitia James paralyzed the once-mighty NRA with a multi-year bid to try and break up the organization and seize all its assets.[194]

It was clearly meant to be a lesson to Republicans. Don't talk about holding your political opponents accountable when they've broken the law. Either say nothing, or when you have the power to act, do something!

Too often the right acts like this is a play and the only reason to point out wrongdoing by the Left is to catch them in an act of hypocrisy. Don't bring a whistle to a knife fight, please. If Hunter Biden deserves to go to jail, he deserves to go to jail. If the DOJ won't find a way to make it happen, then red state AGs should look for a way, just as the New York AG's office has made the destruction of Trump and his allies a full-time mission, quite divorced from actually punishing any real crimes in the state.

Think aggressively, and act aggressively. Never be afraid of *using* power, where you have it, to win victories in the unfolding conflict this nation is in.

For an example of how to get things done, look north.

Despite a razor-thin majority from the 2022 elections, the Democrats in Minnesota adopted the attitude to govern by the slogan "What if this is the last time you ever held power?"[195] They put that slogan into effect with incredible energy. They spent all of 2023 pushing through a left-wing Democrat's Amazon wish list of political desires: Formalized abortion rights, mandated background checks on private gun transfers, carbon-free electricity by 2040, voting rights for felons, legalized pot, more power to teacher unions, increased taxes (of course), and even a "refuge program" for trans people who don't feel enabled enough in their psychosis by the government of another state. I could go on and on. The bottom line was that Minnesota Democrats saw an opportunity and decided to just go for it. Legislate now, contest elections later. If you fuss over the next vote, you've already lost. And the result is a long list of accomplishments to boast to their voters about. No liberals in Minnesota are complaining that their legislature are "Democrats in Name Only." In Minnesota, the DINO is as extinct as its namesake.

In America, we should make the RINO go extinct as well. And in the next part of this book, we'll explain now.

PART THREE

CHANGING
THE COUNTRY

CHAPTER NINE

Unmasking The "Civil Rights" Scam

In June 1964, Goldwater delivered a speech on the floor of the U.S. Senate. The subject was the Civil Rights Act of 1964. As a senator, Goldwater had consistently attacked all forms of racial and religious discrimination. He had voted for civil rights legislation in 1957 and 1960. But the bill before the Senate in 64, he said, was a bridge too far.

Goldwater's objection, specifically, was to Title VII of the act, which barred racial, religious, and sex-based discrimination by all large private employers. Goldwater's first objection was constitutional. Nothing in the Constitution even hinted at the federal government having such sweeping authority, he said, and so a law creating such authority, if upheld, would supersede the Constitution. But Goldwater then proceeded to make several additional practical criticisms of the law, and the impact he foresaw it having on American life in the many decades to come:

> "Fifty years from now, if this law is passed, you will be permabanned from TikTok for saying that men shouldn't use women's restrooms. You will be demonetized on Youtube if you notice patterns to who commits the most violent crimes. You will lose your podcast deal if you say police should use force to stop looters. By the time this law has its full effect on the culture, you won't even feel comfortable shooting the sh*t with your bros in a frat basement or an Xbox lobby."

Okay, okay, Goldwater obviously didn't put it quite like that. But he wasn't as far off as you'd think! Here's what Barry did predict:

> To give genuine effect to the prohibitions of this bill will require the creation of a Federal police force of mammoth proportions. It also bids fair to result in the development of an "informer" psychology in great areas of our national life—neighbors spying on neighbors, worker spying on workers, businessmen spying on businessmen, where those who would harass their fellow citizens for selfish and narrow purposes will have ample inducement to do so. These the Federal police force and an "informer" psychology, are the hallmarks of the police state and landmarks in the destruction of a free society.[196]

The concept didn't even exist yet, but Goldwater had anticipated woke tyranny.

Goldwater's vote made him a pariah to most of the country (though ironically, a young Hillary Rodham was a supporter). While he won the Republican presidential nomination a month later, he went on to lose the fall election to Lyndon Johnson in a gruesome landslide, winning just six states and losing the popular vote by almost 23 percent.

But sixty years later, I'm going to say something that you will never hear a modern Republican say, but it needs to be said if we want to reverse the woke virus on our nation. When it came to civil rights, Barry Goldwater was right.

I can't claim that this is an original thought of mine. Increasingly among conservatives, there has been a realization that so much of what ails America, and so many of the reasons that conservatives consistently, systematically lose one culture war after another, is rooted in the emergence of "civil rights law" in the 1960s.

The pioneer in making this observation was conservative writer and Claremont Institute senior fellow Christopher Caldwell, in his 2020 book *The Age of Entitlement*. In his book, Caldwell argues the ideology of civil rights has become so powerful that it has, effectively, replaced our original Constitution with a new one. Where we once had equality under the law, we now have affirmative action. Where we once had freedom of expression, we now have political correctness (and its successor, "woke"). Where we once had a restrained, limited federal government, we now have a regime of perpetual social reengineering. In the words of writer Helen Andrews, who reviewed Caldwell for the *Claremont Review of Books*, the 1964 Civil Rights Act has become "the law that ate the Constitution."[197]

> If you doubt the infinite adaptability of civil rights to any subject under the sun, consider the multifarious uses to which it has been put. Last year, the University of Missouri-Kansas City took down student art supporting the Hong Kong protests after pro-Beijing Chinese students complained it was discriminatory hate speech. The Second Circuit Court of Appeals ruled that a New York ban on euthanasia violated the civil rights of patients who wanted to be euthanized by treating them differently than "similarly situated" patients who could arrange to die simply by refusing further treatment (the U.S. Supreme Court reversed). There are pavilion-sized homeless encampments on the streets of Los Angeles, employers can hire illegal immigrants with relative impunity, gay marriage is the law of the land—all because of civil rights law, directly or indirectly.[198]

Political conflict in America, Caldwell says, is essentially a perpetual clash between those who believe in our official Constitution (conservatives) and those who follow our post-60s unofficial one (liberals).

"Affirmative action and political correctness were the twin pillars of the second constitution," Caldwell writes. "They were what civil rights was. They were not temporary. Affirmative action was deduced judicially from the curtailments on freedom of association that the Civil Rights Act itself had put in place."[199]

That's all easy to say, but what makes the Civil Rights Act so powerful, and so immovable? It's actually not the text itself, per se. As Caldwell makes clear in his book, the creators of the Civil Rights Act believed that it only banned intentional and overt discrimination, and that it required equal treatment rather than equal outcomes. The plain text of the bill supports this.

Yet now, we live in a world where the government demands the exact opposite. Today, our government tells states, businesses, and schools that they must engage in *reverse* discrimination, attempting to engineer equal outcomes, or else they will run afoul of the law, and be vulnerable to dev-astating lawsuits.

So, what changed? It's precisely what Goldwater warned of. The Civil Rights Act empowered an army of *bureaucrats* to "interpret" the law. And, adhering to the latest left-wing values as bureaucrats tend to do, they utterly remade the law to mean the exact opposite of what it says—and the courts have played along.

Think back to Chapter 3: The left has taken civil rights and put it in drag!

DISPARATE IMPACT

The centerpiece of civil rights law as it exists today is a concept called "dispa-rate impact." That concept has its roots in a little-known 1971 U.S. Supreme Court case, *Griggs vs. Duke Power Co.* Duke Power was a North Carolina electric company with five departments, four of them of which paid well and a fifth, "Labor," which paid poorly. During Jim Crow, blacks had only been allowed to work in the Labor department, but as segregation ended, Duke adopted a policy of allowing Labor employees to transfer to other depart-ments if they either had a high school diploma or performed well enough on two basic intelligence tests.[200] As it happened, blacks on average scored worse on the test, leading to a lawsuit. When the Supreme Court heard the case, it ruled that while Duke's test was outwardly neutral (and not even designed by the company), because it produced different outcomes based on race (a "disparate impact"), and simply testing employees' general ability wasn't sufficiently related to specific work duties, it violated the Civil Rights Act's ban on racial discrimination in employment.[201]

Over the past half-century, *Griggs* has utterly remade every aspect of American life. It is, in essence, the *Roe v. Wade* of federally enforced, bu-reaucratic wokeness. Once it was allowed into federal law, disparate impact became the skeleton key that unlocked almost every facet of wokeness that we've seen since. In Chapter 2, I mentioned that wokeness is fundamentally bureaucratic. Disparate impact is by far the strongest factor creating that bureaucratic power. In the words of the Manhattan Institute's Gail Heriot, the doctrine of disparate impact "makes almost everything presumptively illegal."[202] In a remarkable passage of a paper she wrote, Heriot describes the sheer insanity of what the law has become.

> [D]isparate impact liability is incoherent. *All job qualifications have a disparate impact. . . .* On average, men are stronger than women, while women are generally more capable of fine handiwork. Chinese Americans and Korean Americans score higher on standardized math tests and other measures of mathematical ability than most other national origin groups. They are also more likely to hold a B.S., B.Eng., M.S., or Ph.D. in one of the hard sciences or engineering.
>
> There is a lot more. South Asian Indian Americans are disproportion-ately likely to have experience in motel management than the rest of the population. . . . Native Americans are less likely to have access to high-speed internet service. They are hence less likely to learn of jobs that are posted only on the internet and less likely to be able to comply with requirements that job applications be submitted through the employer's web site.[203]

As Thomas Sowell once said, "Nobody is equal to anybody. Even the same man is not equal to himself on different days."[204]

Armed with disparate impact, the Equal Employment Opportunity Commission (the group charged with enforcing the Civil Rights Act) has spent half a century roaming America waging war against, in essence, any-thing its own bureaucrats decide is "racist." In 2012, the EEOC warned that companies could not categorically refuse to hire convicted felons because black Americans are more likely to have a felony conviction.[205]

But notice the key fact: It's not that *literally* everything is illegal. Rather, what is illegal is always simply *whatever EEOC decides.* As Heriot puts it, "Since all job qualifications have a disparate impact on some group, all employer decisions are subject to second-guessing by the EEOC (or by the courts in the case of a private lawsuit)."[205] It's a perfect recipe for tyranny: Woke bureaucrats have made everyone a criminal, and then they simply decide who they feel like prosecuting.

For example: Different races all graduate college at different rates, yet requiring a college degree for a job has never been targeted by the EEOC.

Why? Because the EEOC has simply decided that such requirements are fine—probably because colleges are run by liberals. Yet at the same time, the EEOC looks very critically at any employer who simply gives job applicants a written test, with no degree requirement, because of the "disparate impact" of the test.

And so, in a roundabout way, civil rights law is driving students to spend tens of thousands of dollars getting degrees from woke universities, rather than going right into the workforce. Civil rights law is creating the college scam! Not even Goldwater could have predicted that one.

THE HR INDUSTRIAL COMPLEX

But it's not just about Supreme Court rulings empowering the courts and federal bureaucracy to muck up your life. What you know today as "woke capital" is, substantially, the creation of this civil rights regime.

Most Americans believe that hormones and surgery can't magically turn a man into a woman, so why is this borderline impossible to say in a workplace? In fact, why is almost *anything* that goes against wokeness dangerous to say at any large American company? You know what it is: Human resources, and DEI.

But why does every company have such militant HR and DEI inside them? It's precisely because of what I said just above. Since the government can decide at any time to go after *any* organization for some policy with a "disparate impact," the way to avoid being targeted is to show slavish devotion to the cult of wokeism. Imagine a town run by a gangster where anyone who slobbers the gangster with praise is spared, but anybody who criticizes him gets murdered, and you start to get the idea.

And so, as the Soviets had commissars and Mao had his Red Guards, America has its DEI and HR professionals, monitoring every company for ideological offenses. When America was at its apex, these people did not exist. Companies were once able to hire and fire the way you would want to be able to do it if *you* ran a business (or the way you wish you could if you run one right now): By simply soliciting applications and hiring whoever seems like the best fit, by whatever criteria you think is best. It's a system that empowers business owners and entrepreneurs rather than parasitic government employees who have never worked a real job in their lives.

Now, that's all changed. In the 1950s, less than a third of American employers had an HR office. By the 80s, more than 70 percent did.[207] In 1963, no companies had "equal employment opportunity" officers (the forerunners of today's DEI staff). By the 80s nearly half of companies had one, and today a large company without DEI staff might as well be an Egyptian house without lamb's blood over the doorway, waiting for a visit from the federal government's Angel of Death.

Why do so many people fear being fired from their job for a single bad joke? Why are you forced to attend tedious workplace trainings every year that sound like political lectures and are designed to make you feel racial guilt for being white? It's because federal civil rights law is kept vague, and there is little standard for what corporations can do to comply other than show total loyalty to the unholy trinity of Diversity, Inclusion, and Equity. And so, companies have done that. In the immediate aftermath of George Floyd's death, hiring for DEI roles increased by a whopping 55%.[208] It wasn't because the world suddenly needed more do-nothing diversity hires. It was companies reading the zeitgeist, and making sure they weren't the ones caught not applauding for Stalin.

It all reminds me of a quote from one of my favorite writers, Theodore Dalrymple:

"Political correctness is communist propaganda writ small. In my study of communist societies, I came to the conclusion that the purpose of communist propaganda was not to persuade or convince, not to inform, but to humiliate; and therefore, the less it corresponded to reality the better. When people are forced to remain silent when they are being told the most obvious lies, or even worse when they are forced to repeat the lies themselves, they lose once and for all their sense of probity. To assent to obvious lies is in some small way to become evil oneself. One's standing to resist anything is thus eroded, and even destroyed. A society of emasculated liars is easy to control. I think if you examine political correctness, it has the same effect and is intended to."[209]

TO INFINITY, AND BEYOND

However, we aren't being held hostage by a single law; rather, it is a whole constellation of laws, policies, court rulings, and so on. The 1964 act that Goldwater opposed set a template that has been copied all over the place.

Over the course of the 1960s, Presidents Lyndon Johnson and then Richard Nixon issued executive orders that required both federal contractors and the government itself to be non-discriminatory in hiring. But then, a twist: Both orders defined "non-discrimination" as requiring "affirmative action" to remedy the supposed effects of discrimination. In other words, they required discrimination and preferential treatment, based on race.

At a glance, affirmative action—giving a person a boost specifically because of their skin color or their chromosomes—obviously violates the Civil Rights Act, which bans discrimination in hiring, firing, or promotions when based on race or sex. It also violates the 14th Amendment, which guarantees American citizens the equal protection of the laws. But the liberal Supreme Court of the time—the same Court discovering rights like abortion—rubberstamped this radical reinterpretation. And ever since, this revision has been allowed to stand virtually unchallenged: That "civil rights" is not treating all citizens equally, but instead radical social engineering for the sake of creating whatever woke bureaucrats think society *ought* to look like.

In 1972, Congress passed Title IX as part of the Higher Education Act. The text of the law is brief: "No person in the United States shall, on the basis of sex, be excluded from participation in, be denied the benefits of, or be subjected to discrimination under any education program or activity receiving Federal financial assistance." Taken literally, this should just ban things like, say, requiring women to get a higher test score to gain admission to a school. But just like the Civil Rights Act, bureaucrats have instead used the law to give themselves a general mandate to engage in social engineering to eradicate supposed "discrimination." Schools have abolished popular male sports teams and created unpopular women's teams that they struggle to even recruit athletes for, just to comply with Title IX mandates. During the Obama years, schools were ordered to create special kangaroo courts with low standards of evidence to police sexual assault (rather than just leaving such cases to the courts, where they belong), and if they didn't, bam, Title

IX violation. And in 2015, a professor at Northwestern University, Laura Kipniss, was subject to a lengthy investigation on the grounds that she had violated Title IX by . . . criticizing Title IX![210]

In 2015, the Obama White House ordered American K–12 schools to scale back suspensions for violent or disruptive students because suspended students were more likely to have some kind of disability (whether there was a lucid diagnosis to support their so-called disability or not) and so (the Administration said) too many suspensions violated the Rehabilitation Act of 1973.[211]

I could cite examples for an entire book (and other people have). Why are so many police departments becoming so much less aggressive in enforcing the law? It's not just because of Soros DAs and blue city governments. It's also because of pressure from the federal civil rights bureaucracy. In 2009, the DOJ's Civil Rights Division launched a two-year investigation of Seattle police, accusing them of violating the constitution and civil rights law because of "excessive" use of force and because their police stops showed racial disparities.[212] In 2013, this investigation resulted in Seattle police placing themselves under federal oversight. Seattle cops had to endorse constant anti-bias training. Their stop data, arrest data, and use-of-force data were subject to constant scrutiny (requiring, among other things, vastly more paperwork).[213] In 2023, the Biden DOJ congratulated Seattle for "consistent compliance" with the decree—and coincidentally, Seattle's violent crime rate hit a 15-year high.[214, 215] Many other bloodstained cities across America, from Baltimore to Chicago to Ferguson, Missouri, have had the same experience, which already overstretched police hobbled by federal investigators policing their every action for phantom "racism."

It's not all at the federal level either. States and cities, including conservative ones, have passed their own civil rights laws with the same flaws as the federal ones.

By now, just about everything imaginable can become a "civil rights issue." When AIDS emerged in the 1980s, nearly 30,000 Americans were infected by blood transfusions tainted with HIV.[216] The FDA responded by barring men who have sex with men from donating blood, due to their astronomically higher rate of carrying HIV (knowingly or not). That fact has never changed and gay men are still vastly more likely to have HIV than other potential blood donors. Of course, blood is tested for HIV and other pathogens, but since no blood test is perfect, it seemed logical not to run the risk of passing on HIV via a lifesaving procedure in a hospital.

Yet the Biden White House decided to add this unnecessary risk back into the lives of patients, rolling back this prohibition, saying blood donations from gay men are fine, just as long as they haven't had multiple partners within the last three months.[217]

"The implementation of these recommendations will represent a significant milestone for the agency and the LGBTQI+ community," an FDA director said when the change was made. Health is nothing compared to the all-consuming force of civil rights, though. And this disregard for public health in the name of political correctness is all the more ironic because these same liberals, who disregard the risk of AIDS donations, are probably still wearing masks and would seek to have you fired, today, for not getting COVID vaccines.

In the civil rights era, identity politics is *everything* and more important than anything else. In the words of Lenin, it is all about, "who will overtake whom."

TAKING THE PLUNGE

I'm sure you're not surprised to hear any of this, and you don't need me to tell you that all of this is bad. You all know this is bad. So why am I taking the time to talk to you all about it, especially this far into my book?

Because, quite simply, *no campaign against wokeness has a shot without confronting civil rights law directly.* Conservatives have learned to complain about wokeness in schools, in corporate America, and in government, but few conservatives know where this wokeness is actually coming from. It's coming from our nationwide patchwork of civil rights laws.

This knowledge is crucial. Imagine if conservatives had spent fifty years complaining about abortion, but without actually understanding where it came from. Imagine if they simply complained about schools promoting abortion, about countless clinics offering the procedure, and about the government funding it, yet somehow remained clueless of *Roe v. Wade,* the legislation in place mandating it, and various laws and policies propping it up. If that was the case, then abortion-on-demand would still be the law of the land in America.

Fortunately, pro-life activists knew better. They knew that to turn the tide on abortion, they needed to pass new laws, and they needed to appoint judges who would pave the way for overturning *Roe*.

To beat wokeness, we need the same attitude.

Want police to enforce the law rather than worrying about the skin color of who they handcuff? You need to change civil rights law. Want schools to stop penalizing white and Asian applicants? You need to tweak civil rights law. Want to make woke capital obsolete? Adjust the law so they don't have to center their plans around avoiding a civil rights lawsuit. Want your daughter's locker room free of leering 40-yo men wearing bad wigs? Gotta change civil rights law.

There is a vast federal bureaucracy of civil rights enforcers, who even under Republican presidents have relentlessly pressured private and state-level institutions to be more woke. From now on, conservatives have to see obliterating these bureaucrats as a top priority.

Along with *Griggs vs. Duke Power*, there are dozens of other court rulings that have upheld the "woke" interpretation of civil rights, fixing discrimination to somehow requires *more* discrimination. Conservatives need to be vetting and appointing judges who will overturn those rulings, and affirm the common-sense, originalist version of civil rights, that all people are to be treated as individuals rather than identity-group categories.

We have to slay the dragon. Go for the head, and the body will follow.

I recognize this is hard, for basically one single, overriding reason. Because it involves the word "civil rights." The left has turned the various laws of the 1960s into a kind of American sacred scripture. If your children attend public schools, the 1964 Civil Rights Act is guaranteed to be in bold print in their history textbooks. It is treated as an unambiguously good development for America, as important as the 13th Amendment 100 years before it.

The legal regime we live under is one of the strongest examples of the left exerting its power to define America's moral horizons and its sense of right and wrong. Breaking that conditioning is tough, but essential. The Left screams when someone criticizes "civil rights" because it is sacred to their agenda. Eric Hoffer said decades ago, "To know a person's religion we need not listen to his profession of faith but must find his brand of intolerance." The Left tolerates no criticism of civil rights because it is the edifice that countless dogmas and destructive policies of the last 70 years have been built on. The respect they do not have for our own Constitution they have infused into their second, far more precious sham constitution that has misappropriated the term "civil rights."

Overturning this is going to require basically all the attitude adjustments I advocated in Part 2. We have to reject the left's framing of the issue, which is designed to give them everything they want and let them control us. We have to get imaginative with tactics and think like liberals would. We have to be ready to not blink as horrible, dishonest people call us racists for wanting to *get rid* of racist laws. We have to be active and aggressive, instead of inert and complacent. And finally, we can't be doomers. We have to realize that *winning is possible.*

Because if we do this right, winning absolutely *is* possible. In fact, we've already won on something very similar in the past. The Civil Rights Act isn't the only law of the 1960s that gets bold print in every textbook. Another one is 1965's Voting Rights Act. The VRA had several positive aspects, like banning the literacy tests that were used to deny so many black Americans the vote for a century after the civil war. The law played a central role in finally, definitively ending Jim Crow in America.

But the law had many other side effects which only became clear to conservatives over the decades that followed. One part of the law, for instance, singled out specific states and counties and required them to obtain clearance from the Department of Justice before changing any of their election laws. Over time, this law simply became a way for Democratic administrations to prevent red states from making changes they saw as harmful to the left. In 2011, Eric Holder's DOJ used the provision to block Texas from implementing policies as basic as voter ID.[218] In Arizona, the Obama Department of Justice vetoed Arizona's electoral maps for not being friendly enough to Democrats.[219] And most incredibly, in 2009, Holder blocked the town of Kinston, North Carolina from switching from partisan elections to non-partisan ones, on the grounds that blacks *obviously* always vote Democrat, and so removing the ability to vote specifically for a Democrat was an attack on their voting rights.[220]

There were other impacts too. In 1982, the DNC sued the RNC, accusing them of violating the VRA for actions such as striking voters from the rolls for having non-working mailing addresses and hiring off-duty police to stand outside voting precincts (you guessed it: *Raaay-cist*).[221] Inexcusably, rather than properly fight the case, the RNC entered a consent decree simply agreeing not to conduct all kinds of election-related activities. Of course, the Democrats were still allowed to perform these activities themselves!

Within just a few years of its passage, just like the Civil Rights Act, the VRA had gone from a tool to end Jim Crow to a tool for helping Democrats perpetuate fraud and win elections. Yet for decades, any criticism at all of the VRA act was essentially unthinkable. After all, it had "voting rights" in its name.

But eventually, Republican leaders learned to ignore the left's magic spells. They ignored the cries of "racist!" They mounted a serious legal and legislative campaign to roll back the law's worst excesses. In 2013, they got the Supreme Court to strike down the VRA's preclearance regime, no more letting Eric Holder or Merrick Garland micromanage election laws. In 2018, Republicans finally escaped the ridiculous consent decree.[222]

And that was a weaker GOP! The GOP of Mitt Romney and John McCain checked the Voting Rights Act. If that's the case, then the GOP of Donald Trump can blow up the left's totalitarian "civil rights" sham.

STRIKING BACK

The good news is that, once we accept what needs to be done, taking action is a lot easier than you might think. Precisely because conservatives have thought so little about it, the "woke" version of civil rights has been able to penetrate deep into even red state governments. Waking up from that is easy. Red states can, practically overnight, abolish DEI at their state universities. They can ban affirmative action and ban awarding state and local government contracts based on race or sex rather than merit.

At the federal level, huge amounts of institutional wokeness are propped up by executive orders, or by "interpretations" of federal law that can be gutted and removed. Win back the White House, and it's all there for the taking. Other woke aspects of the law are propped up by the courts. So when we appoint judges, we can have the Federalist Society vet for nominees who will overturn those precedents. We don't have to repeal the 1965 Civil Rights Act, or even change it very much. We just have to change how it's interpreted.

Don't fret about this sparking a backlash. In reality, one reason the left has to use "civil rights" as a shield so much is that so much of the specific policies it mandates are overwhelmingly unpopular. Whenever affirmative action is given a straight up-or-down vote for what it actually is—differential treatment based on race—voters reject it decisively. Voters have endorsed bans on government affirmative action in Michigan, Washington, Nebraska, and Oklahoma. In California, they've done it twice. In 2020, despite a massive, richly funded propaganda campaign looking to re-legalize race-based discrimination in the state, voters weren't fooled, and rejected it by 15 points despite also voting easily for Joe Biden.[223]

In fact, as I write this, the opportunity for an aggressive campaign against discriminatory affirmative action is right before us. In June 2023, the Supreme Court decided *Students for Fair Admissions v. Harvard*, which threw out as illegal a wide array of the practices colleges used to racially discriminate in their admissions. But while the ruling didn't explicitly say so, its reasoning strongly implied that the Court's conservative majority would be open to throwing out other facets of the woke civil rights regime.

Conservatives need to recognize the opportunity and seize it. And fortunately, some are. Just days after the Harvard ruling, thirteen Republican AGs led by Tennessee's Jonathan Skrmetti sent letters to several Fortune 100 companies, warning them that they would face legal action if they continued to hire, promote, or dole out contracts based on race rather than ability, citing the new Supreme Court precedent.[224]

We can't let such threats be bluster. Where we find policies like this, we need to be ready to sue. Where we can pass laws at the state level, we need to pass them.

The ground is ripe. Conservatives can and should start to expose the sham civil rights regime. Rip off the dress of civil rights in drag and show it for what it really is—the gross face of discriminatory wokeness.

CHAPTER TEN

The Federal Revolution

"Those who make only half a revolution dig their own graves."
—Georg Buchner

DAY ONE

" . . . and will, to the best of my ability, preserve, protect and defend the Constitution of the United States."

It's noon on January 20, 2025, and with that line, America has its forty-seventh president, a Republican. Joe Biden has been tossed from office after a single ignominious term, after a close but clear rejection by the Electoral College.

Is that President Donald Trump? Tim Scott? Vivek Ramaswamy? Someone you've never heard of?

The name doesn't really matter. What matters is what happens next.

The new president's first executive order drops at about 4:00 pm, mere moments after the new president returns from the traditional wreath-laying ceremony at the Tomb of the Unknowns at Arlington National Cemetery. Fittingly, the president's first order is to restore a directive from President Trump's first term directing the Department of Justice to prosecute rioters who vandalize or damage statues and monuments during protests.[225] When Joe Biden took office four years earlier, repealing that order was one of his first actions.

The press shrugs. Is that all? Then, at 4:10 pm, another announcement arrives: In a terse press release, the new president announces that Christopher

Wray, halfway through his ten-year term as FBI director, has been dismissed, and he will be appointing a new FBI director.

At 4:25 pm, another press release arrives, this one announcing that the president will be cutting short the term of the incumbent Chairman of the Joint Chiefs of Staff, Charles Brown Jr. The nation's military, the president says, should not be led by a General who released a weepy video about George Floyd while the nation convulsed in riots.[226]

Those firings aren't the last ones. At 4:50 pm, another release announces that the president will be dismissing *all* the various inspectors general within federal agencies and placing his own appointees in their place.

By now, the yelps on Twitter are getting loud. But the blows don't stop. At 5:30 pm a bombshell drops.

"Executive Order 11246 is hereby repealed," a short press release from the new Administration announces. Reporters at *Politico* exchange confused looks. "Order 11246? What's that?"

After some frantic Googling, they learn exactly what it is. For half a century, Order 11246 ordered federal contractors to engage in "affirmative action" to make sure they filled job positions with "diverse" hires rather than merely the best ones. Now, at a stroke, it's gone.

Before reporters can even process that one, another notice arrives at 6:10 pm: Executive Orders 13950 and 13957, issued by President Trump in fall 2020 and repealed by Biden three months later, are once again in force. Order 13950 bans sensitivity training in the executive branch, as well as for federal contractors. Order 13957 creates a new category of federal employee, Schedule F, which can be fired far more easily, like the president's other political hires.

At 6:30 pm, cameras monitoring the White House pick up a surprising sight. Dozens of White House employees marching out of the Eisenhower Executive Office Building which sits next to the White House. Career staff at the Office of Management and Budget, and at the National Security Council, have been told they're getting relocated, permanently.

By the end of dinner time, Washington is in a frenzy. Journalists sob on Twitter that "our democracy" is gone, it's *finished.* AOC has already introduced articles of impeachment, which will sit impotent in the Republican House. It is the most momentous and diverse day of political action in American history.

And there are still 1,460 days of the term to go.

THE MAN WHO WOULD BE (LIKE A) KING

*"It is an approved maxim in war,
never to do what the enemy wishes you to do."*
—Napoleon

The scenario above might be a work of fiction, but that doesn't mean it's outlandish. Everything mentioned there is something that a well-prepared Republican administration really can (and should) implement on Day 1 of a new administration. In fact, striking hard right away is crucial to seriously rolling back wokeness at the federal level.

Every second of a presidential term is precious. The federal government is a leviathan. Changing it is difficult and will always involve unexpected delays and setbacks. While I believe Donald Trump to be one of the greatest presidents in American history, much of his vision was left incomplete for one simple reason. Trump and his team were overwhelmingly political outsiders, it took them a very long time to figure out just how much power they actually had. In terms of appointments, executive orders, and memoranda, Trump's very best year was his last one, yet almost all of that year's agenda was repealed by Joe Biden before it could take effect.

If we use Donald Trump's final year as the blueprint for year 1 of the next Republican presidency, we have the groundwork for the most effective conservative administration in history.

It's a common dream for Americans regardless of their politics, to dream of their ideal candidate winning a dramatic presidential victory, sweeping into office with a powerful mandate, and fixing the country's problems virtually overnight.

Needless to say, it typically doesn't happen. America is, fortunately, not a monarchy, and not a military dictatorship. We're a republic, with coequal branches of government that check and balance one another.

That's a good thing, but of course it's also bad news. America has a lot of problems, and even if we win the 2024 election, no president can snap his fingers and restore America to the height of its glory.

But I have some good news. For many of the worst poisons and afflictions in America, the president actually *can* fix things and get the country back on the right path, virtually overnight. His power has always been there. What conservatives have lacked is not power. What we have lacked, too often, is the right knowledge, the right targets, the right ambition. As President Lyndon Johnson said, "Doing the right thing is not the problem. Knowing what the right thing is, that's the challenge."

But above all, what we've lacked is the *self-confidence* to use the powers we have. Where the left has made, we have seen ourselves as unworthy of unmaking. That must change.

This is a pragmatic chapter. You will not find this chapter filled with constitutional amendments that I wish Congress would pass. That's because amending the Constitution *will not happen.* Amending the Constitution requires two-thirds of Congress and three-fourths of the states. The last time Republicans had two thirds of both houses of Congress, Ulysses S. Grant was president. It's not going to happen. If a Republican politician is campaigning on constitutional amendments he wants to implement, he isn't being serious and he is wasting your time.

This is a chapter of things that *can* happen, right away. I want to lay out a vision of what conservatives can and *should* demand that their next president do. I want to present the things that there are *no excuses* for not doing, because the president's ability to do them is beyond question. The president is not a king, but on a lot of matters, he has the power of one. And to undo the mess that Washington has created, he is going to need to use that power. Only at the end of this chapter will I dare to suggest what a unified Republican Congress, feeling emboldened to improve America's future, might accomplish.

In any game of strategy, a good thought exercise for choosing your next move is to think "what does my opponent fear me doing?" This maxim is also a good rule for fixing up wayward superpowers.

The left has spent the better part of a century building the U.S. federal government into the single largest, most complex, most powerful, and most impenetrable organization on Earth. They fear that this organization might be torn down in a manner that cannot be quickly rebuilt, and that this organization might be turned *against them* as it has been turned against so many Americans.

Surface-level reforms are not what they worry about. They do not fear agency heads who reverse some policy that can be restored the moment a

Democrat is back in charge again. They don't fear symbolic attempts to fire a single person which can be fought over endlessly in court.

What the left fears is a Republican president who plays to win, not just on one issue, but on everything.

In summer 2023, *The New York Times* warned about the sweeping acts that a second Trump administration (but really, *any* aggressive Republican administration) could carry out:

> Mr. Trump and his associates have a broader goal: to alter the balance of power by increasing the president's authority over every part of the federal government that now operates, by either law or tradition, with any measure of independence from political interference by the White House. . . . Mr. Trump intends to bring independent agencies . . . under direct presidential control.
>
> He wants to revive the practice of "impounding" funds, refusing to spend money Congress has appropriated for programs a president doesn't like—a tactic that lawmakers banned under President Richard Nixon.
>
> He intends to strip employment protections from tens of thousands of career civil servants, making it easier to replace them if they are deemed obstacles to his agenda. And he plans to scour the intelligence agencies, the State Department and the defense bureaucracies to remove officials he has vilified as "the sick political class that hates our country."[227]

As always, strip away their ominous warnings about the End of the Republic and read the deeper truth. The left fears a Republican president who acts like a chief executive.

So why don't we give them one?

RECONQUER THE WHITE HOUSE

Chances are, you remember how much of a struggle President Trump's term in office was. The president could call for any number of things, issue any number of executive orders, but for all four years he was hobbled by an executive branch that was unhelpful and unenthusiastic at best, and an active sabotage operation at worst.

You've also heard the term "Deep State" thrown around a lot, but what is it? You might think it's the intelligence apparatus: The CIA, NSA, and FBI. You might think it's the security state: The figures in the military and the State department who maintain America's geopolitical outlook of "invade the world, invite the world" going without end.

All of those are parts of the Deep State. But the actual nerve center of the Deep State is a far less prominent piece of the government, the Office of Management and Budget.

OMB's origins lie in the 1920s, when the Bureau of the Budget existed as a small arm of the U.S. Treasury, tasked with (wait for it) making the president's budget. Under FDR, the Bureau of the Budget was moved into the Executive Office of the President, and under his expanded New Deal version of the federal government, its obligations expanded rapidly. Under Nixon, it was given the name it has today.

OMB is, in essence, the culmination of 20th century academic progressivism. It was meant to be a technocratic army, providing "expert" control of government that continued from one administration to another.

As it currently exists, a core part of OMB's job is coordinating among various agencies, and making sure the president's policies and plans are implemented. Yet, crucially, other than a handful of people at the top, OMB is *not* staffed by a president's political appointees. Instead, it's staffed by career bureaucrats. The word "bureaucracy" comes from the French for "rule by desk workers," so take a guess what kind of politics those people hold.

A veteran of President Trump's White House once explained to me, at length, how much of an obstacle OMB had been for his administration. It was, in essence, the Deep State's way of controlling the White House itself.

"They're a management barrier between the president and all his agencies; they have all the institutional knowledge," he said. "They're in everything. You can't do anything without OMB. They're on top of your ass. They have representatives at every agency, watching it. Because they're located in the physical White House, they claim that they speak for the President, even though they're routinely telling federal agencies to do the opposite of what the President actually wants."

On more than one occasion, the staffer told me, President Trump would order certain regulations to be cut or amended, but OMB would block or water the order down once it went up to them for approval (among other things, OMB has final approval over every regulation enacted by agencies!). If staff appealed to the political appointees atop OMB, far too often they would side with the bureaucrats out of fear of upsetting them.

The former staffer described one bizarre scene where a Trump appointee was summoned to the Eisenhower Executive Office Building to be chastised by an OMB bureaucrat for his efforts at draining the swamp. The OMB official chastised him and then pointed towards the nearby West Wing and said "See that? That's the President's office. When I give you an order, that's where it's coming from."

Fortunately, this appointee had the confidence to hit back.

"Is that so?" he said. "Well, President Trump is a friend of mine. And I'm pretty sure he doesn't know who the f*** you are. In fact, I was in the Oval with him yesterday and he told me he's thrilled with the job I'm doing."

Sadly, though, scenes like that were the exception, not the rule. Most appointees didn't have the personal relationship with President Trump necessary to counter OMB's interference.

"The only people that know how to move the bureaucracy are the bureaucrats at OMB," my friend continued. "And the thing is, they don't actually have any real power. They've just *taken* power by knowing all the routes through the maze of government and getting the president to delegate to them."

The solution, he said, isn't to commandeer OMB, but to eliminate it.

"If you try to control them, they just run circles around you. They're career bureaucrats, and we're not. You have to completely bucking destroy it," he said (okay, he used a slightly different word). "Just return to cabinet government—The President has to have a real, weekly Cabinet meeting with secretaries, where he tells them what to do, and they go to their agencies and do it."

But if that's not possible, he told me, there is at least a simple starting step.

"Send them out of the White House. Shove them back into the Treasury building if you want. But make a symbolic statement and get them away from the president." At every step possible, he said, the next Republican president must shove OMB aside in favor of directly managing the agencies with political appointees.

OMB isn't the only other permanent White House organ that needs to be brought to heel in a new, more assertive GOP presidency. Another is the National Security Council. Remember the sham 2019 impeachment of President Trump? You might remember that impeachment was over Trump calling Ukraine's President Zelensky and asking him to take a look at possible Biden family corruption in his country (imagine!).

But why were President Trump's private diplomatic phone calls leaking to the public? Well, that feat happened because the National Security Council's Eric Ciaramella, a Democrat and CIA employee detailed to the White House, listened in on the call, then leaked what happened to the intelligence community's inspector general, who in turn leaked it all to Congress.[228]

My friend described the NSC as another mass of would-be saboteurs who must be moved out of the White House and away from the president, in favor of trusted, politically loyal personnel who will carry out the president's vision instead of overriding it.

My friend flagged the many inspectors general as another office in need of sweeping turnover on Day 1 of a new GOP admin.

"Inspectors general are supposed to be agency watchdogs to prevent waste and fraud," my Trump Administration friend told me. "Instead, they've become Congress's spies inside the executive branch. They open investigations every time a cabinet secretary does something they consider 'questionable.' Trump should have fired them Day One."

Trump didn't fire them Day One, because neither he nor any other Republicans understood the danger. Now, we do. There is no need to make the same blunder again.

THE RETURN OF SCHEDULE F

One asset for remaking OMB, and countless other domains of government, will be the revival of Schedule F.

During the final months of the Trump Administration, the Trump White House laid the groundwork for an entirely new category of federal employee, christened Schedule F.

Out of the vast federal workforce of about 2 million people, currently only about 4,000 people are considered political appointees, subject to being replaced every time the White House changes hands.

But the reality, of course, is that far more than 4,000 employees are involved in actually concocting U.S. policy. The Schedule F plan, in short, would reclassify as many as fifty thousand additional executive branch workers, those related to crafting federal policies, as political employees subject to at-will employment.

An article by Axios lays out what could happen if Schedule F returns:

> Trump, in theory, could fire tens of thousands of career government officials with no recourse for appeals. He could replace them with people he believes are more loyal to him and to his "America First" agenda.
>
> Even if Trump did not deploy Schedule F to this extent, the very fact that such power exists could create a significant chilling effect on government employees.
>
> It would effectively upend the modern civil service, triggering a shock wave across the bureaucracy.[229]

Does that sound exciting? Remember, we must do what the enemy fears! The left has gotten very used to a "non-partisan" civil service that is, of course, totally in their corner on almost every issue. Conservatives must stop taking that problem for granted.

The next conservative administration shouldn't save Schedule F for the last days of a term. It should revive it day one and hour one.

BRING THE MILITARY TO HEEL

One of the most dangerous moments of the Trump presidency came during the George Floyd summer of 2020, but didn't get nearly as much attention as it should have. As rioters rampaged throughout American cities, President Trump was publicly mulling whether he should deploy U.S. troops to restore order in Washington, Minneapolis, and elsewhere. He would have been categorically in the right to do so, just as George H.W. Bush was in the right to deploy the National Guard to suppress the Los Angeles riots of 1991.

But as Trump considered what to do, the chairman of the joint chiefs, Mark Milley, put out a very strangely worded letter.

"Every member of the U.S. military swears an oath to support and defend the Constitution and the values embedded within it," Gen. Milley wrote. "This document . . . gives Americans the right to freedom of speech and peaceful assembly. We in uniform—all branches, all components, and all ranks—remain committed to our national values and principles embedded in the Constitution."

Milley then continued: "As members of the Joint Force—comprised of all races, colors, and creeds—you embody the ideals of our Constitution. Please remind all of our troops and leaders that we will uphold the values of our nation, and operate consistent with national laws and our own high standards of conduct at all times."

Handwritten next to his signature on the letter, Milley added a postscript: "We all committed our lives to the idea that is America—we will stay true to that oath and the American people."[230]

What is odd about this letter? In a word, context. Just one day before this letter was written, President Trump had publicly suggested he might invoke the Insurrection Act of 1807 to order active-duty U.S. troops to quell the chaos in America's cities.[231]

In the end, he didn't, and the moment passed. I can't prove it, but I think Milley's words signal that America came very close to a dramatic constitutional crisis. I believe that Mark Milley was laying the groundwork to defy the orders of his commander in chief. I believe he was on the brink of launching a military coup d'etat.

According to self-serving leaks from Milley or his close staff, Milley nearly resigned in June 2020, but instead backed away. Instead, he vowed to "fight" Trump "from the inside," even if it ended in his court martial.[232]

Well, that court martial never happened. Instead, Milley outlasted Trump. I've already described the military he helped create, one where domestic social engineering is the highest priority, far ahead of any priority rationally related to the national defense.

As I write this, Air Force General Charles Brown is set to take over for

Milley. As head of the Air Force, Brown signed off on diversity target quotas for his branch, calling for radical cuts to the number of white men for the sake of precious diversity.[233]

Sure, a Republican president could order Brown to stop worrying about race quotas and start worrying about America's security. But you know the drill by now. Ideologically hostile actors *will* undermine a genuine America first, anti-woke, MAGA agenda in favor of their own priorities. They can't be ordered around. It's time to reverse course, instead.

While changing the civilian government might be full of obstacles, shifting the military in a positive direction is more straightforward. The U.S. president is, after all, commander-in-chief of the armed forces. The current military leadership signed off on vaccine mandates, transgender troops, renaming historic bases, diversity-based promotions, and more. It's time we gave them the heave-ho. While the president can't necessarily kick any general he wants out of the military, he has absolute authority to strip them of their commands and exile them to irrelevant positions where they can't do damage. The next president should clear out the Joint Chiefs, and any of their subordinates he doesn't have rock-solid confidence are on board with restoring the military's dignity and its mission. Once the military has real commanders again, have them stop paying for the gender reassignment surgeries for trans people and stop obsessing over diversity quotas. Then, announce an immediate amnesty for any soldiers pushed out of the military due to vaccine mandates, and allow them to rejoin the service if they wish without penalty. This isn't just about undoing that particular injustice. Kicking out vaccine refusers was partly a project to politically remake the military. It *must* be undone.

Finally, have the military actually fulfill the only mission they exist to do, and order them to secure America's borders.

The press, and plenty of retired generals who have grown fat and comfortable from the current system, will moan that our "national readiness" is being damaged. Conservatives in Washington and across America should ignore them. Remember, don't get tricked by the left's drag military, and don't fall for their framing. Remember that our pro-woke generals have done nothing but lose for the past twenty years. They are discredited. Treat them like it.

TAKE COMMAND AT THE DOJ

If any arm of government has grown drunk on its power and sense of entitlement, it's the FBI.

The FBI likes to cultivate the impression that it is somehow an autonomous arm of government, not subject to the elected chief executive. Based on this, it does things like launch investigations of active presidential campaigns because its personnel don't like the campaign's position on Russia. It does things like entrap lockdown opponents in a cockamamie plot to kidnap Gretchen Whitmer. It dispatches agents to target Latin Mass attendees. It labels anti-CRT parents as domestic extremists.

The next Republican president can't simply fire Christopher Wray, name a replacement, and hope for the best. That's what we did with James Comey, and we all saw what happened next.

Instead, it's time to have an attorney general and FBI director who will actively monitor what the FBI is up to. Former Trump staffer James Bacon came on my show in summer 2023, and described a surprising role model conservatives should look to, Vice President Dick Cheney. Cheney was such an active presence at the Defense Department that he had his own office set up at the Pentagon. Cheney, he said, understood that the only way to make sure the administration's priorities were executed was to give bureaucrats orders face to face.

"Once a week, have the Attorney General walk across the street to the FBI building, and review all the cases they're working on," he told me. "If he finds a weird case like targeting a conservative group for partisan reasons, he should say 'This case is closed, thanks. And who thought this was a good idea? Pack your stuff and get out.'"

Active management is the order of the day. Boss people around!

LAY OFF THE STATE DEPARTMENT

Hungarian Prime Minister Viktor Orban is one of the world leaders that American conservatives identify with the most. Despite colossal pressure from the European Union, the UN, and expatriate billionaire George Soros,

Orban's government has secured its borders, implemented pro-family policies, and taken the decidedly radical position of being pro-Christianity instead of treating it as a relic of the past.

The Trump Administration, understandably, was friendly with Orban. Yet even as Trump sent them friendly overtures, the U.S. State Department had its own ideas. In 2017 and 2018, it was moving forward with plans to spend $700,000 to support "independent" (i.e. left-wing) media in the country. Only in summer 2018 did the Trump Administration notice what was afoot and successfully cancel the grant.[234]

This small episode illustrates an important reality. Whatever might be going on at home in the U.S., the American State Department is *always* pushing woke nonsense overseas. During the Floyd summer of 2020, the U.S. embassy in South Korea put up both a Pride flag *and* BLM flag until the Trump White House ordered them to take it down.[235] Of course, during the Biden years, the Pride flag has become the de facto second American flag, flying at U.S. embassies all around the world during Pride Month.

What do Americans get in return for all of this? Well, some of them get killed, fighting in the wars that the State Department helps suck America into. Others get to watch as their tax dollars spread the woke religion worldwide.

Many conservatives at this point understand the value of pulling back America's military presence around the world. But it's time to recognize the value of pulling back America's *diplomatic* presence, too.

So, let's do it. Cut off all nonsensical foreign spending to "promote independent media" or whatever stupid labels they give it. Then, bring the diplomats home. America does not need nearly 14,000 overseas Foreign Service personnel. Keep enough around to help out U.S. citizens who have passport problems, and get the rest home. If our global neighbors need to negotiate something important, they can call us up on Zoom.

REVOKE THE ORDERS

Once the president has prioritized crafting an executive branch that actually obeys him, we can turn to the realm of policy. At the outset of this chapter, I mentioned the president repealing Executive Order 11246.

Yes, I know, "Order 11246" sounds like something from a Star Wars movie. But there's nothing fantastic about it. The order is, quite simply, one of the skeleton keys that makes the federal government so woke.

Have you ever thought how odd the term "affirmative action" is? What does "acting affirmatively" have to do with race quotas? The term's use, as we know it today, largely stems from E.O. 11246.

Issued by Lyndon Johnson in 1965, E.O. 11246 bars all companies receiving federal contracts higher than a trivial amount from engaging in discrimination based on race, sex, religion, or the like. So far, so good. But then, crucially, the order also required companies to "take *affirmative action*" to ensure "equal" treatment of various protected groups.[236]

You know, and everybody knows, what the outcome of this "equal opportunity" push was. Instead of becoming an order that *banned* racial discrimination, E.O. 11246 has been reinterpreted, by both companies and by the government itself, as an order that *mandates* discrimination. Fearful of losing immensely important government contracts, companies have created de facto racial quota systems, hiring, and promoting based on skin color to avoid any risk of losing lucrative federal contracts.

So, it's time to get rid of it. And while we're at it, repeal Executive Order 11478, the order that orders the federal government itself to practice affirmative action in all of its hiring decisions. In the place of both orders, the next conservative president can issue replacements, making it official that the government now (correctly) interprets U.S. civil rights laws as banning *all* discrimination, including reverse discrimination.

REVIVE EXECUTIVE ORDER 13950

Along with Schedule F, Order 13950 was another executive action from President Trump that would have been momentous if he'd issued it in his first year. Instead, it became a historical what-if by virtue of rolling out in the final months of his term, only to be immediately junked by President Brandon.

Well, we won't make that mistake again. Order 13950 was President Trump's decree banning aggressive, critical theory-infused "sensitivity training" within the federal government within any companies receiving federal contracts. The moment it was issued, it sent diversity rackets across the country into a panic.[237] The DEI racket survives, despite being utterly worthless, because companies fear being sued or losing contracts if they don't pay their protection money. If they have to fear the opposite—*losing* federal funds for inflicting woke propaganda lectures on employees—the practice will melt away.

DEFUND THE NGOS AND THE DEI RACKET

Imagine if I told you that the federal government gives away your money for the explicit purpose of helping liberals sue you. Across America, there are hundreds, maybe *thousands* of organizations that are politically left-wing, yet heavily or even completely dependent on subsidies from the federal government in order to pursue a political agenda.

For instance, in the Department of Housing and Urban Development, there is an annual program known as the Fair Housing Initiatives Program.[238] Every year, HUD makes tens of millions of dollars in grants to groups as part of the program. In spring 2023, 182 organizations collected a total of $54 million in FHIP grants.

One of the dimensions of FHIP is grants for the "Private Enforcement Initiative"—AKA, simply handing out taxpayer dollars so that left-leaning "housing non-profits" can sue landlords for alleged discrimination. One of the 2023 recipients of these dollars, for instance, is the Chicago branch of the Lawyers' Committee for Civil Rights Under Law. As I write this, the Lawyers' Committee's national arm is suing Donald Trump, on the grounds that January 6 was a "white supremacist" attack that violated the Ku Klux Klan Act.[239]

Some federal grants are dressed up as paying for a service yet are no less political. In 2022, for instance, the Biden Administration's Department of Agriculture forked out almost $13 million for various DEI "services," such as $931,000 to the consulting firm Accenture to do an equity audit of the food stamps program.[240]

It's easy to blame this DEI spending on Democrats holding the White House, but it's not that simple. Much of this spending was happening even while Trump was president. That FHIP program, paying lawyers to sue Americans? Biden might have paid out $54 million in 2023 . . . but the Trump administration paid out $40 million in 2020.[241]

These are just a handful of initiatives in a handful of agencies, but giveaways like this gut the entire federal government. The American left has a big enough monetary advantage from its dominance of well-funded universities and major foundations like the Aspect Institute, yet they get an even bigger financial cushion courtesy of the U.S. taxpayer.

The next Republican president must make it a priority to shut down these grants *en masse.* In fact, a very reasonable action would be to pause *all* grants until they can be vetted to make sure conservatives aren't funding a war against their own values and livelihoods.

And what about DEI in the government? Simple! Shut it down. For all its problems, the Office of Personnel Management does have one excellent feature. It has provisions for large-scale government layoffs through so-called "Reduction in Force" exercises. Use that to wipe out every DEI office government-wide in one stroke. If that fails for any reason (if there's one thing we learned 4 years ago, it's that federal judges feel entitled to block whatever they want), then get creative, and simply put them all on permanent paid leave. It would literally be better to pay DEI slugs to do nothing than to keep them around ruining things for the people with real jobs.

KILL THE DISINFORMATION OCTOPUS

Since their 2016 election upset, the left has steadily built up a worldwide infrastructure to fight "disinformation" that is little more than a dressed-up, decentralized ideological censorship bureau. Nevertheless, the U.S. federal government sits at the center of this apparatus. The government funds, the government tracks, the government assists, the government asks, the government threatens, and then lo and behold, "disinformation" and "hate speech" gets suppressed by "private actors." No First Amendment issues here!

In just the first two years of the Biden White House, the administration funneled nearly $40 million into grants and contracts that propped up the "disinformation" industry.[242] In the context of federal funding, $40 million isn't a lot, yet it can go a very long way. $20 million per year can mean jobs for 200 people at $100,000 apiece, more than enough to produce a whole bunch of "reports" and "warnings" that justify a wider censorship crackdown.

Mike Benz, head of the anti-censorship Foundation for Freedom Online, emphasized that while this whole system is designed to look independent of Washington, it actually cannot function without it.

"You have to go department by department, and break every single lever they have," he told me. "This industry can't survive without federal backing. It's millions from HHS, millions from the State Department, and so on."

Benz also recommended an even tougher, more scorched-earth tactic. Rather than just shutting down funding wherever possible, the government should announce a new policy of defunding any institution hostile to free speech in America.

"Oh, Stanford has a disinformation center?" Benz told me (they do). "Well, now they no longer qualify for DARPA grants."

SELL THE LAND!

This latest point crucially intersects with what is needed for thriving, conservative cities.

Look anywhere in America, and a pattern is consistent. Density is the death of conservatism. Dense areas are blue areas. Cramped apartments are blue. Detached homes, the kind that families can comfortably live in, breed conservative attitudes.

One excellent way to make sure more of those single-family homes go up, instead of high-rise apartments, is to free up land to build them. East of the Mississippi, almost all land is owned by the private sector or state and local government. But in America's western states, gargantuan amounts of land, even right outside cities, is owned by the federal government. In Utah, Nevada, and Idaho, it's more than sixty percent. In my own state of Arizona, it's about half.[243]

One report estimated that freeing up federal lands for sale could lead to the construction of 300,000 additional homes in Maricopa County,

Arizona alone.[244] More homes over more space means more people buying more affordable single-family homes, and that means more conservatives.

THE COURTS, DUH

This practically goes without saying, but appointments to the federal courts will continue to be one of the most important things any president does. But the next conservative administration will be in an interesting spot, because many of the things conservatives have fought the hardest for have actually been delivered recently. Thanks to President Trump's three Supreme Court picks, *Roe v. Wade* has been overturned, religious liberty has been enormously strengthened, and gun rights are reasonably secure. So, what's next?

The last chapter pointed toward one of the most important priorities. The next conservative president, and the people advising him, should make tearing down the apparatus of "woke" judicial rulings their next target. If the Supreme Court were to throw out *Griggs v. Duke Power*, and label "disparate impact" as the illogical and unconstitutional mess that it is, then the whole federal apparatus that props up wokeness would be gravely damaged. Judicial candidates should be vetted for a willingness to overturn it, the same way we once vetted judges to overturn *Roe*. When hunting for lower-court nominees, we should prioritize judges who will aggressively enforce the recent *Students for Fair Admissions v. Harvard* decision, using it to smash apart the biased admissions policies of America's thousands of federally funded colleges.

OKAY, BUT IF WE HAVE CONGRESS

I've focused so far on what conservatives can do the moment we have the White House again. All of what has been discussed so far requires winning just a single election and is therefore the most attainable. It just requires planning and a small team of visionary people to carry it out.

But our Founders did, in their great wisdom, give us a legislative branch as well, *intending* it to be the nation's most powerful branch.

Granted, for the past few decades it's instead been our most paralyzed branch. But still, what should the agenda be if the American people do entrust us with a Congressional majority once again?

Answering that question starts with answering what kind of person we should be sending to Congress.

In terms of electing lawmakers, our priority should be what I like to call the Four Bs: Boring, Bright, Based, and Brave.

Boring: Yes, you heard right. Legislators should be low on antics, low on theatrics, low on drama. A Republican president can and should be exciting and charismatic. But we don't need fifty or a hundred mini-presidents, all trying to outcompete each other.

Bright: Members of Congress should be clever. They should recognize that they hold power, and constantly be looking for opportunities to use it. There are more than you think, and clever lawmakers with clever staffs will find those opportunities.

Based: This word gets used a lot by conservatives these days, without knowing its full meaning. Based doesn't simply mean "good" or "awesome" or "cool." It means someone who is assertive, and doesn't take marching orders from the media, the bureaucracy, the "intelligence community," or any other arm of America's regime. In short, a "based" person is one who is fully resistant to the moral imperialism of the enemy. This will be crucial, because if our next president is as bold and assertive as he needs to be, there will be *immense* pressure on Congress to act to make him stop. The Willard Mitt Romneys of the world would probably do it. We need Republicans who won't.

Brave: Even if you're boring, a genuinely conservative Congress is going to be absolutely savaged by the public, and maybe even physically threatened. Don't believe me? Remember 2017 when the mere prospect of a border wall and other America-first policies caused a lunatic lefty, James Hodgkinson, to try and murder Republican lawmakers practicing for the Congressional baseball game? Only his poor aim, a rapid response from police, and luck prevented a bloodbath.

Bluntly, we are probably not getting a Congress where both houses have a 4-Bs majority any time soon. It will be good enough to have a Congress that doesn't actively derail the presidency. Still, in case I'm wrong, and some Congressmen are looking for ideas, here's a few:

- Confirm all the next president's nominees *quickly.* One hundred days into President Trump's term he only had 26 of his 1,200 Senate-confirmed appointees in place! This was far behind Obama and George W. Bush, and its effects hobbled his entire presidency. The Republicans let themselves be distracted by the Russia election interference hoax and cowered in the face of Democrat obstruction and harassment of Trump's nominees. Mitch Mc-Connell refused to use up Senate floor time to confirm Trump's nominees because he didn't view it as important. This must not happen a second time. All other legislative business can and should take a back seat to a rapid confirmation operation. Also, Congress should simply not allow itself to go into recess while there is a single nominee still outstanding.

- No grandstanding, period. Holding stunt hearings that otherwise achieve nothing legislatively might be fine when your party holds Congress but nothing else, but when your party holds the White House the emphasis should be on getting things done, whether it's ramming through nominations or ramming through legislation. Every hour spent on members reading random nonsense into the Congressional Record is an hour wasted.

- Play hardball on budgeting. Give the president a boost in shuttering the toxic bureaucracy by simply writing out its funding. It will be politically difficult for Democrats to explain why they are filibustering a budget that *saves* the American taxpayer money by folding up the federal government's equivalent of the HR departments they hate so much at their own jobs.

In fact, this is one of the things worth doing even as I write this, in a world where Republicans have the House and nothing else. One badly underused power of the House? Defining the roles and compensation of specific federal employees.

Consider the case of the infamous Sam Brinton. If that name doesn't ring a bell, perhaps this phrase does, "Cross-dressing non-binary nuclear luggage thief." Yes, that Sam Brinton, the man who served as deputy assistant secretary of energy, with a focus on nuclear waste disposal.

Even before he lost his job due to his repeated luggage thefts, Brinton was a minor celebrity purely due to his freakish appearance and behavior.

What could Republicans have done? They could have played politics with Brinton's compensation. Literally!

Brinton was a political appointee of President Biden. Republicans couldn't control who Biden picked for that job. But they could have simply folded a simple segment into the next piece of must-pass legislation to roll through the House. Simply reclassify Brinton's job into a volunteer position with no government salary.

• Repeal the Nixon-era Impoundment Control Act of 1974, giving the president the power to selectively not spend money even if Congress has appropriated it.[245] There are countless cases throughout the federal government where money is mindlessly funneled into a void. Virtually without exception, mindlessly spent money is money that is propping up the left. So, give the president the power to not spend it.

Could this law, in theory, be used against conservatives in the future as well? Certainly, but on balance, it's a change that is friendlier to us than to the left. Whether it's funneling grants to left-wing non-profits or bloating up the size of a left-wing Washington bureaucracy, the left is a far greater beneficiary of maximizing federal spending on various programs and agencies. Enhancing the president's power to unilaterally curb that spending would be a boon to conservatives. Not only that, but with the right barriers removed, slashing the size of the bureaucracy will be easier than expanding it back out again, even should we lose the White House again.

But truthfully, I'm not too fixated on what Congress can be doing. They've been practically paralyzed for decades, and that won't be changed in a single election or even several. America needs to be turned around now, and only a decisive president can do that. For better or for worse, the White House has to be where we look for righting the American ship of state as quickly as possible.

CHAPTER ELEVEN

The States

Settle in. This chapter is going to be a long one.

During his days as a young radical, Saul Alinsky would ask students why they wanted to organize. When they responded with selfless blather about selflessly helping others, Alinsky would bark back that this was completely wrong. *Power*, he said, "You want to organize for power!"[246]

The left-wing radicals used every maneuver they could to obtain power, and once that power was obtained, they used it to remake all of America.

The first prerequisite for *un*making what the left has made is to get power. And there is one place in particular where we already have a lot of it: America's state governments.

Of all the ways to turn the tide against wokeness, this is the most important. The battle to slow down, halt, and turn back wokeness will be waged, above all, at the state level. That is where we have by far the greatest capacity to act right now, and it's where we will have the most power to act in the future, *even if* we win the White House back.

Why are states the key battleground? For four critical, interlocking reasons.

1. That's where we run things.
Republicans run states, dozens of them. At the moment I write this, twenty-three out of fifty states have total Republican control of the state government. That's both houses of the legislature, and the governor's mansion. By the time you read this, Louisiana and Kentucky will hopefully have become the 24th

and 25th. If they don't, it's not the end of the world. Republicans dominate the legislature in both states so thoroughly that they can override a governor's veto.

In these roughly two dozen states, we don't need to win a single election to get to work. We just have to get to work. The great news is, we've got a lot to work with. Red State America has more than 140 million people. If it were its own country, it would have a larger economy than every other nation except China.

2. That's where we will keep power.

Even if you can win the White House or the U.S. Congress, holding it is tough. This is a sharply divided country where every national election is closely contested. Keeping power for long is never a sure thing. This makes federal lawmakers a cautious and hesitant bunch, as they fear any sweeping change will create an equally sweeping backlash. States are different. Several states are very conservative places, and whatever the efforts of the left, they are not going to change their stripes overall. That means lawmakers can afford to be more aggressive, take more risks, and try out more experiments, knowing that in all likelihood, they will still hold power in the state afterwards. If you watch sports at all, you've seen games where a team blows a lead by playing it too safe, and we certainly have to be vigilant not to let that happen. We must play aggressively, gain the lead and play *to win*. In states where voters are in our corner, we should be thinking long-term, and dreaming big.

3. That's where government is.

America's federal government has grown massively in size and authority over the course of our country's history. But even now, far more Americans work for state and local governments than work for the feds. Whether it's police or schoolteachers or the ladies at the DMV, state-level government is the kind of government people interact with, and consequently the kind of government that has the biggest impact on our quality of life. Our military going woke may place our country in existential danger . . . but until an existential crisis actually materializes, your local police or public schools going woke has a much bigger impact on life, and preventing either of those eventualities is a state matter, not a federal one.

4. State politics is more responsive.

Want to lobby your federal lawmaker? Get in line. If they're a House member, they represent about 760,000 people. If they're a Senator, they probably represent several million. They're being lobbied by every interest group, every corporation, and every shady foreign actor that has set up shop in the world's most influential city. Federal lawmakers have big egos and big to-do lists.

State lawmakers are better. They represent fewer people—in some states, just a few thousand. In a state like North Dakota, if you want to really get to know your local state house or senate member, you probably can! And frankly, in my experience, state lawmakers tend to be more idealistic as well. Few of them are career politicians, and most aren't perpetually calculating the next stage of the ascent up to the White House that they've had planned since high school. They're people who, if you present them with a good legislative idea, may very well go for it. And because this isn't Washington, it might actually pass!

5. States have more freedom of action.

As powerful as the federal government is, it's still a creature of enumerated powers. It can only do what the Constitution actually allows it to do, and at least *occasionally*, our Supreme Court strikes down a federal law for that reason.

But at the state level, things are very different. America's fifty states have the police power, meaning they can pass any law or pursue any policy that isn't *explicitly forbidden* by the federal Constitution or by their own. And while our federal Constitution is essentially frozen in place, impossible to amend, state constitutions are typically far more changeable.

So, despite being far smaller than the federal government, states can actually concoct far more ideas.

We have the political leeway, and the legal leeway. It's just a matter of exploiting it.

YOUR ROLE MODEL: SCOTT WIENER

There are more than four thousand Republican lawmakers in America. Some of them are, sadly, stuck as powerless minorities in states like New York. But most of them, thankfully, are part of Republican majorities in red states. They have the power to conceive, draft, and pass whatever laws they can imagine. What should they be looking to do? Who should they be looking to as a model?

I have a suggestion: California state senator Scott Wiener.

The more alert among you may have just gagged. But I'm serious!

As a lawmaker, Wiener represents San Francisco. In 2017, he co-authored a bill that lowered the criminal penalty for intentionally spreading HIV from a felony to a misdemeanor. In 2020, he authored a law that reduced certain criminal penalties for anally raping a minor. He wrote and passed a law requiring California women's prisons to house male inmates—just so long as they "identified" as female (many rapists do!).[247] He wrote the bill creating California's third "non-binary" gender designation.[248] In 2022, Wiener crafted his most infamous bill yet, becoming the primary force behind California's bill making itself a "sanctuary state" for transsexualism:

> According to State Sen. Wiener, the law prohibits enforcement of other state laws that allow a child to be removed from parents or guardians who allow their child to receive "gender-affirming health care." It would also bar California from complying with out-of-state subpoenas seeking information on families who seek that care in California, and put criminal arrest warrants against people who violate these out-of-state laws on the "lowest priority for law enforcement."[249]

In the words of Revolver News, "Under Wiener's law, a parent who loses a custody battle could flee to California, claim that their child requires sex change treatments, and then enlist California's courts and police to protect them in a de facto kidnapping."[250]

Wiener's interests go well beyond LGBT issues. He sponsored legislation in 2017 forcing solar panels to be included on many newly-built buildings.[251] That same year, he wrote California's Senate Bill 35, which compels local communities to approve new housing developments if they are otherwise not constructing enough housing.[252] A few years later, he co-authored the notorious SB 9, which essentially abolishes single-family zoning in California, allowing for up to four homes to be built on lots previously zoned for one home.[253] And, in a move aimed exclusively at Donald Trump, he co-authored legislation requiring presidential candidates to publish their tax returns to appear on California's ballot (this bill, at least, was thrown out even by California's ultra-left Supreme Court, perhaps so as to not embarrass Gavin Newsom when he eventually runs for President).[254]

So why do I call Wiener a role model? You may have started to guess by now. Scott Wiener is so enthusiastic about writing, and then passing, left-wing laws that he has become a *national* celebrity, the subject of sputtering rage from conservatives all over the country. When he drafts laws, he doesn't just look at the impact on his own state. He aspires to affect policy in neighboring states, and even politics at the national level.

In *every* red state, I want Republicans who want to be like Scott Wiener. Every year, every legislative session, they should be looking for opportunities to take legislative ground. They should ask themselves questions like, "How can I make my state more of a haven for those with conservative values?," "How can I dull the aggressive attacks of the left?" A politician like Scott Wiener doesn't just play to win, but to run up the score.

The watchwords should be energy, aggressiveness, and constant action. *Not* showboating, though. Never introduce a law just so you can get the publicity hit of introducing it. Every piece of legislation that is introduced should have a serious purpose and should be seriously intended to become law.

You may have heard of the phrase "mission creep." It's when an organization or a bureaucracy adds new goals that go far beyond ones, either to justify a bigger budget or simply to perpetuate its own existence once the old goals become obsolete. NATO was founded to contain Soviet expansion, but 30 years after the fall of the USSR, NATO is still around, sending troops to the Middle East and getting enmeshed in Ukrainian border disputes. That's mission creep.

• • •

Most mission creep is bad. But in politics, mission creep is good! Politics is literally never going away, so our eyes must always be scanning the horizon, imagining "what's next?" It's the best way to keep your opponents on their heels. Progressives are themselves masters of this. When the Supreme Court imposed gay marriage nationwide with *Obergefell v. Hodges*, there was barely even a pause to catch one's breath before the new fads arrived like trans-sexualism and polyamory.

A radical in Students for a Democratic Society once wrote that, "The issue is never the issue. The issue is always the revolution."[255]

Democrats have a whole state, California, that serves as a test model for just about all of their long-term plans. What is the Republican version of California? You might say Florida, or Texas, but while conservatives have won many victories in both states, neither of them is the full-on laboratory of bold conservatism that we need. There should be red states that are so deep red in execution that they make Florida and Texas look as purple as the Minnesota Vikings.

So, let's do it. Let's build the laboratory. In fact, let's build twenty of them. But enough buildup. Let's talk about what we can do.

THE SCOURGE OF TRANSGENDERISM

The flood of new state laws to protect children from insane castration cult would-be mutilators posing as "doctors" is one of the most uplifting developments to have happened with conservatism in my lifetime. It's as if, all at once, all over the country, conservatives snapped out of a daze and realized, "Wait a minute! We don't have to sit helplessly while the latest whack job liberal idea destroys our children! We can do something about it!" It was proof that the moral imperialism of the left can be turned back.

But there is no reason to stop with the wins of 2022 and 2023. In fact, we can't afford to rest. Certainly the left won't. As I write this, many of our anti-mutilation laws are being challenged in court. Some of them have already been blocked by liberal-leaning judges. More of them eventually will be. The whole thing is ripe to end up at the Supreme Court, and the Court might rule against us, enshrining the right to irreversibly mutilate children as a core constitutional liberty. It's our duty to be *ahead* of the curve, anticipating possible setbacks so that when they arrive we are already rolling out our next attack, rather than restarting our entire political operation from scratch whenever a new setback happens.

As I write this in late summer 2023, a 24-year-old girl, Prisha Mosley, has brought a lawsuit in North Carolina.[256] Like far too many girls, as a teenager Prisha struggled with depression and anxiety. And like far, far too many girls, instead of receiving real help, Prisha was funneled into the toxic lie that her problems were rooted in being born in the "wrong body," and her "real" body was different from her physical one.

Doctors told Prisha that her problems were caused by "gender dysphoria" and would go away if she received treatments like cross-sex hormones and a double mastectomy. One of these consultations was just two minutes long. At one point, a professional told Prisha that taking testosterone shots would put her through male puberty, and allow her to "grow a penis."

Now, nine years later, Prisha has been left physically mutilated, with a deep masculine voice, facial hair, missing breasts, and more. She will most likely never be able to have children.[257]

I hope Prisha succeeds in her lawsuit. But conservatives also shouldn't passively watch and hope. We should pave the way for more Prishas, all over the country, because sadly there *will* be more as the consequences of the past decade's social contagion play out. In short, we need a legal and regulatory backup plan if outright bans on child mutilation don't hold up. (I cannot stress enough the importance of planning for all these different scenarios, good and bad. Every football coach hopes for 2nd and 1 but has plays drawn up in case they face 3rd and 14. Remember this, for *every* issue!)

Fortunately, the trans issue is one where almost *infinite* creativity is possible, just as long as conservatives are willing to engage in it. Here are just a few ideas for what to try as supplements to more sweeping bans on child sex changes or as backup plans if the courts get in the way.

- Create a state registry of all doctors who have performed castrations on children ("gender-affirmation surgery") or hormone treatments on minors, or who have recommended such treatments, so parents can find them with a quick search and know to avoid them.
- Take inspiration from the pro-life movement and raise procedural hurdles. Pro-lifers cut down on abortions by requiring ultrasounds

and imposing waiting periods. Do the same for gender insanity. Require disclosures about the actual side effects from sex-change treatments and impose long waiting periods before escalation in treatment.

- Make being a pro-mutilation doctor a profoundly miserable experience. One of the simplest ways to do this is by making it easier to hold them legally accountable for what they do. Make child-mutilating doctors easier to sue by passing laws saying if a child seeks to detransition after undergoing hormone therapies or surgeries as a child and suffering permanent damage to their body as a result, they can sue the "doctors" responsible for letting this happen. Taking a play out of New York's playbook that got the statute of limitations lifted, draft a law called something like the Surgical Justice Act that rules all waivers the child or their parents signed for such surgeries to be legally nullified. Make it explicit that transitioning a child who later regrets it is a form of malpractice.

- Require mutilating doctors to carry extra health insurance. Or even better, make it so that malpractice related to child sex changes cannot be covered by insurance at all. If post-transition regret and detransitioning are as rare as advocates say, then they should be just fine with doctors paying out huge malpractice judgments if grown adults decide that the irreversible procedures they received as children were a mistake.

- If courts look askance at stripping a doctor of his malpractice insurance, try going the other way. Make doctors who stand for child transitioners carry cartoonishly large amounts of malpractice insurance to raise the cost and difficulty of working in such a sickening specialty.

- Many liberal jurisdictions (and also Utah, for some reason) have bans on so-called "conversion therapy," treatments or counseling that try to help a person change their sexual orientation. Well, red states should feel free to copy the concept. Relabel the sham "counseling" of gender radicals as "gender conversion therapy" or "sex conversion therapy," and then ban it. If sexual desires are innate at birth and immutable (as liberals say), then how much more innate and immutable is the body you are born with?

- Are there any drugs or tools in the surgery for child castration, or in the treatments that follow, that are unique? Take a page out of the anti-gun lobby and find ways to make those tools artificially scarce or wildly expensive. Put regulation and red tape over them like the anti-gun lobby does with ammo.
- Go to war against the word "gender" itself! Comb through state laws and rules, and revert them back to referring only to two "sexes," without any concession to the "gender" nomenclature of the past 70 years.

Too often, conservatives see a failure to achieve a total victory as being total defeat, and a justification for giving up. It's not. Small victories and partial victories are all still victories. If you'll allow me one last football analogy: sometimes a game changes momentum because the defense didn't give up a touchdown but held the opponent to a field goal.

YOUR AG IS A WEAPON

Red state AGs have gotten pretty good about suing against the worst excesses of the Biden Administration. In just the first twenty months of the Biden Administration, for instance, Missouri AG Eric Schmitt filed or joined 25 different lawsuits against the Biden White House.[258] One of those lawsuits brought down Biden's vaccine mandate for companies with more than 100 employees. Another brought down Biden's forcible pause on new oil and gas leases. But Schmitt's boldest play, and one that may eventually prove his best, was when he and Louisiana AG Jeff Landry sued the administration in May 2022 over its collusion with social media companies to suppress freedom of speech in the guise of preventing "disinformation." In July 2023, that suit temporarily resulted in a national injunction on the Biden regime communicating *at all* with social media companies.[259, 260]

Obviously, red state AGs should keep finding reasons to sue Democrat administrations. But what AGs do shouldn't just be limited to suing the feds. There is more than they can and should do.

If Scott Wiener is the model state legislator, then Letitia James might be the model state attorney general.

James lucked into the job as New York's top cop after her predecessor Eric Schneiderman MeToo'd himself out of it. Since then, James has seen her job as, substantially, delivering wins for the *national* liberal movement. She is well-placed to do so. As the state overseeing not just America but the entire planet's financial nerve center, New York's legal system has unparalleled reach and influence. No red state can match it, but we can at least feel inspired to try.

James, for instance, inherited from her predecessor an entire legal machine for bringing down the National Rifle Association, which has the misfortune of being incorporated in New York (gun politics were a lot different in the 1800s, when it was founded). In 2020, James filed a suit to dissolve the NRA completely and confiscate its war chest of donations. While James' bid to destroy the NRA totally has failed, other parts of her lawsuit have continued. Fighting back has cost the NRA millions and largely sidelined it politically.[261] An organization that was a major force in U.S. politics throughout the 80s, 90s, and 2000s, doing major work to keep Republican politicians in line on gun rights, has been rendered impotent and borderline irrelevant. So far, the NRA still exists, but when was the last time you heard much about them? That's no coincidence. The endless legal battle in New York has cost the organization tens of millions of dollars in legal fees and utterly hobbled it. But there is no pause button on the battle over gun rights. The NRA sits hobbled and useless while the war rages.

James has also made herself into a backstop for federal prosecutions, just in case those fail to put away the left's designated enemies. President Trump pardoned Steve Bannon for politically motivated charges brought against him by DOJ prosecutors . . . so in 2022, James simply brought her own charges against Bannon on the same set of facts, to drag him back into prison.[262] And since they're state charges, the only possible pardon would have to come from New York's governor . . . and good luck winning that governor's mansion back any time soon.

And of course, James has been perfectly happy to use civil charges against individuals, too. Even as Donald Trump has battled the various criminal indictments brought against him by Alvin Bragg and Jack Smith, he and his children have also battled Letitia James' multimillion civil fraud case.[263] Not only that, but James' office acted as a supplement to Biden's DOJ, sending multiple referrals to Biden's DOJ and IRS accusing Trump of criminal misconduct.[264]

So, where's our Letitia James? If Letitia James can be a nightmare to the NRA, which has done nothing wrong except build a reputation for policy success, then think about what red states *ought* to be doing to America's most glaring charity scam, Black Lives Matter. The Black Lives Matter Global Network Foundation Inc. collected more than $90 million in its first year of operations, riding high on the link between its name and the chant shouted by George Floyd rioters.[265] The charity, from the beginning, was a scam. It spent $6 million on a luxury home in the Los Angeles area, justifying the purchase by saying it could be used by black social media influencers (seriously) or serve as a "safe house" for people receiving "death threats" (seriously). In reality, the house was enjoyed by founder Patrisse Cullors for her personal use, while being monitored by her brother, who was on BLM's payroll.[266]

I could dig into the crimes of BLM in more detail (in fact it could be its own separate book), but the above is all we need to call it a criminal scam. Buying an entire luxury house with dollars donated to fight racism is much worse than anything Steve Bannon has ever been accused of doing. So Republican AGs ought to act like it. The people of their states were defrauded by BLM—so investigate them! Indict them! Convict them!

And then, find more. For decades, the Southern Poverty Law Center has collected revenues well in excess of its spending.[267] In 2022, it collected $140 million, and spent just $110 million, for a surplus of nearly $30 million.[268] It has amassed a pool of assets totaling more than $700 million.[269] The Center's lavish headquarters is nicknamed the Poverty Palace. Even other, more principled liberals find the group completely loathsome; in 1996 one of them called SPLC founder Morris Dees "a fraud and a conman."[270] In a 2019 piece, former staffer Bob Moser said the group was "ripping" off donors and was, essentially, a "con."[271]

Well, the SPLC is headquartered in *Montgomery, Alabama*. So, I ask, where is the war room in the Alabama AG's office investigating the SPLC the way New York investigates the NRA?

If Trump can be harassed everywhere from Fulton County to the Financial District, why can't Hunter Biden, whose lifetime of sordid criminal behavior has literally been released for the entire planet to see? Biden has written *in his memoir* about a four-day crack bender he went on in Nashville in October 2016, part of a "crack-fueled, cross-country odyssey."[272] His infamous laptop, meanwhile, has damning proof of Biden buying tens of thousands of dollars worth of prostitute services from Florida-based madam Ekaterina Moreva.[273] What can Florida do in response to that? I don't know the answer, but I know that if the Democrats discovered a Trump family member sent thousands to a madam in one of *their* states, the answer would not be "nothing."

States shouldn't just look for ways to use their existing laws to target the left's wrongdoing. They should consider creating *new* laws. As I write this, Donald Trump is fighting out a defamation lawsuit against E. Jean Carroll over a sexual assault she says occurred in the 1990s. We don't need to get into what an absurd sham Carroll's allegations are (she can't even remember the *year* it supposedly happened!). What matters for our purposes is that Carroll shouldn't have been able to bring her lawsuit at all, because New York's statute of limitations on civil lawsuits related to alleged sex assaults is three years. But in 2022, New York passed a special law creating a one-year window to sue over decades old cases . . . a law essentially tailor-made for Carroll, who sued within *minutes* of it taking effect.[274]

Consider that a possible inspiration. Maybe it's time states reconsidered the statute of limitations for certain offenses, civil or criminal. Maybe it's time for a Prostitution Prevention Act that conveniently ensnares a whore-mongering First Son. Remember Chapter 8! When we live in a world playing by the left's rules, we should look to the left's tactics.

REMOVE YOUR OWN ROADBLOCKS

Like the rest of the South, Florida was largely a Democrat state for most of the 20th century. But that all changed in the mid-90s, when Florida moved decisively into the Republican column at the state level, where it has remained ever since.

But there was a major lagging factor that kept conservatives from changing the state more dramatically, and that was the state court system. In the 1970s, Florida created a series of judicial nominating commissions to pick potential judges, with many members chosen by the Florida Bar instead of the governor.[275] The result was predictable. The Florida Bar was more liberal than Florida, and so Florida ended up with courts more liberal than the state. Even as conservatives won election after election, Florida's supreme court shot down conservative priorities like school vouchers or restrictions on abortion.[276]

Republicans under Jeb Bush(!) took the first step to fixing the problem, by giving the governor a majority of all appointments to the nominating commissions. But it took until Gov. Ron DeSantis for them to be appropriately aggressive about making sure judicial nominees were genuine, reliably conservative picks, every time. DeSantis ensured every one of his appointees to the supreme court nominating committee was a member of the conservative Federalist Society, and he's done everything in his power to make sure that the commissions nominate the conservatives he wants. He's rejected Florida Bar nominees to the commissions (as he has the power to do) to compel them to propose somebody else. By summer 2023, *The Washington Post* was writing articles whining that DeSantis used "secretive panels" to "flip [the] state Supreme Court."[277] Now, Florida has the Supreme Court it ought to have, after a quarter-century of Republican dominance.

The lesson in this? Every state is different, with variable ways of choosing all kinds of offices. In red states, conservatives must adjust those processes as much as possible to make sure that *conservatives* fill those offices. Don't stand pat, and don't be complacent. A "nonpartisan commission" is a liberal one by another name. Where we can, we should adjust the law (or amend state constitutions) to make it so "nonpartisan" appointments are political ones, where conservatives can be chosen. And no matter what the office, *every* opportunity must be taken to maximize the conservative credentials of the officeholders. No being lazy!

GET RID OF DEI EVERYTHING

Seriously, if you're in a red state, why does a single DEI job exist with tax-payer support in your state? I don't care what high-minded excuse is given for them. I don't care how your state's version is super-special and different and thus less likely to be woke. Don't submit to the left's frame! "Diversity," from its very inception, has been a con to inject the left's values of racial discrimination and undermining merit. Stop valuing it, save taxpayers money, and restore the better world where DEI didn't exist. If a red state has DEI officials in any departments, eliminate the positions. If a red state's colleges have them, order them to be eliminated. If local governments have them, either ban the positions outright, or inform cities that they are ineligible for any state funding until they change course.

THE RED STATE SANCTUARY PROJECT

On March 30, 2023, Manhattan DA Alvin Bragg crossed a legal Rubicon and became the first prosecutor in American history to criminally indict a former U.S. president. Even *The New York Times* said the charges were based on a "novel legal theory."[278]

Most conservatives fixated on the spectacle of their president being dragged into court on trumped-up charges that had (quite literally) never been attempted against anyone else before.[279]

But Mike Benz, executive director at the Foundation for Freedom Online, was focused on the big picture. Specifically, he was focused on Alvin Bragg, the prosecutor for deep-blue Manhattan, plucking Donald Trump out of south Florida and extraditing him to New York to face criminal charges. If that could be done to the former president on the flimsiest possible allegations, then Benz knew literally any conservative in the country was vulnerable. And so, he went on Twitter and called for the solution.

"We need a sanctuary state for conservatives," Benz tweeted.[280]

Benz was right then and remains right now. It's time for conservatives to craft a "red state sanctuary project." What does that mean? As a matter of policy, in states where they securely hold power, conservatives should tweak, modify, repeal, or replace their laws and policies in order to protect the rights, property, and basic liberty of their citizens from tyrannical over-reach by America's ruling regime. That means protecting them from "novel legal theories" concocted in far-left states, and it means sheltering them as much as possible from the intrusions of the federal government as well.

The model should, of course, be the left's own tactics creating sanctuaries from American immigration law. But there's ample room for growth. Here's just a few starting ideas:

Protect Citizens from Persecutory Blue States

Because a single far-left jurisdiction accused Donald Trump of a made-up crime, he was compelled to leave his base in Florida to face the charges, which could (in theory) result in years of prison time.

Experts will say that there was no choice in the matter; U.S. states have to extradite the accused criminals of other states upon request. But in real-ity, it's hardly that simple. At a minimum, red states can make it maximally difficult to secure extraditions in cases where political motives are suspected. A red sanctuary state could, for instance, prohibit its own police from conducting arrests on behalf of a state or other jurisdiction that has proven itself prone to politically motivated criminal cases. This is much like how current immigration sanctuary laws works. States prohibit their own police forces from cooperating with federal ICE agents in any capacity, forcing the federal government to muster all the manpower and resources itself to enforce American immigration laws. State governments already have near-total leeway in deciding which arrest warrants to focus on and which ones to ignore. Blue states use that leeway to avoid prosecuting actual criminals, so why not have a red state use that leeway to protect the politically persecuted?

This could apply to civil cases as well. A red sanctuary state could pass a law that voids, for collection purposes within the state, any legal judgments rendered in another jurisdiction that violate public policy. A lawyer suggested I write that previous sentence, so I wouldn't be surprised if you got a bit caught up in the legalese. So, what does it mean in layman's terms? Well, as I write this, Kyle Rittenhouse is facing two different civil lawsuits stemming from his justified self-defense shooting during the 2020 Kenosha riots.[281] Suppose he loses those lawsuits and is hit with a judgment for fifty million dollars. Our red sanctuary states could have laws saying that, in their territory, no person will ever be held civilly liable for a valid use of self-defense, and no out-of-state judgment for the same conduct will be enforceable. Then, the state could invite Kyle Rittenhouse to live (and relocate his assets) there, shielded from any out-of-state seizure or garnishment.

Shelter Conservative Non-Profits

As mentioned above, the New York AG's office has spent years attempting to shut down the National Rifle Association, ideally seizing its assets as part of the bargain. A red sanctuary state could help fix this kind of persecution. Allow corporations and charities to relocate from other states (or perhaps specific, politically hostile blue states) without getting the permission of their prior domicile. If the blue state comes along and complains that funds were moved illegally or improperly, ignore them.

A Secure Right to Self-Defense

Remember the sad story of Jake Gardner from earlier in this book. Jake used force to protect his business, his father, and himself from criminal looters. His reward was a murder charge from a left-wing prosecutor. One of the reasons this was able to happen is due to the fact that Nebraska doesn't have a Stand-Your-Ground law. That means that, despite the destruction falling upon his business, legally speaking, Gardner had a "duty to retreat" in the face of his livelihood being menaced by violent predators.[282]

There is no reason for a single red state to keep laws requiring law-abiding citizens to retreat in the face of predators. Strengthen castle doctrine, stand-your-ground, and other self-defense laws to make sure they can never be abused by urban left-wing prosecutors to target those who defend themselves from left-wing terrorism. Even in states with stand-your-ground laws, the letter of the law may need work. The McCloskeys in St. Louis, Missouri were on their own property, defending their own home from a braying mob, and the guns they exhibited weren't even loaded, but they were still criminally charged by the city's radical left-wing circuit attorney Kim Gardner, and eventually pleaded guilty. Such outcomes have to be treated by conservatives as a failure, requiring tweaks to the law to ensure they don't happen again. Clarify the law as needed to make it clear that brandishing weapons against a mob is not a criminal act. Make it clear that force can be used against a robbery or to stop looters. Make sure that those who defend their property and their lives are defended not just from criminal prosecutions, but also lawsuits after the fact.

In fact, don't just limit things to looters. An increasingly common tactic of the left, both in the U.S. and globally, is to disrupt ordinary life by blocking roads or otherwise being a bother. Red states should pass laws making it clear that in such cases, forcibly pushing or dragging a person out of the way isn't assault, it's commendable.

Strip Power Away from Blue Cities

Even in the most conservative states, it's well-known that large cities are dark blue islands. Repeatedly, this has resulted in calamitous harm being inflicted on people who should have been safe from the worst overreaches of blue state liberalism. I've talked about specific examples like Jake Gardner, but there are plenty more, including policies that affect millions and not just unlucky lone individuals. The McCloskeys protect their home from a riotous BLM mob, and get slapped with felonies for their trouble by St. Louis's radical pro-crime prosecutor. Texas is a tough-on-crime state, but the DA of Dallas County can simply announce he'll stop prosecuting thefts of less than $750, which is exactly what DA John Creuzot did from 2019 through 2022.[283]

It doesn't have to be this way. The way states organize their cities and counties is almost entirely up to them, and by extension, states have near-total authority to rework the powers held by local governments. Some governors are fortunately starting to realize this. In 2022, Tampa's prosecutor announced that he wouldn't enforce Florida laws barring late-term abortion or transgender procedures on children, so Governor Ron DeSantis removed him from office. Was it a bold move? Certainly. But it was precisely what was needed in that moment, and, most importantly, removing the prosecutor from his position was entirely within Governor DeSantis' power.[284] The prosecutor sued, and a federal judge ruled that DeSantis's firing was unconstitutional . . . but that as a federal judge he was also powerless to do anything about it.[285] Too bad!

Similarly, in Texas in 2023, the state legislature passed House Bill 17, allowing for DAs who refuse to prosecute certain crimes to be removed for misconduct.[286]

But we can dream even bigger. Instead of just making dereliction of duty grounds for removal, states could make it a criminal offense, or make it easier to sue prosecutors in a personal capacity for crimes committed by those they refused to prosecute when police provided clear evidence of a crime. Make it so even the wealthiest Soros-backed DA has to face personal consequences for unleashing mayhem on the public!

And that's just in the realm of stopping blue city DAs. Obviously, red states also have enormous power to dictate what school districts do in their states (more on that in a couple chapters) and can boss around blue city administrations to the best of their abilities. They can quash any use of CRT or racially discriminatory contracting all the way down to the city level, and they should. While police departments are typically relatively conservative forces even in majority blue cities, red legislatures shouldn't use that as a reason to become complacent, remaining vigilant to find those areas where conservative values aren't being upheld like they should. This way, communities can be ready to act quickly and, if necessary, expand the power of state police at the expense of local ones if needed to make sure that laws are enforced instead of ignored.

Protect Citizens from Doxing, and Punish Doxers

In early 2023, the Southern Poverty Law Center doxed a completely random Texas A&M grad for attending an event organized by white nationalist Richard Spencer five and a half years prior.[287] Set aside your personal feelings about Spencer and his movement. To be clear, I think he's loathsome, and I'm sure you do, too. But Spencer isn't the point of this story. Remember what we talked about in part 2 and don't submit to the left's framing! Look past Spencer and focus on the important party: the A&M grad who was doxed by the Southern Poverty Law Center for attending an event over half a decade ago. Do we dox random people for attending Marxist events half a decade ago? We don't, and we shouldn't. The graduate did nothing criminal or otherwise noteworthy, and it wasn't even clear he was still politically active. Why did the SPLC dox him? Only to terrorize the public. "Step out of line and this could be you," was the message. Similarly, during the trial of Douglas Mackey for making "illegal memes," the SPLC used potentially hacked private emails to dox and intimidate one of Mackey's expert witnesses, pressuring him out of testifying.[288] Courts would hold the SPLC in contempt in a fair jurisdiction, but there are fewer and fewer of those in blue states. A red state sanctuary project could change that.

There are, in fact, several things states can do to protect their citizens from doxing and other kinds of targeted harassment. For starters, make it easier for people to create companies and corporate bodies without revealing their identities. Pass laws allowing individuals to create an LLC and obtain an Employer Identification Number (for paying taxes), without actually needing to put their actual identities into a state database. This would allow for the creation of businesses and political operations that can operate without being exposed to doxing by sinister actors on the left. But a more straightforward option is to simply create a tort against doxing. Using anonymous and private statements to wreck a person's life is one of the left's favorite tactics of social control. A red state could make it legally punishable. They could pass a law allowing a resident to sue the SPLC, the ADL, or any other organization that publishes reputation-destroying hit pieces against them, based solely on private or anonymous speech, if they are a non-public figure. And don't worry, all of this is compatible with the First Amendment. Torts for "public disclosure of private facts" have a long tradition in American law—most notably, it's how Hulk Hogan was able to take down the repulsive left-wing gossip rag Gawker.[289]

Modify, But Don't Eliminate, Qualified Immunity

"Qualified immunity" is when government actors are immune from being personally sued for their behavior while acting on behalf of the state. A recent passion project of the left has been eradicating qualified immunity for police, so that police will avoid using force against criminals out of fear of being personally sued later.

But police aren't the only beneficiaries of qualified immunity. In many states, qualified immunity also protects government bureaucrats who might harass a Christian business owner for "civil rights" violations, or public school teachers who foist anti-white or transgender propaganda onto their students. In Texas, for instance, all school employees (including school nurses, counselors, and the like) enjoy qualified immunity for their behavior on the job.[290]

Qualified immunity means that rogue teachers and bureaucrats enjoy an added layer of protection should they ignore laws or abuse their power. And, in fact, as red states pass bans on injecting CRT or other left-wing propaganda into the classroom, many teachers have proudly boasted of their plans to flout the laws in question—and thanks to qualified immunity, the most they have to worry about is (maybe) getting fired.

In the case of police, who have to make split-second life-or-death decisions, the extra protection of qualified immunity makes sense. However, it hardly makes sense to offer elementary school teachers the same protection. If states want to give their CRT and child sex change bans some oomph, they should strip their teachers and bureaucrats of qualified immunity, at least on that specific matter, so those who willfully ignore those laws swiftly face civil consequences for doing so. If a schoolteacher has to worry about facing personal financial liability for injecting race poison into the classroom, they are far more likely to follow the law. People respond to incentives, and it's no surprise that in America, liberalism is an alliance of elites who don't have to face consequences for their actions and a lower class that believes they *shouldn't* face consequences for theirs.

Guard Against Blue State Chokepoints

This point, I'll admit, is a little ambitious. But hey, it's my book. I can say whatever I want!

During the Obama years, the Department of Justice pursued something called Operation Choke Point. The goal was to hinder businesses such as gun retailers by discouraging banks and other financial institutions from serving them, making it harder for such companies to secure financing.[291] It's a tactic the left has gotten used to pursuing in many other domains. If they can't ban a website outright, they'll simply target its webhost, so it struggles to stay online. Part of New York's offensive against the NRA has consisted of pressuring banks and insurance companies to not serve it, on the grounds that it poses a "reputational risk" to them.[292] In states like California, liberals unable to implement enough gun control are experimenting with bullet control, trying to lower accessibility and raise the price of ammunition in order to make gun ownership more challenging and costly than it would otherwise be.[293]

This is a place where states can step up. Now, obviously I believe in free market capitalism and abhor socialism, but one of the key lessons of this book is that conservatives can't reflexively refuse to use government for fear of becoming socialists. Government is a tool, and when the left is using its institutions to sabotage the free market, then we must take our own steps to correct it.

Did you know that North Dakota currently has a state-owned bank and a state-owned grain elevator? It's had them for about a century, in fact.[294] I won't comment on the merits of those, but clearly they haven't turned the state into a socialist hellhole. So, what if North Dakota (or any other enterprising red state) also set up a state-owned webhosting service, with a mandate that it is strictly bound by the First Amendment? Or what if the state had its own ammo factory, with a mandate to glut the market and help lower prices? Running businesses at a mild loss is a small price to pay to make sure that citizens enjoy the same rights to free speech and self-defense their parents and grandparents had.

Pass Some Quality-of-Life Laws—and Enforce Them

From San Francisco to New York, American cities have become filthy, unpleasant, and ugly. This isn't some inevitable fact of city life, and if you need proof, just visit Japan to see what major urban areas have the potential to be. The filth, danger, and disarray that have become synonymous to American cities is nowhere to be found in bigger cities in Japan. So, what happened in America? In short, the filth encrusting America's wealthiest cities is thanks to a collective loss of will to enforce basic quality-of-life laws. Bums build homes on the sidewalk, erect entire tent cities in public parks, and scream at innocent bystanders on the subway or the bus.

Red states shouldn't just be protecting Americans from the hostile excesses of zealous left-wing governments. They should protect them from the entropy and decay that those governments are normalizing. That means actually enforcing laws against things like vagrancy, public defecation, and drug use. It means, if necessary, placing the severely anti-social in institutions, rather than letting them roam the streets like dangerous wildlife, waiting for them to lash out and kill someone. Above all, though, it means insisting that, yes, Americans have the right to enjoy clean and pleasant cities just like their grandparents did, and red states will do what is needed to create those nice cities.

Set Up Obstacles in Advance For When Things Change

No political regime lasts forever. Vermont elected only Republicans for a hundred years, then was briefly a swing state, and is now just about the bluest state in America. Georgia was solid blue from the Civil War to the 90s, then solid red, and is now purple.

Ideally, any red sanctuary state will be secure for a long time. But they might not be, and the best time to prepare for such an outcome is right now. Red states should pass laws and constitutional amendments that may seem unnecessary now, but will make it a pain for a later left-wing governor or legislature to remake a state overnight. Entrench gun rights, school choice, religious liberty, and other priorities in a state's constitution, so repealing them is a tougher lift than simply winning a single election.

Going Over to Offense

The concept of a "red sanctuary state" is inherently defensive in nature, and most suggestions so far have been fundamentally defensive, answering the concern of ensuring red states are good places to be while also keeping them safe from woke poisons. But red states put together are an enormously powerful force, and we have the capacity to weaken wokeness even in blue states, if we are willing to dream big enough, and pass laws accordingly.

Copy Texas's Social Media Law

The impact of Elon Musk's purchase of Twitter, and the platform's subsequent embrace of more radically pro–free speech policies, demonstrates the dramatic value of a freely-operating, censorship-free public square. But we can't count on maverick billionaires to bring similar changes to Facebook, YouTube, or other major platforms. And that's why we should look to laws instead. Texas's H.B. 20, passed in 2021, restricts the power of any social media company with a large user base to censor users' posts based on ideological content.[295] Right now, the law is clogged up in the courts, but if it survives, every red state should adopt a similar bill. In fact, they should all collude to make sure their standards are similar. Right now, tech companies censor because there are no penalties for doing so, and so they pro-censorship voices inside their companies and from woke marketing departments across the economy. Fortunately, as conservatives, we know that companies respond to incentives, so change their incentives! Make the financial consequences of censorship *greater* than those of free speech. America's red states, acting in concert, are an economic bloc that no social media company can dare defy.

Make ESG Legally Anathema

That same incentives-based thinking can bring the cancer of woke capital to heel as well. A key driver of woke capital has been the steady left-wing take-over of pension and investment funds, which then impose "Environmental, Social and Governance" expectations on the companies they invest in. This is dressed up as managing the long-term "risks" faced by companies from climate change or the like, but everyone knows this is a sham. It's a means of exerting political pressure on companies.

So ban it. Fortunately, this is one field where red states are already getting the message. In Idaho and North Dakota, any state-run investment funds are prohibited from contemplating ESG considerations.[296] In Florida's recently-passed law, even *local* governments are barred from engaging using ESG, which could be a useful check on deep-blue cities.[297] Other states have banned giving state contracts to companies that boycott the fossil fuels industry (a common ESG target).[298] In some states where the legislature hasn't acted, the attorney general has still issued an opinion that ESG-based activism by private financial firms violates fiduciary obligations to clients, opening those companies up to investigations or lawsuits.

This is all good, but remember the Wiener rule. We need to be as bold and ambitious as possible! States don't have to limit themselves to their own pension funds. Every red state should follow Florida, and make sure their towns and counties are ESG-free, along with the state. And then, look to swaying the private sector. States can pass laws clarifying that any "ESG" calculations by *any* financial companies serving its residents violate their fiduciary obligations, opening them up to a wave of lawsuits if they persist.

Could blue states retaliate with laws mandating ESG, forcing companies to choose between one or the other? Sure, but that would just lead to an outcome where there is one financial ecosystem for red America and another for blue America. And I think you'd agree that would be an improvement over the status quo.

Weaponize the Contracting Process

State governments don't have the same contracting oomph as the federal government, but they still have a lot of pull. So use it!

In 2019, Los Angeles tried to impose a requirement that all city contractors disclose any connections to the NRA.[299] Courts quickly shot that requirement down as the flagrant First Amendment violation that it was, but the incident still shows how imaginative blue areas can be about curtailing constitutional rights. Well, we can be just as imaginative in bolstering constitutional rights, and thankfully, our methods should pass a court's muster. For instance, states could require that any large employers seeking a government contract must include free speech provisions in their employee contracts, allowing employees to sue if they are fired for expressing their political or religious views outside of work. Or, for web-related contracts, a state could insist on only giving its business to companies that refuse to engage in tech censorship.

The combined value of red state government contracts amounts to hundreds of billions of dollars. Realize that these dollars are a weapon that can be wielded for good.

Mackey's Law

Earlier, I mentioned the case of Trump supporter Douglas Mackey, who in 2016 made memes ridiculing Hillary Clinton by, among other things, suggesting that they could vote by text message, making jokes that fit into a long history of suggesting one's opponents are idiots by giving them laughably stupid guidelines on voting, like the classic, "Be sure to turn out on *Wednesday* to support the Democrats!". Thanks in no small part to holding the trial in New York City, where prosecutors could secure a safely liberal jury, Mackey was convicted.[300]

The specific "crime" Mackey "committed" was a violation of the 19th-century Ku Klux Klan Act, which criminalized any use of threats, intimidation, or force to deprive someone of civil rights. The Biden Administration took this and argued that a meme on the Internet somehow "deprived" a person of their right to vote.

Well, two can play that game, and we can play it with far greater justification. In reality, it is the left that routinely conspires to strip people of their rights through threats and intimidation.

To give an example: Prior to Kyle Rittenhouse's murder trial in Wisconsin, left-wing criminals hacked the donation site Give Send Go and obtained personal information on those who donated to Rittenhouse's defense fund.[301] "Journalists" then published the identities of those who donated to support his defense. At least one person, a Norfolk, Virginia police officer, lost his job over it.[302] Under existing law, the act of hacking Give Send Go was a crime, but traditionally, publishing the actual names was held to be protected First Amendment speech. But in the Mackey case, the court held that engaging in otherwise-protected First Amendment speech (posting memes on Twitter) with the supposed *goal* of chilling the "right" to vote was still a felony. In fact, the court held that merely conspiring to engage in such speech was a crime.

Very well, then. Our new, bolder, red sanctuary state can declare war on conspiracies to crush free speech. Red state AGs can be empowered to investigate the organizations and "journalists" who dox people for the purpose of chilling free speech rights. Investigate, indict, arrest, and imprison them for conspiring against those rights. Call it Mackey's law, for some poetic irony.

· · ·

Whew! That's nine thousand words worth of ideas. I could still easily go on for another nine, because I tried to leave out everything that was a little *too* obvious (you don't need me telling you that red states should ban vax mandates or require voter ID).

But we still have another level of government left to go. It's the one where you, the reader, matter the most, and it's the one where you have a moral duty to act even if you are stuck in the bluest possible area of the bluest possible state (though if you are, c'mon, move!).

It's time for us to take a look at local government.

CHAPTER TWELVE

Fighting Wokeness Means Fighting Locally

Confucius defined a good government as one that makes its people happy.

America, by this metric, has a terrible government, and our worst governments aren't at the national level. They're at the local level. The government closest to the people, the one supposed to be most responsive to their concerns and their needs, routinely makes a mess of our lives instead.

I've spent thousands of words laying out what elected Republicans can be doing in Washington and in their state houses to protect you from wokeness. Obviously, we should all be pressuring and lobbying them constantly to make sure that those measures happen, and don't simply become another set of forgotten and abandoned campaign promises.

But there is one field of politics where the Republican Party cannot fail us. We can only fail ourselves.

It's time for us to talk about local politics. It's time for us to talk about all of you reading this book.

Fighting wokeness means fighting locally. It means the duty of all of us, no matter where we live, whether it's the reddest rural town or the bluest big city, to step up and stand against the madness gripping our nation. Conserving the things we care about is not about sitting in place. It requires radical action. We—and that includes YOU—have to make the change close to home.

Here's how.

ARE YOU WOKE?

I have some uncomfortable news for the Christians reading this book. Want to know why atheist liberals get what they want in American politics? They want it more.

The stereotype promoted by the mainstream media is that evangelical Christians are particularly political and aggressive in pushing their views onto the public. It's a lie. For the most part, we're disengaged.

Political scientist Ryan Burge polled members of different American religious groups about how often they engaged in six basic political activities, such as attending a local political meeting, contacting a public official, or working for a campaign. The results weren't close. In Burge's study, atheists engaged in political acts at roughly twice the rate of evangelicals.[303] Fifty percent of atheists donated to a candidate in the past year. Less than a quarter of evangelicals and Catholics had. Atheists were roughly three times as likely to have attended some kind of protest or march. Atheists were more likely to be politically engaged at all levels of education, too. Higher levels of education generally predict more political involvement, but atheists with only "some college" were actually more engaged than Catholics and evangelicals with post-graduate degrees.

Survey work from Pew Research backs up Burge's findings. According to a 2018 poll, liberals were more likely than conservatives to have contacted an elected official, attended a local government meeting, or worked on a campaign.[304]

But you probably didn't even need me to recite stats like the ones above. You've probably noticed this pattern yourself already. If there's a protest ("mostly peaceful" or otherwise) at your local college, is it more likely to be a conservative one, or a liberal one?

Do you want to win? Well, you have to start to love what is good more than the adversary loves what is evil. You have to want it more. And that means going out and doing the work to win.

Early in this book, I mentioned the original origin of the term "woke" was used by black Americans to describe someone alert to what was going on (in their case, racial injustice). Well, be honest with yourself, when it comes to your own town and neighborhood, are you woke? How aware are you of what's actually going on in your town? And I don't mean simply being aware of all the things that annoy you like the Pride flags outside city hall, the police department that takes 40 minutes to respond to a robbery, or the Critical Race Theory worksheets that your elementary's 5th grade teacher is making kids fill out. I mean the actual organs of government. Do you know what system of government your city has? Do you know if it has a strong mayor, or a weak ceremonial one who shares power with the city council? Speaking of which, do you know when your city council holds meetings? Have you ever attended one? Do you know the name of your city councilman? Do you know when elections are held?

If you answered "no" to any of those questions, then frankly, you are not involved enough in your community. And make no mistake: The enemy will answer "Yes" to all those questions. Precisely because the left so desperately crave power, they naturally know where it is held and how it is exercised.

GET THERE FIRSTEST WITH THE MOSTEST

Today, Nathan Bedford Forrest is known as the namesake of Forrest Gump and the founder of the Ku Klux Klan. But before that, Forrest was one of the most successful Confederate generals in the American Civil War. Forrest's doctrine for winning battles was simple, "Get there first with the most men," or as he's more often misquoted, "Git thar firstest with the mostest."

It's a good rule of warfare, but an even better rule for politics. If you want to win in local politics, you want people getting involved and speaking up *early*. A single person being engaged and involved at the very beginning of a political battle is worth five hundred people who only get involved after something is a national story on Fox News.

I'm not saying that you need to read the minutes of your local city council meeting, but if you aren't willing to do that, make sure somebody in your social circle does. Division of labor is exactly how the left gets it done, and you need to do the same. Find out who is politically engaged in your church, in your group of friends, or among the parents at your child's school (and if it's not many people, *get* them politically engaged). Then, make sure everything is being covered. Someone is watching the city council. Another person tracks everything the school board is up to, and another follows what's going on with crime in the city, and what the police are doing about it.

Organizing this sort of circle is easier than ever today, thanks to the Internet. Twitter and Facebook don't just exist for sharing Let's Go Brandon memes. They are powerful tools for local political action. Make a Twitter or Signal group chat for people in your area who think like you do. Create a Facebook group for parents at your school worried about opposing CRT and utilize sites specifically dedicated to local communities, like NextDoor.

The step after being informed is to be involved.

It's not just city council and school board meetings either. Especially in larger cities, the calendar is absolutely full of civic events that are nominally neutral but in fact are woke-dominated. For instance, major city police departments are constantly holding "listening sessions" with the public. The typical listening session ends up like this one:

> The City of Kenosha and its Police Department must take "dramatic and practical steps" toward police reform in order to build community trust.
>
> This was the theme foremost on the minds of participants at four listening sessions held over a two-month period this fall, according to findings compiled and released by the city this week. The listening sessions were held at Kenosha churches and the Public Museum. . . .
>
> The listening sessions drew 207 people in total and 38 people also engaged by participating online to give feedback, with a goal of identifying strategies intended to address systemic racism.[305]

That's the immediate aftermath of the Kenosha riots, in which Kyle Rittenhouse shot dead two rioters who were attacking him. The riots were sparked by the police shooting of wanted criminal Jacob Blake, which an inquiry found to be entirely justified.[306] And yet the big takeaway of the "listening sessions" was the need to prevent "police brutality" and work against "implicit bias."

What share of Kenosha residents felt that the city needed *tougher* law enforcement after the riots, and wanted *more* assertive police, not less?

I suspect it was greater than the number of Kenoshans who saw police as the villains. But it was woke activists who showed up and had their voices heard. That is inexcusable—only 207 people participated in total, and Kenosha has a hundred thousand people. Outnumbering pro-crime voices with anti-crime ones should have been easy. But instead, because they actually showed up, one five-hundredth of the city set the tone to make their city worse off.

Oh, and while this may be rather obvious, make sure you and everyone you know is also turning out to vote. Thousands of American counties, cities, and school boards hold their elections separately from the big national elections, and if they do turnout is guaranteed to be low. Often, it's less than twenty percent, and for a standalone school board election, turnout might be as low as ten or even *five percent*.[307] That means each marginal vote matters far more. Turning out your friends to vote for president might be more exciting. But in purely practical terms, getting a few dozen of your friends and neighbors to vote in local races is far more likely to make a difference in your life.

Okay, so you're getting engaged locally. But what should you actually be doing?

KEEP THE STREETS CLEAN AND SAFE

Every day in America is a battle to preserve civilization against the entropy of liberalism. The left genuinely believes that crime is caused by putting police on the streets, rather than criminals in jail. Even in hyper blue cities, though, the most radical anti-cop attitudes of the left are outliers, and only becoming more so as more and more urban liberals wonder why their car keeps getting broken into and why their local drugstore has moved everything behind glass.

At a bare minimum, you must have the guts to demand that your local government fulfill the *first* duty of any government, which is protecting the public from evildoers. Show up at city council meetings or "listening sessions" to say, loudly, that you want the police out in the streets, enforcing the law.

PROTECT YOUR COMMUNITY FROM UGLINESS

At its heart, wokeness loves what is ugly. It abhors the beautiful and it wallows in what is filthy, disturbing, and off-putting. That's one reason it's adopted drag queens and homeless drug addicts as some of their greatest heroes. It's no surprise that during the period where wokeness seemed most unstoppable, in the summer and fall of 2020, America's major cities became vastly more repulsive right before our eyes. Tent cities popped up in parks and under overpasses just blocks from the U.S. Capitol in Washington. Cities filled with burned-out, smashed, and looted storefronts. Mobs ripped historic statues from their pedestals and left only wreckage in their place. Afraid of being called racist, police abandoned basic qualify-of-life law enforcement, letting open-air drug use, graffiti, and vagrancy explode.

Some of this happened because of the national political vibe, but much of it was simply local pressure, manifesting in the same place all at the same time. Arrogant woke maniacs claimed to speak for everyone when they spoke only for themselves, but in that moment of national psychosis and terror, few people were willing to openly speak *against* them.

One form of ugliness feeds on another. When graffiti covers every surface you'll get more petty crime, too. When homeless camps flourish, so does murder. That's one reason crime rose *everywhere* in America during George Floyd. It was as if a spell had been cast on the country, and in a sense, one actually had been. People saw looting in Minneapolis and Chicago and D.C. and thought, why not loot our own neighborhood Foot Locker?

We should never allow a trauma like 2020 to occur again, and the first line of defense is local. People like us have to be the voices attending city council meetings and rallying support for local candidates who pledge to keep streets tent-free, drug-free, and lunatic-free.

It's not just about stamping out petty crimes of ugliness, though. You should pay attention to the aesthetic hygiene of your town.

As America has declined, so has the beauty of our public spaces. City halls built a hundred years ago are without exception lovely buildings. The ones being thrown up today, not so much. The Old City Hall building of Boston, built during the Civil War, is one of Boston's prettiest buildings. The city's current City Hall, built in the 1960s, is one of planet Earth's ugliest, with Twitter users rating it the fourth worst in the world in 2023.[308] Here in Phoenix, our city hall is better, but still inferior to the one we had before. The skyscrapers New York built at the height of the Great Depression are iconic international symbols of American greatness; the ones it is building right now are proof that billions of dollars can't buy taste.

If your town is growing, chances are it's putting up new buildings pretty often, be it new schools, new government buildings, or new public housing.

Always fight to make sure that what is built is beautiful, rather than ugly. This is one example of where paying attention early is invaluable. By the time an ugly building is going up, it's probably too late to stop it. But when it's in the planning stages or the architectural contract is being rewarded, it's much easier to make a fuss. If your town is paying an architect a million dollars to design a new city hall or a new high school, and their portfolio shows a track record of being ugly, make a fuss! Complain, and agitate for hiring a firm that designs on time-tested, classic architectural principles instead.

Of course, most buildings aren't put up by the government. Make sure your own home looks pleasant and that the property is well-maintained. If you build a new home, make sure it is aesthetic, fits in with the area, and is not an ugly, bloated McMansion showing poor taste. Is your church building a new building? Make sure it is beautiful, and that it looks like a church rather than a community college campus.

MAKE A STINK ABOUT WHAT'S IN THE CLASSROOM

Chances are you're familiar with the Twitter user LibsOfTikTok. The account's creator, Chaya Raichik, has instigated volcanic amounts of hate and vitriol from the left, even though her account does almost nothing except link to videos, images, or educational materials created by liberals themselves. Nothing drives the woke nuts like when you "shine a little light" on what they do. The casual grooming and propaganda that takes place in so many classrooms gets rolling because in far too many cases, parents simply aren't paying attention. The moment there is any publicity or scrutiny, it evaporates, both because of parental outrage and because, for every true believer radical in the school system, there are many bureaucrats who simply don't want trouble. Make being woke a pain in the butt, and schools will stop letting teachers get away with so much unsupervised.

But don't just be on the lookout for porn masquerading as pedagogy. Pay attention to how your local schools handle real subjects, too. Ask for and demand serious standards. Don't let your local school board cancel advanced classes in the name of equity (as they've done in some blue areas).

SUPPORT LOCAL CONSERVATIVE BUSINESS OWNERS

There is no business too small for the woke in your area to make into a target. They will repeatedly sue a Christian baker to try and make him bake a gay wedding cake. When the small family pizzeria Memories Pizza in Walkerton, Indiana voiced support for a state religious freedom law and told a local reporter they wouldn't cater a gay wedding (who caters pizza to a wedding, anyway?), President Obama himself ridiculed them. The business received hostile reviews from across the country and closed for more than a week due to threats.[309]

It's not enough to just boycott a beer because it made an ad you don't like. Building a thriving conservative community means helping other conservatives earn a living as independent entrepreneurs.

Find out the conservatives in your own community who work in the skilled trades and be sure to call them up when you need a leak fixed, a pool dug, or a deck built. Fast food is bad for you, but if you're going to get it anyway, pick out a franchise owned by a conservative. You may be surprised by the number of businesses in your town run by proud conservatives and Christians. And especially today, there's no excuse not to know where they are. If you're not sure where to start, the PublicSq. app is a great place to start, as it helps people find conservative, Christian, and pro-America businesses. Put it on your phone and use the businesses that are on it.

PROTECT SINGLE-FAMILY HOMES

Have you ever noticed that the same liberals who say it's inhumane to keep animals in a zoo see no limits to urban density and cramming Americans on top of each other?

The modern liberal has a surreal hatred of the single-family home as a concept, at least when said home is occupied by anyone but themselves.

"Single-family zoning preserves century-old segregation, planners say" is an article run by *The Washington Post* in 2021.[310] The same year, *The New York Times* published an opinion piece by the head of the left-wing Century Foundation calling single-family zoning "the new redlining."[311]

The left offers many explanations for this loathing saying things such as, single-family housing raises inequality, single-family housing is too expensive, or single-family housing is bad for *the climate*.[312]

The real reason that liberals loathe single-family zoning is also the reason conservatives should support it. Lower-density, single-family housing creates conservatives.

"As you go from the center of cities out through the suburbs and into rural areas, you traverse in a linear fashion from Democratic to Republican places," Stanford professor Jonathan Rodden said in 2017, and the trend is even more true today.[313]

Why? Honestly, I don't entirely know myself. I have some theories. I think it's logical to think that owning your own plot with your own standalone house makes a person feel greater ownership of their surroundings, which they are more protective of. Or maybe it's that living with lower density means you know a greater share of your neighbors, and that makes a person more conservative. Maybe high-density living increases stress, makes people feel atomized and unhappy, and causes them to turn to liberalism to fill the void.

Those are all just guesses, but the reality is indisputable. And liberals are very aware of it, and so they're always looking to jack up density wherever they can.

In my own state of Arizona, Phoenix remained a red city even as it grew and grew and grew, but in the last couple elections Maricopa County finally flipped blue. What happened? Among other things, it went too vertical!

The density battle is a federal and state issue, too, but above all it's a local one. The main theater where the left battles to bulldoze small homes and erect new high-rise tenements is in cities and their suburbs. Every year, liberals are lobbying cities, towns, and counties to increase density, to let developers toss up ten-story high-rises in the middle of happy, safe, functional neighborhoods.

Want to protect your town? Here's a simple maxim: Trust nothing over three stories.

BECOME AN ELECTION WORKER OR POLL WATCHER

Are you worried about election fraud in your area? After 2020, it'd be crazy if you weren't. But don't just fume online about it, do something! The elections that are the bedrock of America's system of government are largely run by volunteers and temporary employees, and ever since the Covid pandemic delivered a body blow to American civil society, there's been a shortage of them.[314] If you want elections that you can trust, one big step is to be a participant in those elections yourself. Monitor your local polling place to make sure the election rules are being followed, or be a poll worker and enforce them yourself.

In many states, the lowest level of political office is the precinct leader (or precinct committeeman, or precinct chair; there are many names!). Precinct leaders help monitor polling places, but also take a local lead in registering voters, collecting signatures for ballot initiatives, and more. In 2022, Turning Point Action helped recruit more than 2,000 precinct leaders. I want to muster more than five times that number for 2024. Why not consider being one yourself?

And while you're at it, you can also try to influence the form that these elections take. In many states, the very way that ballots are cast and counted is decided at the country level. Do you want physical paper ballots instead of all-electronic voting systems? Pressure your county's election authorities to use paper ballots, or if you already use them, be on the lookout for someone trying to change things.

RUN FOR OFFICE YOURSELF

The best way to get lawmakers who pursue the policies you care about is to be one of those lawmakers yourself. If you have the time to do it properly, run for a local office yourself, or help run a friend's campaign to do the same.

When you're running for office at the state level or in a big city, it's money that matters. But in your average suburb or small town, making a competitive electoral run is often simply about putting in the work. Literally go door to door and conduct politics the old-fashioned way. Do it enough and you can meet most of the people choosing whether to vote for you.

IT DOESN'T MATTER WHERE YOU LIVE

"But Charlie!" some of you are crying. "Because of my job/family/being too lazy to move, I have no choice but to live in Portland/the Bay Area/Cambridge/Chicago/Gomorrah! This city is so liberal that even bothering to participate in politics is hopeless."

Sorry, but no dice. Sure, if you live in California, state politics may be a lost cause. If you live in the downtown of a major city, your U.S. House race probably isn't worth voting in. But local politics is *never* worth ignoring, because even in the bluest parts of America, you can move the needle to make life better for yourself and for your neighbors.

One of the worst of the Soros prosecutors was Chesa Boudin. Boudin is the son of two members of the Weather Underground and grew up with fellow Weathermen Bill Ayers and Bernardine Dohrn as his foster parents while his parents spent decades in prison for their role in a fatal armored car robbery in 1981.

In 2019, Boudin won the race for San Francisco district attorney, boosted along by several non-profits funded by George Soros. Immediately after taking office, Boudin flexed his progressive muscle by firing seven of the city's prosecutors.[315] Boudin then announced that his office would no longer prosecute cases for possession of illegal contraband if he believed the police had made a "pretextual" stop.[316] Boudin's office also stopped seeking enhanced jail sentences for gang membership or multiple prior offenses, because doing either of those things was something that starts with "r" and ends with "acist."

When Covid rolled around, Boudin used it as an excuse to release 40% of San Francisco jail inmates.[317]

When 17-year-old Deshaune Lumpkin shot and killed 6-year-old Jace Young, Boudin's office tried Lumpkin as a minor, resulting in a sentence of just 7 years. Factor in the chance of parole, and thanks to Boudin, Lumpkin might spend fewer days in prison than little Jace got to spend alive.

The results spoke for themselves: By the end of 2020, San Francisco's burglary rate was up 46%, in large part due to a handful of serial burglars who kept being arrested, only for Boudin's office to let them go immediately.[318]

It would have been easy to completely give up on San Francisco, to shrug and go "well, they voted for this." After all, it's San Francisco.

But it turns out that, even in San Francisco, it's possible to win victories on the margins. While the city is understandably filled with fanatics, not every resident of the city by the bay wanted to live in an apocalypse of crime and filth. San Francisco's Asian community, in particular, didn't see why they needed to suffer because of Mr. Boudin's crippling white guilt.

Citizens organized a recall campaign against Boudin. And despite the opposition of the San Francisco Democratic Party, the state's top officeholders, and the local press, the recall succeeded.

Is San Francisco tough on crime now? No. Is it still a liberal hellhole in countless ways? Sure. But is the city better now than it would be if Che Fan Chesa were still in charge? Absolutely.

And guess what? This wasn't a one-off! Until 2020, San Francisco's Lowell High School was one of the best public high schools in the country, with a demanding merit-based admissions process that rewarded top test scores and GPAs. But following the death of George Floyd, using Covid as an excuse, San Francisco administrators switched Lowell's admissions process to a luck-based lottery. The very next year at the school, grades crashed. Nevertheless, the city's school superintendent wanted to stay the course for at least one additional year. But under pressure from parents, particularly in the Asian community, the San Francisco school board reversed course, and narrowly voted to make merit matter at Lowell again.[319]

That's two substantive wins, in America's most notoriously blue city. I don't want any excuses that getting involved in your town is "hopeless." It's your duty as a citizen and as a conservative to be hopeful and spread that hope to others. The enemy wants you defeated and hopeless. Refuse them on both counts.

LOOKING THE PART

A quick word about your demeanor as we close the chapter. Remember that we oppose wokeness, and want to preserve our towns, because we love our neighbors.

Don't simply be a gadfly of your town, obsessed with politics and nothing else. It is far more important to be a good neighbor, not a good Republican. Don't only watch your child's school for ideological poisons. Be involved with its non-political activities, too, so that other parents will know you, trust, and regard you positively. Be an active public citizen, not a recluse. Always remember that, when you speak out at a protest or at a school board meeting, you are a representative of everyone who agrees with you. Dress well. Be clean. When you are attacked, maintain your composure and be polite. Resist the temptation to land a low blow. Be the kind of person you want running your city, because then others will want you doing the same.

CHAPTER THIRTEEN

Toppling the Education Goliath

"Give me four years to teach the children
and the seed I have sown will never be uprooted."
—Vladimir Lenin

"Train up a child in the way he should go,
And when he is old he will not depart from it."
—Proverbs 22:6

We just finished a grand tour of the federal, state, and local governments. But so far, I've had very little to say about education. There's a very simple reason, which is America's education system is by far the *biggest* source of woke poisons. The issue is so large it warrants its own dedicated chapter.

What we call *woke* was developed and nurtured in the universities, and to this day it is from those universities above all else that its tendrils spread. College students are told to take classes that promote a woke view of the world. Schools of education pump out woke teachers, who are more than ready to turn their high school, grade school, and even kindergarten classes into woke petri dishes.

But it's not just what they teach. Roughly 5% of all U.S. GDP goes into the education system.[320] That's enough money to employ a lot of people, and that's exactly what happens. Besides pumping woke poison into the classrooms themselves, America's schools are like a vast monetary reserve for woke parasites. People with degrees in grievance studies or specializations in

DEI, who will be purely negative for any company stupid enough to hire them, can instead achieve middle class incomes by taking jobs at America's lavishly funded schools.

At the individual level, the threat from America's toxic woke schools can be mitigated. But this is not a problem that can be solved through individual initiative. It's simply too huge. We can tout homeschooling or private Christian academies *ad infinitum*, but the blunt truth is that the vast majority of American parents will send their kids to public schools, because that's the cheapest, simplest, and easiest option. I can write an entire book exposing how college is a scam, but most upwardly mobile young Americans are still going to go because too many desirable jobs in America require it.

So, there is no evading the education issue. If we want to beat woke permanently, we *must* assail its stronghold in the academy. Fortunately, the attack is already well underway. Here's what has to be done to keep it going.

THE LIMITS OF DIRECT ACTION

Recently, red states have started to step up more when it comes to fighting the worst far-left obsessions that have infiltrated the classroom. Conservatives have passed laws against radical gender ideology or anti-white critical race theory being used in the classrooms. They've started evicting inappropriately sexual or anti-white books from being featured in school libraries.

I support all these laws and will be happy to see more of them. I also support every coalition of parents competing in school board elections, to try and change their local school policies and curricula.

But these actions aren't a solution by themselves. Every law regulating public schools and colleges has a basic shortcoming, which is the law's attempt to boss around the woke forces in education, rather than displacing them. All of these laws will be interpreted by hostile, radical left teachers, and they will have to be enforced by their equally radical superiors.

When Florida Gov. Ron DeSantis started demanding that the University of Florida provide him a full inventory of what their DEI work was, they gave him a list of 30 programs and initiatives adding up to about $5 million in spending. But according to Chris Rufo, who compiled his own list using open records requests, the real number of programs was closer to a *thousand*.[321]

A red state can pass laws banning CRT, but that just means the left will do its best to simply deny that whatever anti-white crap it is pushing is "not really CRT" and that conservative claims otherwise are a "conspiracy theory." A red state can pass bans on promoting transgenderism in the classroom, but if there's one thing that Libs of TikTok has proven, it's that there are countless teachers who see said promotion as their sole mission in life.

Imagine if a school had a paranoid schizophrenic as a teacher, and we tried to control him by passing a law saying he couldn't talk to children about the voices in his head or about how the CIA was sending him secret messages through his television. Pass all the laws you want, it doesn't solve the core problem, which is the children are being taught by a crazy person. The same principle applies here.

There can't be a narrow focus on bossing around teachers and professors about what they can or can't teach. It's similar to the medical problem of treating a symptom rather than the actual disease. The disease isn't simply that woke race and gender politics are in the classroom. It's that our public schools are infested with so many deeply committed extremists in the first place, and the vast majority of parents will be entrusting their children to them.

Fortunately, there is more we can do.

IT'S ABOUT MONEY

As mentioned above, one in every twenty dollars in America each year is going to education. Where does that money *come* from? The question is rhetorical, of course. It comes from you. The vast majority of money spent on K–12 schools, more than 90 percent overall, is collected at the state and local level.[322]

It's easy to say this, of course. The crucial thing is realizing how much leverage can be derived from this mastery of education dollars.

Woke schools get away with their shenanigans because *your* dollars are sent to fund them. They are able to act with impunity when they are confident that the money will keep coming no matter what. If that assurance goes away, they will change their behavior. The entire reason that free market capitalism succeeds as an economic system is because human beings respond to incentives, even self-proclaimed Marxists and socialists. If you want to change how schools and teachers behave, change their incentives.

Everything intolerable about the public school system is able to exist because public schools are allowed to avoid real competition. True, there is a market in education, but the market is not equal. Attending a private school costs thousands of dollars, while public schools are free. For most people, the choice is regrettable but automatic. If they don't have the time to homeschool, and don't have the money for a private school, then a public school is the only option.

But there is absolutely zero reason this state of affairs needs to prevail. It exists because of the assumptions we operate under for our schooling system. Currently, Americans are taxed, and then (typically) their tax dollars are handed over to public schools on a per-student basis to cover the cost of educating them.

But a revolutionary idea is taking root right now in America. What if instead of viewing education dollars as the property of principals and teachers, we viewed them as the property of the actual *students* being educated? This leads to a natural conclusion, which is rather than being forced to spend their child's education dollars at a public school they may despise, a parent should have the right to spend the education dollars at whatever school they believe is best for their child.

This revolution kicked off here in my own state of Arizona. Since 2011, Arizona has had Empowerment Scholarship Accounts, which allow a parent to receive up to 90 percent of their child's educational tax allotment to pay for private school tuition, tutoring, or other educational services of their choice outside the public school system. The program was initially available only to children from specific categories, such as those requiring special education, those on Indian reservations, and those who would otherwise have to attend chronically failing public schools.[323] But in 2022, conservatives took the bold step of asking why a program that was good for the most vulnerable couldn't also be available for everyone. Now, the ESA is available to everyone, with a benefit of up to $8,000 for the average student. Lawmakers expected $450 million worth of demand for the program in 2024. Within months, demand exceeded $900 million. More than a hundred thousand children sought to participate.[324]

Arizona's bold step has inspired conservatives all around the country. In Iowa, lawmakers passed a $7,600 voucher benefit, open to every child for any school of their parents' choice. In Florida, the benefit is roughly $8,500 per student, and once again open to everyone. In Indiana, not all students are eligible for its $5,400 vouchers . . . but more than 96% are.[325] Arkansas, Utah, and West Virginia have massively expanded vouchers as well.

In my opinion, literally every red state should follow as quickly as possible. The full effects of this policy might take decades to fully manifest, as parents adapt to a world where they have far more agency and control over what their children learn. But the possibilities are limitless. It could be that our entire understanding of education is completely wrong, and just needs the freedom of universal vouchers to show how. Maybe it makes sense for children to only spend a couple days a week in a traditional classroom, while spending the rest of their time learning practical skills or working in an apprenticeship. Maybe children learn far better if they're in class three hours a day, every day, instead of spending five days on and two off each week? I'm just making some wild guesses, but that's the beauty of a real free market in education. We get to find out, instead of being hidebound by what a few statist progressives decided education should look like a hundred years ago.

Defending these programs will take political courage. The sky-high demand for vouchers will cause liberals to shriek that the programs are costing taxpayers billions, as if throwing billions at worthless public schools so teachers could instruct kids how to have gay sex was not a far greater waste.

Critics argue that the massive expansion of parent-controlled vouchers might kill public schools. The obvious answer to that: Good! Why on earth should parents be forced to send their children to schools with shoddy outcomes at best, that teach values they abhor, when for *less* money they could enroll in a school they actually prefer? Literally everyone wins, parents, students, taxpayers, except for teachers so incompetent that they can only find employment at a public school, but not a private one.

But while red states can move toward total educational freedom, it's a safe bet that blue states won't. How can we help parents in those states? Well, fortunately, there are federal ways to leverage the money question too to change how schools behave. About 8% of public school dollars come from the federal government, and it has the power to cut these funds off in some circumstances. In fact, liberals themselves are already worrying that Republicans might do this. Let's revisit *Blowback,* the book we mentioned in Chapter 10:

> A former senior official at the Education Department under Trump said "Don't Say Gay" policies—prohibiting educators from talking about same-sex marriage—could be implemented without legislation. The former aide explained how it could be done: the department has the power to restrict funding from school districts that are on probation.
>
> "They would tell the Office of Civil Rights at the Department of Education that any complaints of 'grooming' automatically open a systemic investigation," he noted, "and put school districts under consent orders."
>
> Knowing this, right-wing figures will try to gin up false allegations. That paves the way for the department to open investigations and withhold education dollars, or attach conditions to them, such as forbidding discussions of same-sex marriage in the classroom.
>
> "It's the 'Don't Say Gay' version of entrapment," the official deadpanned.[326]

Once again, skip past Taylor's spin about "false allegations" and dig into what he's really saying. A Republican administration can cut off funding to schools that are putting inappropriate, radical gender ideology into the classroom! Thank you for the tip, Miles!

This is all equally true for the collegiate level. Remember in Ch. 10, where we suggested cutting off federal grants to any school running a center dedicated to "disinformation"? Well, this power can be used far more aggressively, often thanks to the very same civil rights laws that until now have been used as weapons for enforcing wokeness. Title VI of the Civil Rights Act bans racial discrimination for any school getting federal loans or grants. Even a *whisper* that a school might lose cash from its government sugar daddy for practicing racially discriminatory admissions, or holding segregated graduation ceremonies, or forcing students to submit to anti-white diversity trainings, would immediately make those practices vanish. So let's make it happen!

SHOCK AND AWE

The New College of Florida never knew what hit them.

Until the early days of 2023, New College was remarkable mostly as a display of what it was possible to get away with as a public, taxpayer-funded school in America. Established in the 1960s, New College was truly left-wing in its very essence. The school had no grades, instead relying exclusively on written evaluations. Its website was a hodgepodge of DEI buzzwords. *The New York Times* simply called it the "most progressive" school in the state.[327]

And then, practically overnight, that all changed. In a single day, Florida Gov. Ron DeSantis appointed six new trustees to the school's board of trustees. Among them were anti-CRT journalist Chris Rufo, Hillsdale government professor Matthew Spalding, and Charles Kesler, editor at the conservative *Claremont Review of Books.*

Within a matter of days, the new majority on the board fired New College's president and installed former Florida House speaker and education commissioner Richard Corcoran as her interim replacement. In March, they fired the school's dean for diversity, equity, and inclusion.[328] In April, the trustees denied tenure to five professors.[329] In May, they dismissed the school's librarian. Other faculty at the school left in despair.

The new board hasn't been secretive about what it wants to do. In essence, they want to turn New College into a new college, a public iteration of Hillsdale College in Michigan, with a revamped core curriculum that places an emphasis on a classic liberal arts education.[330]

What Florida Republicans did was finally treat a public college the same way the left has been treating them for decades: As, among other things, political operations, which embody the values of the public. Florida voters don't like woke, which is why they've elected conservatives consistently for decades. So, why should the colleges their taxpayer dollars fund an overtly left-wing school with ideologically left-wing programs that go directly against their values? The refreshing answer from DeSantis's administration: They shouldn't.

What can be done at one college can be done at others. It's not that every college needs to be a copycat of Hillsdale (though a few more certainly wouldn't hurt). But the strategies used to remake New College can be applied just about anywhere. There are more than 1,600 public colleges and universities in America. Seventy-three percent of U.S. college students attend a public school.[331] For decades, it's been taken as a matter of course that even public colleges will be liberal places, with overwhelmingly liberal faculties, administrators, course offerings, and policies.

It's time that conservatives stopped accepting this as the status quo. Ethnic or gender studies departments (the "grievance studies" majors) can be abolished at public colleges by simply passing state laws abolishing them. New departments with more appealing curricula can be created from scratch. There is no reason, except defeatism and laziness, for accepting that campuses have to be ideologically left-wing.

REMAKE THE BOARDS

Here's a question: What's the difference between a U.S. Supreme Court justice, and an appointed regent at a public university?

Trick question! There is no difference. Both are appointed by politicians. Therefore, both are fundamentally political positions.

In Chapter 6, I described how insidious woke content has been allowed to exist at both the University of Oklahoma and at the University of Tennessee. Woke organizations, woke policies, and woke personnel flourish at those schools, even though they are state-run, state-funded institutions in red states.

The first step toward improving the dozens of public colleges existing in red states is to treat their senior positions as what they are, inherently *political* jobs. That's not to say that just any Republican should be appointed as a college regent. Just the opposite in fact (you wouldn't pick a random person to be a Supreme Court justice, either!). Far too often, the regency of a state university is treated as an afterthought, a political plum to reward a supporter, or as some kind of lifetime achievement award for distinguished citizens. It should be none of those things. The regent of a state university is, in many cases, an individual with enormous, though rarely exercised, power.

For instance, here is an incomplete list of some of the powers held by the board of trustees for the University of Tennessee:

- "Monitoring nonacademic programs, other than athletics, including programs related to diversity, and monitoring compliance of nonacademic programs with federal and state laws, rules, and regulations."
- "Overseeing and monitoring the operation of the intercollegiate athletics programs, including proposed actions reasonably anticipated to have a long-term impact on the operations, reputation, and standing of the intercollegiate athletics programs or the University."
- "Approval of policies governing student conduct and disciplinary actions."
- "Approval of policies and procedures, including campus handbook provisions, governing academic freedom [and] appointment, retention, promotion, tenure, evaluation, and termination of faculty members."
- "Approval of the termination of academic programs when termination of tenured or tenure-track faculty members is involved."
- "Approval of the annual operating budget and thereby confirming the salaries of all University employees."[332]

In addition to all of the above, the board has absolute authority to hire and fire the University of Tennessee's president at any time. That president in turn has absolute authority to hire and fire the chancellors of specific campuses, as well as other senior positions in the university.

Clearly, the board of the University of Tennessee has all the ingredients necessary to manage the University of Tennessee completely in accordance with the values actually held by Tennessee voters. The board itself is hand-picked by the governor. The board can name whatever president it wants, and fire him if he refuses to hire or fire the right people.

Taking all of the above into account, it becomes clear that whatever woke-ness exists at the University of Tennessee is not some fact of nature. It is an affirmative choice, made every year that Tennessee conservatives fail to act. And the same is true all over the place. In Idaho, the state board of education has 8 members, one elected and seven picked by the governor for five-year terms, and it oversees *all* public colleges in the state.[333] In Indiana, the governor appoints the state higher education commission, as well as a majority of seats for separate boards of trustees at each public university in the state.

Sometimes, there are obstacles. In Iowa, the governor appoints trustees to oversee the state's public universities, but a trustee must be confirmed by a two-thirds vote in the State Senate, putting a limit on how political a nominee can be—but that said, as I write this, Republicans actually *do* have a two-thirds supermajority in the Iowa Senate.

The point here isn't to run through every single red state and lay out what, exactly, each of them should be doing. Rather, I want to make the point that *knowing* what powers a board of trustees holds, and exercising those powers, should be a core objective of conservatives everywhere they hold power. A trustee seat at a college is a political position, with immense long-term impact. Act accordingly!

MAKE IT UNNECESSARY

One reason that fixing how our colleges operate feels so pressing is because of how necessary most of America considers a college degree to be. With only a tiny number of exceptions, if you want to join America's elite, you're expected to get a degree, or two or three of them. The most respected jobs in America require a degree. But it doesn't have to be that way. I'm not saying that education is bad—just the opposite. Education is excellent, but *credentialism* is toxic.

Everywhere possible, red states should look into removing degree re-quirements for jobs. In 2023, Virginia Gov. Glenn Youngkin eliminated degree requirements for 90 percent of Virginia's state jobs.[334] I'd say that's a good start, but the goal ought to be 100 percent. I'm not calling to lower standards. In fact, it's *colleges* that have lowered their standards, to the point where getting a degree from one barely reveals everything except the ability to show up to class on time for four years straight. Everywhere we possibly can, we should aim to replace the demand for a degree with a demand for actual demonstrated ability.

Instead of requiring an expensive degree to hold a job, allow people to show mastery through an apprenticeship, or by simply taking an online, pen-and-paper, or practical test of the relevant skills. If a student can learn the material just as well by tutoring themselves online instead of forking over a hundred grand to a cartel, we should let them do so. *Encourage* such paths by providing funding to apprenticeship programs.

One of the best places to reduce credentialism, in fact, is for education itself. Especially over the past twenty years, the education cartel has thrown up many barriers to becoming a teacher. Every state requires a bachelor's degree, and many strongly encourage a master's as well. I haven't seen a single piece of evidence that American education improved thanks to these requirements. That's no surprise, because these requirements are a joke. America's education majors have some of the lowest standardized test scores of all college students, yet they finish college with the highest grades.[335] In other words, their coursework is a joke.

So why even bother requiring it? Instead, get rid of that requirement, and instead make prospective teachers pass a test demonstrating that they understand the material they are going to teach.

Could a few grossly incompetent teachers slip through this system? Sure. But tons of grossly incompetent (and predatory) teachers *already* slip through. The fix is easy: Instead of making teachers virtually unfireable, make them *easy* to fire if they show evidence of incompetence.

MASTER THE ACCREDITATION RACKET

American schools operate on a system of accreditation: Various outside oversight bodies assess schools and pronounce that their diplomas and degrees are valid reflections of the competency those credentials are supposed to reflect.

If we start to turn the tide against campus wokeness, it's inevitable that the left will try to counter by weaponizing the accreditation racket. The lie will go out that, if schools aren't properly promoting diversity, or respecting the "academic freedom" of Marxist charlatans, or pushing the latest left-wing woowoo in the guise of science, then they are no longer valid academic institutions.

In early 2023, trustees at the University of North Carolina began moving forward with plans to create a School of Civic Life and Leadership. The center's intent would be to "explore American civic values with the full freedom of expression, intellectual diversity, and open inquiry that such studies require"—in other words, the plan was to hire professors of political science, history, and similar topics who actually reflected America's full ideological spectrum, rather than the narrow band that is able to clear the typical faculty hiring committee.

Almost immediately, UNC began receiving vague threats from its accreditor, the Southern Association of Colleges and Schools.

> At a meeting Tuesday of the Governor's Commission on the Governance of Public Universities in North Carolina, accreditation official Belle Wheelan declared that the UNC board would be getting a letter from her agency. Ms. Wheelan is president of the Southern Association of Colleges and Schools Commission on Colleges (SACS), which accredits UNC, and she referred to "a news article that came out" on the plan to create a new school.
>
> "We're waiting for them to explain that, because that's kind of not the way we do business." she said, according to a report by HigherEd Works. "We're gonna . . . either get them to change it, or the institution will be on warning" with SACS.[336]

These threats are nothing to be scoffed at. The accreditation racket is, in fact, a central component of how the federal government is able to hold so much sway over American colleges and universities. Federal student loans are only available for schools that are accredited by a federally approved accreditor. Similarly, tax plans, which allow parents to save up money for their children's educations tax-free, may only be used for accredited schools.[337] Accreditors, in turn, are recognized by the federal government. For the great mass of undergraduate colleges and universities, there are only seven accreditors. For specific professional schools there are even fewer. For medical schools, there are only two approved accrediting bodies. For law schools, there is only one, the American Bar Association.

The American Bar Association having a total stranglehold on accrediting law schools becomes more worrisome when one knows more about how the ABA operates. In early 2022, the ABA passed a requirement mandating that all accredited law schools educate students on their duty to "work to eliminate racism." The requirement also mandated a professional responsibility course, covering "the obligation of lawyers to promote a justice system that provides equal access and eliminates bias, discrimination, and racism in the law." At the same meeting, for good measure, the ABA issued a call for law schools to accommodate "lactating individuals"—but never once used the word "woman" in the process.[338]

The continuing power of these accreditors is a weapon the left uses for institutional domination. Conservatives should be looking to break it up. Thankfully, this is something 2024 GOP candidates are already talking about.[339] The Trump Administration already liberalized regulations, making it easier for a school to switch which accreditor it uses. But the next GOP administration could go further. It could approve new accreditors, to increase competition. It could ban them from imposing DEI or other woke requirements on schools seeking accreditation. Or, best of all, it could simply devolve the question of accreditation to the states themselves. Then, red states could band together, collectively creating and using a new accrediting agency purged of the political agendas of currently existing ones.

This is one area where collective action will be critical. If one school or one state rebels against the system, the left will try to ostracize it, and treat it as illegitimate (it's very possible to imagine a blue state refusing to recognize degrees from a red state that reforms its colleges too much). But just like it's easy to cancel one person but not a thousand people, the left may be able to bully one college but can't go to war against dozens of them.

SHOW UP ON CAMPUS

Turning Point USA is focused on America's college campuses more than anywhere else. No matter what the promising signs are, I know that a large majority of students at college campuses lean left. They dominate student governments and they dominate student activism.

But just like in big cities, a left-wing majority is not an excuse to give up and not show up at all. For one, student government elections aren't partisan the way almost all other U.S. elections are, nor are the issues easily mapped onto state and national politics. It is entirely possible for those holding conservative values to win by simply working harder, organizing better, and having a more positive, organic appeal.

At Turning Point, we've created the Campus Victory Project, with the aim of identifying and recruiting potential campus leaders to run for student government positions, and even roles like student body president or vice president. We also train them on how to campaign for their rights and values on campus.

If you're on campus yourself, there's no excuse to be checked out! Join one of our chapters and learn the ins and outs of how your school chooses its leaders and sets its policies. Just like local government, there are massive advantages to simply caring more and being prepared. Don't let the left win on your campus because they face no dissent!

CONCLUSION

Throughout all of this, as we remake our schools from something treacherous and wretched into something useful, there will be howls, and not necessarily just from the left. For a lot of people, the status quo has been around so long that any change at all feels extreme. Libertarians will complain that telling teachers not to bring anti-white hatred into the classroom, or pornography into the library, is a brand of "authoritarianism." It's not. Saying that schoolteachers have the right to show pornography or CRT to children, with no opposition or limitation from parents or voters, is to say that teachers have a legal right to commit child abuse. They don't. Period.

Our schools do not exist above or outside the political process. As parents and as citizens, we have the right to decide what our schools exist to do, and what they exist to teach.

PART FOUR

CHANGING YOURSELF

CHAPTER FOURTEEN

Beat the Woke

In 2001 one of my favorite writers, Theodore Dalrymple, published *Life at the Bottom*, a book assessing the state of the working class in his own country, the United Kingdom. Well, "working class" is the wrong term, because as Dalrymple explained, they increasingly didn't work. Not because of economic collapse, not from physical infirmity, but from something different.

"Having previously worked as a doctor in some of the poorest countries in Africa, as well as in very poor countries in the Pacific and Latin America, I have little hesitation in saying that the mental, cultural, emotional, and spiritual impoverishment of the Western underclass is the greatest of any large group of people I have ever encountered anywhere," Dalrymple says in the book's prologue.[340]

In a climate of superficially unimaginable prosperity, Dalrymple, a psychiatrist, found unimaginable decay.

It's time for the final part of our game plan for defeating the woke. We've laid out what the threat is. We've described how to change our attitudes, so we can be more aggressive and less boxed-in by limits defined by the people who hate us. We've delved into how to change our strategy. We've explained the ways we need to change the law.

But in the end, wokeness is not just about the country and civilization. It's about the battle between good and evil that, as Solzhenitsyn wrote, is fought within each individual human heart.[341]

Wokeness creeps in where normal human relationships have gone sour or crippled. It thrives where people have forgotten or given up on their obligations and duties to God, their family, their friends, and their community. It triumphs where men and women are cowardly, neurotic, and weak. It wins recruits among the broken, the unhappy, and morally sick, who want to blame an outside cause for what ails them within. It has gained so much ground in America precisely because so many people have decayed from the kind of person they should be.

Think about what the most committed wokeists are like, deep down: They're petty. They're consumed with resentment of what is beautiful and successful. They are constantly on the hunt for some outside force that is to blame for everything wrong in their lives. They're miserable and mentally unwell. They deface and mutilate and bloat up their bodies, as if willing their exteriors to become as hideous as what lies within.

Defeating woke isn't simply about changing our attitudes, our strategy, or our laws. Winning a final victory requires that we change ourselves.

Let's be honest here: Liberalism could vanish tomorrow and this would still be a badly ailing country. We would still be crippled by obesity, addiction, and broken families, and we would still be spiritually adrift, because all these problems are far worse among self-identified conservatives than they were for *all* Americans, liberal or not, half a century ago.

Let's be even more honest. Look at yourself, your friends, and your extended family. Do you *really* feel like the inheritors of America's greatness? What would your great-grandparents make of you? Would it be entirely positive, or would they find many ways you fall short?

I know, I know, it's easy to spout off advice. I'm not saying this to claim I'm perfect. Instead, take everything I say in the spirit of acknowledging that every one of us is flawed and imperfect.

But even if we are all imperfect, all of us can be *better*. And in fact, that is the single most important thing all of us can do to fend off the woke threat.

The following chapters will explore how to improve yourself in more detail, but for those who want a quick and dirty list, here's a few short suggestions, divided up by age and sex.

IF YOU'RE A YOUNG ADULT (18–27)

Men:

- Learn at least one skill that will let you consistently make money well into adulthood.
- Get into the best physical shape you reasonably can without getting vain about it.
- Learn how to dress properly for a date, a business meeting, and a wedding.
- Find a religious community that appeals to you and attend regularly.
- Help your younger siblings get off the ground of young adulthood. Don't leave them to fend for themselves.
- Call your mom back, even when you're a bit busy.
- Volunteer for something thankless and demanding, like a political campaign.

Women:

- Date seriously right away, with an eye towards marriage and family. Make your future family a top priority *now*, not something you'll worry about later.
- If your goal is to put family and children above your career, avoid an educational path that involves large amounts of debt.
- Watch your weight and do your best to maintain your attractiveness.
- Listen to your parents, especially your mom, and don't be afraid to ask her for advice.
- Volunteer to help out with your Sunday school nursery

IF YOU'RE A LITTLE OLDER (28–45)

Men:

- Become well-acquainted with all major types of saving and investments. Especially if you're still single and have money to spare, save and build wealth for the future.
- Develop a career that will let you support a family on a single income.
- Volunteer as much as you're able in your place of worship. Be involved in the men's group and be a spiritual companion to other men in the parish.
- Help your parents better plan for their retirement and look for ways you could help them save money by being economical.

Women:

- If you are married, have whatever kids you plan to have sooner rather than later. If you wait, it will be harder than you think.
- Make a plan for homeschooling your children, or find a school your children can attend that will match your values.
- Keep your home life active. Don't outsource parenting to screens, and don't let your family time consist of family movie nights.
- Follow what your city government and school board are doing. If something is amiss, contact political allies and raise hell, sooner rather than later.

IF YOU'RE IN LATER ADULTHOOD (46–65)

- Be a mentor. Be the man who can offer a job, an opportunity, or a leg up to someone younger who needs it. Be the woman who tells girls what they need to hear, not what they want to hear.
- Impress on your children the value of taking dating, marriage, and family seriously at an early age.

- Take an active interest not just in what your kids and grandkids are learning at school but what they do for fun. Find out their favorite books, music, movies and internet hobbies and do a little research on them. This will quickly help you understand what their mind is really feeding on, and you can save a lot of trouble down the road if you intervene now.
- Be an overall leader in your community. If you have the skills for it, run for office yourself.
- Take your health seriously. Don't let your weight creep up with age. Make your doctor appointments. Age gracefully.

IF YOU'RE RETIRED (65+)

- Stay involved and engaged in your community. Be a respected elder at church. Volunteer for time-consuming political jobs like being an election worker, a canvasser, or a poll watcher.
- If your kids or grandkids are single, consider getting to know other parents with eligible children, and arrange some introductions.
- Don't check out with a lazy, pleasure-chasing retirement. Instead of planning to burn up your entire nest egg and die penniless, think about how you can help your children or grandchildren get started in life. Leave something for your church or a local classical school in your will.
- Be the beloved elderly neighbor, not the busybody or crotchety one.
- Read, do puzzles, or engage in other activities to keep your mind sharp, as long as possible.

Here's my challenge to you, or really, to us: Ask yourself every day, *How can I be better?* Do you honor old things, the things that came before? Are you configuring yourself to the divine? Do you believe in God? If so, do you try to do what is pleasing to Him?

Every micron of improvement in your life, whether it's losing weight, getting to church, being financially independent rather than reliant on a corporate master, or having a better relationship with your children, is a rebuke to what the woke value, and to their ability to colonize your mind and the minds of those around you. Every improvement is a small step toward victory in the great battle for this country.

That might sound weighty and ominous, so I want to emphasize that all of this should be done with a joyous spirit. Wokeness is miserable, so happiness itself rebukes them, and happiness is a choice. Every day, you can choose to wallow in bitterness, or you can reject bad thoughts from your mind. You can stay in a rut of bad habits or make the conscious choice to be happy by doing the things that we know promote happiness.

Yet it's a choice not enough make. The famous psychiatrist Thomas Szasz, in an article for the British medical journal *Lancet*, described happiness as a psychiatric condition![342] It was a joke, of course, but only barely. In 2023, "pleasure" is everywhere, but happiness is rare.

The key to a happier life is to pour your energies in things outside yourself. Be the person who is happy he fulfilled his duty to others, not the person bitter that others didn't give you what you think you deserve.

In the following smaller chapters I focus on some of the things we can do to be happy and flourish as people, because with that flourishing, we will triumph.

CHAPTER FIFTEEN

Be a Lover of Old Things

In 1992 Bruce Springsteen sang that there were 57 channels, and nothing on. At the dawn of cable TV, 57 channels was a staggering number, but today's reality renders that number quaint. Satellite subscribers might have five hundred channels. Then, separately, a person can subscribe to more than half a dozen streaming services, each worth the equivalent of many TV channels by itself. In 2009, America had 210 scripted TV shows. In 2022, it had 600.[343]

But that only scratches the surface. We live in the age of the "influencer" and "content creator." For every scripted show on television, there are a hundred YouTube documentarians, Twitter political pundits, or TikTok comedians. The world of podcasts dwarfs the old pre-Internet world of the radio.

This torrent of content drives all of us, quite literally, to distraction. As Theodore Dalrymple wrote recently, "entertainment, or rather the ubiquity of entertainment, is one of the greatest causes of boredom in the modern world, [a]nd boredom is itself a much underestimated state of mind in the production of human misconduct and therefore of misery."

The truth, as you know (and really, as everyone knows), is that America is awash in cultural trash, trashy movies, trashy TV, trashy music, trashy games, trashy literature. Ultimately, these make for trashy lives. On top of that, almost every culture product pumped out today is infused with the propaganda of wokeness. Social scientist Charles Murray, who wrote a sweeping survey of human accomplishment up to 1950 fittingly titled *Human Achievement*, predicted that almost no art from the second half of the 20th century will be remembered 200 years from now.

Murray might well be right, or if he's wrong, what is remembered won't be the stuff that is popular today. Because what is popular today is mass-produced schlock. In 1960, the top two grossing films of the year were *Spartacus* and *Psycho*, both regarded as among the greatest films ever made. Not a single film in the top 10 was a sequel, and they ranged widely in genre from horror to rom-com to epic to drama. By 2022, everything changed. Every single top 10 film in 2022 was a sequel or "reboot" of some kind. Four were specifically superhero films. Good films are still made today, but the ones that most dominate the cultural landscape are repetitive, derivative, and frequently terrible.

Sure, consuming trash won't kill you, at least not immediately. But it does rot away at your soul, and it slowly drags you away from the timeless truths.

I don't know how many times I've heard conservatives complain about Star Wars going woke, Amazon ruining Lord of the Rings, or Disney shoving LGBT propaganda into children's movies, and then go back and *keep watching the same things*.

It doesn't matter if you think you're watching something "ironically," or if you say you're "hate-watching" it. It doesn't matter if it's just a "time-waster." First of all, why are you wasting time, anyway? It's the only thing you will never get more of. It doesn't matter if you try to provide your kids moral instruction to counterbalance the lectures they're getting from their favorite cartoons. What you read, watch, and do shapes who you are. Garbage in, garbage out.

Do you want to be a person who adheres to pre-woke values? Then be a person who consumes the art and culture of the pre-woke era. You are the heir of more than three thousand years of Judeo-Christian and Greco-Roman civilization. So don't be a slave to the trendy content of the moment. Be a consumer of old things, the things that built and shaped the civilization you want to preserve.

My advice to you is to *be intentional* in the culture you consume, and what absorbs your leisure time. Take command of your life. Do not mindlessly watch whatever reality show is on TV, whatever book is on the bestseller list, or whatever the online algorithm pukes up for you.

I'm not saying you categorically shouldn't watch anything new, or anything from a big Hollywood franchise. But you should recognize what you are choosing to do, and enjoy it in moderation, the same way you might enjoy the occasional piece of junk food or skip the occasional workout. Pure distraction television, like reality TV shows, is the entertainment equivalent of eating nothing but Jolly Ranchers and should be kept to a minimum.

As conservatives, we value things that have stood the test of time. That applies to morals and political systems, but it applies just as much to art and culture. It's not just that a play or novel written 300 years ago can still possibly speak to us. It's that, by virtue of its sheer timelessness, it can speak to us *better* than almost anything produced today.

So go out and find classic books that are still being talked about a hundred years or more after their release. Watch films and read plays that have endured as classics long after their original runs ended. Ideally, don't watch much television (it's a medium designed for plopping on your couch 8 hours straight), but if you do, look for shows that stood the test of time. Chances are, almost everything coming out this year will be entirely forgotten in a decade.

Do you want to be a better Christian or a better Jew? Then read Scripture, as well as classic religious works in your faith tradition. Do you want to be a better thinker? Read Plato and Marcus Aurelius. Want to understand the American experiment? It's still best to start with *The Federalist Papers* and go from there.

I have a busy schedule, but despite that I do my best to read and study whatever I can. Throughout 2022 and 2023, I spent a lot of my free time working (very slowly) through the Pentateuch (the first five books of the Bible) in the original Hebrew. True, that's tougher than watching ten episodes of *The Bachelor* or marathoning Disney's new Star Wars films, but I think it was more worthwhile, too.

A bit of good news: While modern tech has helped fuel the current deluge of trash, it can also be a great ally if you know how to use it. A half-century ago, finding an old book, or even learning of its existence, could be a genuine challenge. Today, finding just about any book in human history is trivial. Even the most obscure book can be bought from an online store, and if a work is old enough to be in the public domain (anything more than ninety-five years old, more or less), you can get a digital copy for free to read on a portable e-book reader in a matter of seconds. Those e-readers themselves can be had for less than fifty dollars. The only excuse any of us has for not being enormously well-read is our own failure to properly cultivate ourselves.

The same goes for other types of entertainment. Hollywood might be pumping out poison constantly, but for now at least, they're happy to provide their old classics for a small profit. There is literally a century of classic cinema and a lifetime's worth of pre-woke television, so if you must watch something, why not watch that? The Walt Disney Company may be horrifyingly woke today, but their founder and namesake was not. He was a great American, and films the company made during his lifetime are justifiable classics. As I write this many people are looking forward with dread to an obnoxious live-action version of *Snow White,* but when was the last time you watched the original? Have your children even seen it?

Speaking of children, being intentional about what *they* are exposed to is even more important than policing yourself. For far too many parents, screens and algorithms have become their means of outsourcing the job of parenting. But the frightening reality is if you decide to let Disney do it, *they will* raise your children for you, and your children will come out with Disney's values instead of yours.

Young adult books can be even more hazardous. Countless young adult novels that look like harmless fantasy or slice-of-life stories are now packed with explicit left-wing themes and some even feature explicit sex scenes. We've come a long way from the days of *The Chronicles of Narnia* and *The Hobbit.* But given those books still exist, why not make sure your house is filled with those books rather than the alternatives?

When watching entertainment with your children (and if your child is quite young I recommend you watch almost all of their entertainment with them) you shouldn't be disengaged. Talk to them about the story. Explain character motivations and discuss the themes. Cultivate in them an ability to find hidden depth and appreciate aesthetic beauty, rather than enjoying everything on the most superficial level.

Don't let your children fall down a rabbit hole of video games. If you're a young person, don't fall down that rabbit hole yourself. Playing something here and there is fine. But more than any other entertainment form ever created, addictive video games have the potential to eat thousands of hours of a person's life with nothing to show for it.

But free time shouldn't just be for consuming media for fun. It's important to spend your time actively learning about history, and not just for gaining a bunch of fun facts. Actually spend the time reading, learning, and thinking critically about the events of the past. The left itself constantly lies about history, through mechanisms like the 1619 project, and the best way to combat misinformation and propaganda is with knowledge and truth. In Orwell's *Nineteen Eighty-Four,* the perpetual revision of history is a core part of the Party's all-consuming domination. The Left needs to constantly denigrate and lie about our past to make the horrible rottenness of the present look fine in comparison. Chances are, you've heard someone on the left say something along the lines of, "We cannot go back to the way things were. The way things are today may not be great, but to go back to the past is to enter hell." This is a historical distortion, or to put it more plainly, a lie. In the 1970s, the left painted the 1950s as hellish for being racist. In the 1990s, it painted the 60s and 70s as hellish for being sexist. In the 2010s, it painted the 90s as hellish for being anti-gay. And now, we're at the point where it paints virtually everything before just a few years ago as racist, sexist, homophobic, *and* transphobic.

While the left constantly demands that you "educate yourself," they don't mean it. In response, familiarize yourself with the history of America and of Western civilization.

To genuinely understand history is to refute the left's reductive vision of the world. A person who has read about the French and Russian Revolutions will recognize the recurring gaps between what the left promises and what it actually does. A person who knows about Mao's Cultural Revolution will see the parallels in 2020's traumatic Floyd-a-palooza. A person who knows about the events leading up to World War II can confidently ignore left-wing shrieks that every prominent Republican is the second or third or fifteenth coming of Hitler.

If you're a TV and movie fan, think of it this way: history is the story of the prequel. It's the characters and the people who drove the plot in the earlier seasons of the TV show. Unlike the leather and rubber suited superheroes of Hollywood, these people you can learn about in history really existed. They built your world!

I don't presume to be the world's top expert on what to read. I have definitely not read every book I am about to list. But as I said, none of us is perfect. Consider it a starting-off point for serious reading about our shared Western heritage.

LITERATURE:

The Iliad and *The Odyssey* by Homer
The Divine Comedy by Dante Alighieri
Emma by Jane Austen
The Complete Works of William Shakespeare
Crime and Punishment by Fyodor Dostoevsky
War and Peace by Leo Tolstoy
The Thirty-Nine Steps by John Buchan
Wuthering Heights by Emily Brontë
Nineteen Eighty-Four by George Orwell
Scoop by Evelyn Waugh
The Power and the Glory by Graham Greene
The Bonfire of the Vanities by Tom Wolfe
My Ántonia by Willa Cather
Professor Borges: A Course on English Literature by Jorge Luis Borges
The Collected Short Stories by Anton Chekhov

HISTORY:

The Civil War: A Narrative by Shelby Foote
History of the English-Speaking Peoples by Winston Churchill
The Great Terror by Robert Conquest
Parallel Lives by Plutarch
From Dawn to Decadence by Jacques Barzun
A History of the American People by Paul Johnson
The Russian Revolution by Richard Pipes
Citizens: A Chronicle of the French Revolution by Simon Schama

PHILOSOPHY, POLITICS AND ECONOMICS

The Republic by Plato
Meditations by Marcus Aurelius
The City of God by Augustine of Hippo
The Imitation of Christ by Thomas à Kempis
The Federalist Papers by James Madison, Alexander Hamilton, and
　John Jay
Orthodoxy by GK Chesterton
Man's Search for Meaning by Viktor Frankl
The Abolition of Man by C.S. Lewis
The Fatal Conceit: The Errors of Socialism by FA Hayek
The True Believer by Eric Hoffer
Collected Essays by George Orwell
Capitalism and Freedom by Milton Friedman
Genius: A Mosaic of One Hundred Exemplary Creative Minds by Har-
　old Bloom

Appreciating and learning about the art, literature, teachings, and morals of the past aren't just for education, despite the value of properly educating oneself. Engaging with this older content and these older ideals carry many other benefits for an individual and their community. For one, it will give you a better relationship with older generations. If you're younger, say under 40, have you ever thought seriously about things from the perspective of an older person? The world is jarring enough to those who grow up in it, but to be an older person is to see a world that is growing stranger and stranger at blistering speed. People you looked to for guidance die just like anyone else. Institutions that you thought were eternal fade in importance or vanish entirely. In the words of Exodus, "Now there arose a new king over Egypt, who did not know Joseph." Zoomers don't necessarily know Frank Sinatra, Magic Johnson, Richard Nixon, or Katherine Hepburn. Someday, you may be astonished that younger people don't know Taylor Swift, Tom Brady, or Harrison Ford. As hard as it is to believe, you may even live to see the day where young people have no idea who Donald Trump was!

Feeling the world change under your feet is pretty alienating. It's comforting, then, when a young person is not just familiar with the world as it is now but also as it was when their parents and grandparents were younger. This might sound superficial, but it's not. As I said, wokeness is penetrating where old human ties are fading away, and the widening divide between old and young is as much a part of that as anything. We should do our part to close that gap.

Finally, we should engage with and enjoy old things for that most elusive benefit we call perspective. As Ecclesiastes says, there really is nothing new under the sun. The social tumult we face today also faced the 60s generation. The political crisis unfolding in Washington has much in common with the one facing Rome during the late republic. The cowardly, immoral, and downright leaders of our nation have ample parallels in the Book of Kings. Issues we see as peculiar or particularly unique to our own time are in fact ones that have happened again and again. In fact, the mistaken belief that one's era has no comparison in the past is one recurring delusion throughout human history. Knowing more about the past not only helps us from repeating old mistakes, but it can help us gain perspective as we work to carve a path forward to a better future.

So, think carefully about your use of leisure time. Does it enrich your life? Does it improve your perspective? Does it challenge your mind or expose you to beautiful displays of profound truths? Does it strengthen your connection to the great civilization you have inherited? Or does it cause corrosion, distraction, and decay?

CHAPTER SIXTEEN

Log Off For a Bit

"Distracted from distraction by distraction."
— T.S. Eliot

*"There is nothing wrong with entertainment.
As some psychiatrist once put it, we all build castles in the air.
The problems come when we try to live in them."*
— Neil Postman

The rise of woke is inextricably entwined with the rise of the Internet and the creation of the online world. Some of our most important political battles are waged entirely online. When Elon Musk bought Twitter, I remarked on my show that it was the most important single purchase in American history since Thomas Jefferson bought the Louisiana Territory off a cash-strapped Napoleon for just $15 million. I still believe that.

Nevertheless, if the battle against wokeness will be fought online, it will be *won* by going offline and joining the real world.

It's easy to over-romanticize the rise of smartphones and the Internet, and speak about online's influence and how it "connected the globe," put every person in instant contact with an "information superhighway," blah blah blah. Sure. "The web" can still be great.

But deep down, what is the smartphone for most people, most of the time? It's just a television. A television with tens of thousands of channels that you can fit in your pocket. By *far* the biggest use of smartphones, and the rest of the web, is simply to waste time on transient entertainment. Apple and Samsung don't make smartphones. They make tiny TVs that you can, if you want, stick to your ear and use to make a voice call, or tap on to send a message.

This is actually a fairly new development, even when it comes to the Internet.

Back in the aforementioned 1990s, when personal computers first got into people's homes, the Internet was almost exclusively a *text*-based medium. Spending "too much time online" primarily meant reading too many websites and getting into "flame wars" with strangers on forums (if you're younger, ask your uncle about this). You'd read a newsletter or amateurish blog posts (though the very word hadn't been invented yet) to get excited about those upcoming Star Wars prequels, which were surely going to be the greatest films ever made (we were very naive in the 1990s).

In the 2000s, as broadband came around, the internet could afford to show people more pictures (you can guess what kinds of pictures people liked) and let them download music. Spending too much time online in this era might have meant too much time hunting for music to pirate or playing the first online-only games.

But in truth, the modern Internet as we know it is entirely a post-smartphone phenomenon. Internet speeds have become so fast, and machine quality has become so high, that for the past fifteen years, spending "too much time online" now almost always means spending too much time watching videos. Maybe it's called YouTube, or TikTok, or Instagram, but functionally it is no different than spending too much time plopped on your couch watching *The Price is Right*. As I write this in 2023, it is actually the first year in history where the average person's time spent watching online videos each day (more than two and a half hours!) exceeds the time spent watching traditional television.[344]

Many conservatives have talked about restricting or banning the TikTok app because of its links to Communist China, and the inherent security risks that presents. Those risks are real, and it cannot be denied that simply using TikTok means both forking over your contact list and letting the company stick a keylogger onto your phone.

But truthfully, the greatest harm from TikTok is probably not whatever China does with its data. It's the rampant use of TikTok itself. In 2021, American children and teenagers spent an *average* of 91 minutes *per day* visiting TikTok and consuming its endless torrent of new videos.[345] That's *in addition* to the 51 minutes a day on average they spend watching YouTube and its *own* endless torrent of YouTube. That's just TikTok and YouTube. When you add in streaming services, playing online video games, scanning Twitter or Facebook, or any other kind of the countless parasocial activities young people do online, that number goes up fast. As time has gone on, the types of activities that have become popular online have become ever more detached from any kind of activity at all. Video games were already a waste of time, but today millions of people don't necessarily even play them, they *watch other people* play them on YouTube or on streaming sites like Twitch.

All of this is, to say the least, a big waste of time. If you play an hour of video games a day, watch an hour of TV, and then supplement that with two hours of browsing YouTube, Instagram, and TikTok, pretty soon you have exhausted huge quantities of leisure time you will never get back. I'm certainly not calling for a war on leisure, but this sort of leisure is just about the emptiest imaginable. If you're a young person, it keeps you distracted and isolated, sapping real-life relationships (and maybe keeping you from finding a spouse). Since you're plopped in a chair or on a couch, you either shrivel away or bloat up rather than remaining healthy and fit. You pick up none of the skills and knowledge that might come with reading a book or developing a physically engaging hobby.

Life is about opportunity cost. If we're lucky, we'll get to experience about thirty thousand days during our lives. Rich or poor, powerful or powerless, all of us have just 24 hours in each one of those days. Time is never saved, extended, transferred, or found. It is only spent. One day, all of us will die.

Now ask yourself: When you lie dying on your deathbed, will your thoughts be "I wish I'd watched another few thousand TikToks"? Worse yet, when you're on that deathbed, is it possible you'll be alone because of the thousands of TikToks you *did* watch?

Every hour you spent skimming YouTube videos is an hour you weren't exercising, developing a hobby or skill, finding a spouse, cultivating real-life friendships, and above all, being a living, breathing member of a living, breathing community. Put another way, every hour you spend on social media is either making you more liberal, or making you weaker and thus less able to resist liberalism.

Almost all forms of social media, especially any *popular* type of social media, correlates with more left-wing politics. In 2021, among adults aged 18–49, those who leaned Democrat were 8 percentage points more likely to use Twitter, 6 points more likely to use YouTube, 17 points more likely to use Twitter, and *29* points more likely to use Instagram.[346]

Someday in the future, we will grasp the full importance of what the endless stimuli of the Web have done to our brains and our souls, but for now there is too much denial for this question to even be properly researched. Yet there are disturbing signs. I don't think it is remotely a coincidence that the explosion of transgenderism has coincided with the Internet age, and plenty of testimony from actual trans people backs this up.

In 2023, film director Lily Wachowski (formerly known as Andy Wachowski), said in an interview that he got the idea to dress up and call himself a woman from online pornography.[347]

"The first images that really struck a chord with me were trans women in pornography," Wachowski said. "There was something that unlocked in my brain. . . . I saw these wonderful, fearless performers becoming desirable, and in my head I could take the leap where I felt like if I could be desirable, maybe I could be loved."

Wachowski, in essence, groomed *himself* with extreme pornography. And it wasn't just him: Lily's brother Larry has *also* gone trans, adopting the name Lana.

Even if you aren't perverting yourself to the point of self-mutilation, too much screen-time is mangling our brains in other ways. It's no surprise that from 2004 to 2017, as the smartphone took over the world, the share of Americans who read for pleasure dropped by 40 percent for men, and 29 percent for women, and we've reached the point where more than half of Americans read *zero* books in the typical year.[348] The most upsetting part of that is, it's not just a matter of lacking time. It's our minds. Modern website design mangles our attention spans to the point that many people struggle to read even a few pages of a book before glancing at their phone to see if they've received any new notifications, and soon enough, their "reading time" has become another hour wasted on "phone time."

Before the Internet, there was a limit on how much of a specialized niche one could carve out for oneself in life. Unless you lived in a cult compound, the idea of restricting one's social world to only those exactly like oneself was unfathomable.

With the Internet this is out the window. True, the Internet lets us cultivate and maintain friendships across state and even national boundaries. Millions of young people today have close personal friends they have literally *never* met, only spoken with online. But it's easy for this radical ability to craft one's own social group to become a net negative. Before the Internet, if you were a bit of a weirdo—a freak, even—you would probably find out. Family, friends, and strangers, would make you see that maybe you were going down a rabbit hole, were becoming a conspiracy theorist, or that you were obsessing too much about a TV show, a singer, or an actor. In a word, you would get *feedback* that you were acting like a weirdo and be told to knock it off. Thanks to the post-smartphone internet, and social media, people feel emboldened to be weird, not just in oddball ways but in self-destructive ones. All the oddballs are in touch with each other. And I'm not talking about things like Star Trek fan clubs. The Internet has allowed people to spend huge portions of their time with enthusiasts for niche pornography, or in deeply delusional conspiracy circles. I am still recovering from the time my producer Blake informed me of the existence of an entire web forum that exists for adult diaper enthusiasts (no, I don't remember what it was, and I wouldn't tell you if I did).

The online panopticon is also the world where cancel culture thrives and gains power. Websites like Twitter operate like a gigantic high school, filled with gossip, envy, and casual predatory behavior. When you're too online, it's easier to be tricked into thinking that online mobs matter, or worse yet, to become a zealot of an online mob yourself. For millions, the Internet is a distorted mirror that takes even the most warped behavior and affirms it by showing thousands of imitators. It takes your worst aspects and tells you "This is fine. You're on the right track. You aren't a pervert/lunatic/psychopath/loser. You're great." But of course, you aren't great, you are just being degraded by the black mirror of the online world.

The way out of all this? *Log off.* Engage with the world we actually still live in.

The next time you feel moved to binge-watch another set of videos on some dumb social media site, consider trying any one of the following easy alternatives:

- Use the *phone* part of your smartphone, and call your parents or siblings, or a friend you haven't spoken to for a few weeks.
- Go for a walk outside. If you pass a neighbor, strike up a conversation with them. Heck, strike up a conversation with a stranger. You might make a new friend!
- Think of any errand you know you need to do that will take less than ten minutes, and *do it now.*
- Recite a short prayer or read a page from the Bible or a devotional book. Memorize a verse.
- Put your phone in a separate room, pick up a book, set a timer, and read *without interruption* for an hour, a half hour, or even just 15 minutes.
- Clean your bed, your room, your house. Psychologist and author Dr. Jordan Peterson says that a great place to start cleaning up and taking control of your life is by making your bed each day. And he is extremely right. It's showing yourself the bare minimum of self-respect. A dirty or cluttered lifestyle becomes a dirty or cluttered mind.

But don't just vaguely try to be better. I'm well aware of how addicting our phones have become. Just like with losing weight, setting precise goals and rules can go a long way. Don't just think "I should use my phone less." Instead, schedule specific blocks of time where your phone is off-limits. At a certain hour of the day (say, 9 pm), *put your phone away* in a separate room or even a locked safe, and do not take it out under any circumstances until the following morning. Make family meals categorical "no-phone" times, and enforce the rule strictly, on both your children and on yourself.

I live a very busy life that requires being online and connected nearly constantly. But I recognize the harm this does, so I've taken the radical step of logging off completely for one day a week. Every week, I observe the traditional Jewish Sabbath from Friday night to Saturday night, and as part of that I put my smartphone away for a whole 24 hours. That time is to be spent in the real world, with my family.

Even if you don't copy my exact methods, taking deliberate, scheduled breaks from the online and digital world will do you enormous good. And it won't just be that you're spending less time online. Regaining your ability to focus and engage with the real world is a type of discipline with far-reaching benefits. Being better at resisting your smartphone will make you better at exercising consistently, better at completing your work tasks on time, better at being the best person you can be. Better at confronting and beating the people who despise you.

Another viable option? Delete social media from your life, completely. Yes, I know that's a little rich coming from me. I use pretty much every social media platform to spread my messages. You might have learned about this book from a promotional Tweet or Facebook post. All I can say is that, for me, social media is a sadly necessary tool of the trade. But if it's not a tool of yours, consider just deleting it like the useless distraction that it is.

Throughout this book I've peppered in some football metaphors, and I'll leave it with this one: If you're a football fan, have you ever seen a team struggle repeatedly on offense, but once they're finally able to score once, or even pick up a single first down, it's like something was unlocked? Perhaps at the end of the game, a player even commented on how that first first-down, or that initial touchdown, gave them the confidence and momentum they needed? The first victory is always the hardest one, and likewise when it comes to discipline it's that initial fight against your own inertia and sinful nature that will be the hardest fight.

Bad momentum is enormously difficult to escape, but once you start building your way out, good momentum feeds on itself as well. All the more reason to keep your eyes on the prize (and off the screen) and instill that discipline!

CHAPTER SEVENTEEN

Obesity and Fitness

"But I discipline my body and keep it under control,
lest after preaching to others I myself should be disqualified."
—1 Corinthians 9:27

If we are going to obtain mastery over wokeness, then we must also obtain mastery over the self.

For the first time in human history, the poor in most developed nations are distinguished not by their emaciation, but by their obesity. It's a trait they share with more and more of their countrymen. It's a major health crisis, to be sure, but it's also a political one.

Yes, that's right, if you want to win against woke, you have to be fit. I'm not kidding in the slightest.

Let's be honest:, there's an excellent chance that you, the reader, aren't in very good shape. If you're like most Americans, you're overweight. You might even be obese. If you aren't, then many, many of the people you know are. Be it your family members, your friends, and the people in your church.

When this great nation was founded, or when it abolished slavery, or when it fought and won two world wars, obesity was practically unheard of. No more, though. America is a fat country. One of the fattest on earth, in fact, and it's getting worse. In the early 60s, barely ten percent of Americans were obese, and less than one percent were severely obese. Today, more than forty percent of Americans are obese and about one in ten are severely obese.[349]

This is a sign of national decay. Being fat is disgusting. It's visually unappealing. It makes oneself less attractive to one's spouse or to the majority of prospective spouses. Obesity makes a person less self-sufficient, less helpful to their communities, and less fit to defend the nation in a time of crisis. Gluttony and sloth don't just slow the body but the mind as well. When the military complains that most young Americans are too unfit to qualify for military service, widespread obesity is the single biggest reason (no pun intended).[350]

But this goes beyond practical concerns. Obesity is also a physical manifestation of a moral failing. Gluttony, or the failure to responsibly control one's appetites, has been a cardinal sin in Christianity from the very beginning. St. Paul's first letter to the Corinthians calls on Christians to "honor God with your bodies." The book of Proverbs declares that "a companion of gluttons disgraces his father." When we let ourselves go physically, we are displaying a moral failure to the whole world.

As the group that wants to revitalize America, conservatives should want to fix this. And unlike a lot of America's problems, this is very substantially within our power to do, because the fix requires improving only our own bodies, and it requires literally *doing nothing*. Want to fix obesity? Your body is doing it for you with every breath you take. You can only sabotage it by continuing to shovel too much food down your throat.

But wait, Charlie, you might be thinking, *it's liberals who love to babble about "fat acceptance" while condemning "fat shaming." Don't they have a bigger obesity problem than we do?*

You're right that the left's *rhetoric* on obesity is toxic and bad. But as conservatives, we think actions speak louder than words. Now, look at a map of US obesity rates. In 2022, the CDC put out a map of obesity rates by state. Nineteen U.S. states had an obesity rate of more than thirty-five percent. And of those 19 states, *every single one of them* was a red state in 2020.[351]

There is nothing to be proud of in these numbers. Sure, there's a well-earned stereotype of effete, weak liberals eating "healthy" with the diet of a rabbit, and ending up rail-thin. Sure, that's pathetic. But does that mean you're "owning the libs" by eating like a pig and bloating up to 250 or 300 pounds, or even more? No!

As conservatives, we believe that our values lead to a better way of life.

If we want to prove that, then we should, ourselves, live better lives, and that starts with living healthier ones.

Are there explanations for red state obesity besides politics? Of course, it's all the usual suspects, race, average age, disability rates, city design, and more all play a role in the obesity rate.

But you know what? Forget all about that. Making endless excuses and blaming other people is what *liberals* do. As conservatives, we need to confront a raw fact: We are too darn fat.

Heaven knows the left is aware of it. Spend some time around liberals at parties (be careful: Spending more than an hour around liberals at a party raises your risk of stroke to dangerous levels). Wait for politics to come up, and it's nearly a given that eventually someone will ridicule flyover America for being obese.

Liberals routinely mock red states and Trump supporters for their bulging waistlines. In 2021, neocon-turned-noncon David Frum jeered that "The Republican Party, the Trumpy fringes, have special problems with personal physical health . . . I always say to them, 'Stop worshiping these people, go for a walk. Go for a walk and stop eating the fried foods, OK? Go for a walk and order the salmon.'"[352]

The most painful attacks are always ones that are based at least partly in truth. The proper reaction to this isn't to dig in and wallow in obesity. It isn't to own the libs by having a heart attack. The proper reaction is to get mad, then get fit. Just like we believe in national excellence, we conservatives should believe in personal excellence, in being the best people we can possibly be. We want to live in beautiful buildings, listen to beautiful music, and have beautiful nature around us. We should want to be beautiful ourselves as well.

I know this can be a tough pill to swallow. I've criticized obesity on my show more than once, and I've received plenty of hostile emails for doing so. In May 2023, New York City made fat people a legally protected class, similar to one's race or religion (the law was pushed by the National Association to Advance Fat Acceptance—imagine that group's lunch bill!).[353] I said the same thing I've just said to you. Being a few pounds overweight is one thing, but there is no excuse for being dozens or even hundreds of pounds overweight.

The responses I got were immediate, and often sharp. More than one listener claimed that they would never listen to my show again because I had been so disrespectful to obese people such as themselves.

But other listeners shared their own inspiring stories. One man from Chicago said he'd gone from 420 all the way down to 190 pounds, because he decided to stop making excuses for himself.

I hope the overweight people who vowed to boycott our show have since reconsidered. Because I care about them and respect them too much to feed them the same lies that groups like NAAFA do, saying they have no control over their actions, no control over their bodies, and no control over the lives they lead. Many things are out of our hands. But making the most of the bodies that God gave us is achievable for every one of us *if* we put in the effort.

Why am I emphasizing this so much in a book about beating wokeness, though? There are several reasons:

1. Fitness improves credibility.

Conservatives claim to be the party of personal responsibility, yet every one of us looks like a hypocrite if we allow ourselves to waddle around with thirty or fifty or two hundred excess pounds. Each of us should try to be a living example of the responsibility we preach to others. Imagine a preacher who advocated for sexual morality while living openly with a mistress, and you get the idea.

2. Fitness makes conservatism more appealing.

Most people don't want to follow what is ugly and disgusting. They want to follow what is beautiful and appealing. Conservatives are a bell curve on this, I believe. We tend to be the most beautiful Americans, but also some of the ugliest. We should try to move as many people as we can to the right half of that curve. A conservatism of sound bodies and healthy living will naturally attract more supporters than a conservatism that needs a motorized scooter just to do its weekly shopping for Cheez Puffs and Mountain Dew. If conservatives were uniformly in good shape and well-kempt, then the choice between us and the left's blue-haired, tatted-up, nose-pierced freakshows would be more of a no-brainer.

3. Better fitness means more energy.

Being fat and out of shape means you get tired faster. It means you can't keep up with your kids in healthy outdoor activities. It means you can't put as many long hours of crunch time at work or during an election year. Eventually, it means spending less time as an active member of your community. A healthier body eventually means a healthier family life, a healthier community life, and more participation in the causes that matter to you.

4. Fitness makes you live longer.

The planetoids at NAAFA might insist otherwise, but it's a fact: Obesity kills. The obese are at higher risk of diabetes, heart disease, stroke, cancer, and all other kinds of fatal ailments.[354] The obese were in far greater danger of dying of Covid during the pandemic. Overall, moderate obesity lops about three years off a person's life expectancy, and severe obesity lowers it by ten years or more.[355] Get fit, live longer, and that means you're around for more elections to vote against the left and its evil policies!

5. Fitness makes you a better person, across the board.

Most Americans understand the idea of physical training. If you run every day, you will be able to run faster and longer. If you lift weights frequently, you'll eventually be able to lift heavier weights. Your personal willpower actually works the same way. The daily discipline of moderating what we eat and drink will, over time, give us the discipline to resist other harmful temptations, and to undertake difficult and unpleasant tasks—tasks like winning an existential battle for America's future.

6. Fitness literally makes you more conservative.

Last summer, conservatives roasted MSNBC for a tweet claiming that exercise and fitness had become "far-right."[356] Laugh all you want, but thankfully, MSNBC was right!

The very act of getting in shape is, essentially, applied conservatism. It's the application of timeless wisdom and personal effort to achieve a direct result, entirely within your own power. The woke person believes she is miserable because someone microaggressed her on the way to class, and that she's fat because of "genetics" or "PTSD" or something stupid. She places the factors of her well-being outside her control. To instead take command of your life and lift a weight so that you can lift a heavier one next time, is an experience that gives one power over their life, and that directly makes a person view the world from a conservative perspective.

GETTING FIT AND STAYING THERE

So, how do you actually *get* fit? As I mentioned earlier, that's one of the best parts. To reach a healthy weight, you literally just have to do *nothing*. Your body is a machine subject to the laws of thermodynamics. It has to spend energy to power itself, and if no energy is coming in, it must burn its reserves. Those reserves are the fat stores scattered around your body.

"But Charlie!" I can already see the emails in my inbox. *"It's just so hard!"*

True! Any time we have allowed ourselves to profoundly decay, turning things around is a challenge—even when all that is needed is doing nothing. I know that for many people, losing weight isn't easy. Most things worth doing aren't. But again, as conservatives, we should reject taking the easy way out.

But at the same time, ask yourself how hard have you *really* tried? If you struggle with your weight, have you ever gone a full 48 hours without eating? Or even a full 24? Have you *tried?* Have you experimented with cutting out categories of food, like bread, processed carbs, or added sugar? You have the technological advantage of having on your smartphone countless YouTube channels dedicated to fitness tips and exercises you can copy from, for free. To paraphrase T.S. Eliot, "After such knowledge, what fatness?"

The challenge isn't knowing how to lose weight or to get in better shape. The challenge is achieving self-mastery. You need to obtain sufficient control over your willpower so it will keep you going through the temptation to cheat and pig out. How do you obtain that self-mastery? There are a lot of different ways. For some people, a major change in diet helps, such as following a keto regimen that removes nearly all carbs. For others, intermittent fasting is the way to go, because by eating in only a short time window each day, they minimize the chance they will overeat. And for other people, the tactic that works best is total fasting, not eating anything for a couple days at a time.

This is coming from someone who had to make these choices for himself.

I used to be heavier than I should be, and I took steps to get myself healthy. For me, what worked was following a well-defined plan set by professionals. It was like following the blueprints for building a house, or the instructions for a piece of IKEA furniture. Essentially, follow these rules, do not deviate, and you *will* lose weight. Following a step-by-step plan with a guaranteed positive outcome at the end was, for me, a powerful motivator.

No method is a magic bullet for everyone. But I firmly believe that everyone has some kind of method that works. Don't fall for the idea that a strategy is impossible before you have even attempted it.

Lenin once said that socialism meant counting everything. Well, we're not going to go full socialism, but it's not a bad idea to start counting your calories to start a better exercise and diet plan for yourself. Download the free MyFitnessPal app, and for at least a month, log exactly what you ate that day—*exactly* what you ate, including every sugar packet in your coffee—into the app. If you have an Apple Watch, or an iPhone that goes everywhere with you, it will tell you at the end of the day how many steps you did and how many calories you burned that day.

Take advantage of your possibly nerdy and jellybean-counting aspects of your personality by seeing the math on how many calories you are under or over every day. For a man, you want to aim for not eating more than 2,400 calories a day. For ladies, aim for 1,900. Now, of course, how many calories you consume varies by things such as age and pre-existing weight, and it's always best to talk to your doctor about any specific health concerns that are unique to you. However, a good starting point is trying to get under that every day and use your Apple Watch or phone to make sure you walk at least four miles every day. Do that for a month and see what kind of progress you make (weight yourself *every* day, to get an accurate measure).

This might all sound like work, and it is, but at the same time, you already do work! You studied to finish school. You show up at a job. You do the work to raise your kids. Why not throw in a few minutes of extra work for something with benefits as dramatic as being healthier and more beautiful?

Another factor that I think will help, as counterintuitive as it might seem, is shame. Collectively, we ought to set a social standard that people should be fit, and failing to stay that way is a moral shortcoming, or at least worthy of embarrassment. In this regard, all conservatives could learn from groups like the Mormons. Faithful Mormons are expected to follow the Word of Wisdom, a collection of commandments for healthy living. Most people know that Mormons are prohibited from smoking or drinking alcohol, coffee, or tea, but the Word of Wisdom also prescribes healthy eating generally, frequent exercise, and getting sufficient sleep. The resulting good health and fit appearance literally make someone "look Mormon," so much so that at least one study indicates Mormons can be identified by sight alone.[357] Mormons live more than seven years longer than the average American.[358]

You don't have to believe the Word of Wisdom to see this all as an example to be copied. And copy it we should. Parents should compel their children to be in good shape with the same energy they push them to do well academically. Friends should encourage their friends to be healthy, and be honest with them when they are failing.

This isn't just a weight thing.

Conservatives should want to exercise and be physically robust, not just thin. The same rules apply as with avoiding obesity. If you cultivate self-discipline and do the work, you *will* succeed. What plan is best? That will vary. Some people prefer strong cardiovascular health from jogging, cycling, or running. Others want to get strong with weightlifting. Some want to gain athleticism for team sports. And as the rapid rise of Brazilian jiu-jitsu and mixed martial arts shows, a lot of people love getting fit through the primal exercise of fighting. I can't say which is best for you, or what the best plan for getting there is. But as a general rule, the best exercise is the one you *actually do*, rather than fretting about being perfect and then doing nothing at all. Consistently carve out a half hour or 45 minutes a day of real exercise, and you will be well on your way to far greater health and fitness than 80% of those around you.

I began this chapter quoting the Bible's instructions to discipline the body. There's a reason almost all religions practice some commands over diet. This is because there is self-renunciation in dieting and fasting. You are teaching yourself to put some other goal above your own immediate gratification. Think of Jewish and Muslim restrictions against pork, or Christians fasting to show penance during Lent. This applies to politics, too. Think of the Jews observing the fast of the 9th of Av, or Gandhi's fasts. If anything, conservatives could and should make use of fasts not just for spiritual purposes but to promote solidarity amongst ourselves.

This element of cultivating self-renunciation applies to many different spheres. That's for a reason. Failure to practice self-control and abstinence in the realm of food has a strong correlation with a failure to maintain bodily care, restraint, and abstinence elsewhere.

Yeah, you know where this is going next. Go ahead and blush now before turning the page. . . .

CHAPTER EIGHTEEN

Sadly, Porn

"How do I know pornography depraves and corrupts?
It depraves and corrupts me."
— Malcolm Muggeridge

Yep, this book has a chapter about porn. Deal with it!

Do you feel a bit awkward? Good. That's the sort of feeling this topic should instill. I hope you got all your blushing out of the way at the end of the food chapter, because we're attacking this topic directly.

The creation of universal, easily accessible pornography is one of the most dramatic, yet also invisible, societal shifts of the past twenty-five years. It's also one of the most sinister triumphs of the woke age that passed without conservatives acting seriously to stop it. Like obesity, it is yet another example of people not practicing one of the fruits of the Holy Spirit, namely self-control.

G.K. Chesterton predicted all this almost exactly a century ago, "The next great heresy is going to be simply an attack on morality, and especially on sexual morality. And it is coming not from a few Socialists. The madness of tomorrow is not in Moscow but much more in Manhattan—but most of what was in Broadway is already in Piccadilly."[359]

Pornography used to be something that took a little bit of effort and embarrassment to obtain. A teenager still living at home had to buy dirty magazines at a gas station or in some other seedy store (they'd also apparently find them in the woods pretty often; what was up with that?). If someone wanted to see an actual pornographic film, he had to go to a dingy theater that showed them, like the ones that dotted Times Square before Rudy Giuliani salvaged the city in the 1990s (Rudy: From "Get rid of those t**s" to "Give me your t**s" in thirty years. A modern tragedy).

Not anymore. In the age of the smartphone and 5G, literally everyone carries immediate access to a pornographic cornucopia in their pockets. One in every twenty-five websites online is a pornographic page of some form or another.[360] One in every four people has seen porn sometime in the last month—or at least, one-fourth of people admit it.[361] Today, even before they are taught about sex in school or by their parents, a child's first exposure to human sexuality is likely to be seeing hardcore pornography on the Internet.

Nude photos or dingy videos have been replaced by thousands and thousands of high-definition clips. Cam sites let people tune into live shows by "performers." As porn has become ubiquitous, it has also become more extreme, with films catering to more and more niche subgenres involving physical abuse, scatological fetishes, and more. And now, with the arrival of artificial intelligence, computer-generated porn is becoming indistinguishable from the real thing, acting as a harbinger for a future where people can create hyper-realistic pornographic image of their favorite celebrities or personal crushes in real life.

I'm under no illusions. Porn is free, easy to access, easy to hide, and addictive. That means people are using it, including millions of conservatives and Christians, and many people reading this book. I can't make all of you quit, but if you're serious about winning the war on woke, you should be trying to stop.

Conservatives have learned to be radicalized against sexual propaganda appearing in their children's schools. We have rightly revolted against pornographic books being stuck in libraries, and against hypersexual drag queen shows being presented to kids as normal behavior.

But if we're going to be radically against such over-the-top, public pornography, we need to be just as outraged, if not more so, about the poison that is silently seeping into our homes via the Internet.

Porn is corrosive to everything that makes for a happy and healthy family. In the words of conservative writer Ross Douthat, pornography creates young men who are "at once entitled and resentful, angry and undermotivated, 'woke' and caddish, shaped by unprecedented possibilities for sexual gratification and frustrated that real women are less available and more complicated than the version on their screen."[362]

The harm porn causes can be hard to see and sometimes is even harder to even talk about, but it is no less real for that, in my opinion. Porn takes one of the most basic human desires, supercharges it with a hyperstimulus, and then dissipates it against illusory chimeras. Far from being indicative of virility and a healthy sexuality, pornography is a sign of active or eventual sexual exhaustion. It also saps one's will. It is spiritually draining. It's even been linked to impotence at a young age.[363] On the website Reddit, there is an anti-porn subcategory named NoFap (if you don't know, don't ask) that is mostly men posting about their inheritance of mental "superpowers" after breaking an addiction to masturbation. The flipside to that is that many of these same men speak of the brain fog they realized they had when they were on porn.

Porn makes men less interested in the women around them they could be starting families with, and it makes husbands dissatisfied with their wives. Porn use within marriage increases the risk of infidelity,[364] marital strife, and divorce.[365] None of this should surprise us in the slightest. What else would we expect from regularly watching videos of women being degraded or humiliated, which countless pornographic videos show?

Let's quote Chesterton again, "Do not be proud of the fact that your grandmother was shocked at something which you are accustomed to seeing or hearing without being shocked. . . . It may be that your grandmother was an extremely lively and vital animal and that you are a paralytic."[366] I think Mister Gilbert Keith was correct when he said the silent explosion of porn usage is turning men into emotional, romantic paralytics, men who are damaged and warped while barely realizing what has happened to them. No wonder so many struggle not just with relationships, but even something as basic as asking women out.

But I shouldn't just single out men. Porn use by women is exploding, too. Books like the *Fifty Shades* series have been presented as "mainstream" literature, when they are literally just erotica, pornography dressed up with plot to appeal to women. The first book in the *Fifty Shades* series, *Fifty*

Shades of Grey, was the single best-selling novel of the 2010s. The second and third-place books? Its two sequels.[367]

The effects of porn on young girls have partially inspired, in my opinion, the abrupt and rapid rise of female-to-male transgenderism. One such transitioner, who later detransitioned to live as a woman once again, described why she wanted to be male in the first place, "What I've done to my appearance and my body has almost been a survival tactic or a form of protection against unwanted attention from men," she said.[368]

Such accounts are common among teen girl transitioners. The onset of puberty and male romantic attention causes them enormous psychological distress. I think porn plays a big role in this. Young girls exposed to porn as their introduction to sexuality freaks them out, in some cases enough that they want to not become a full-grown woman. Even for the girls who don't wind up mutilating their bodies in distress, the post-porn is one where they must be even more self-conscious of their relative imperfections, and more terrified of what the men they interact with may want from them. Simply put, porn has been devastating for women, perhaps even more so than it has been for men.

A hundred years ago, divorce was incredibly rare in America. Today, it's routine, and red state marriages fail as often (or even more often) than blue state ones.[369] I believe the explosion in pornography access has played a significant role in this trend.

It's not like it would be a surprise. Almost every society that's ever existed has at least stigmatized pornography, if not restricted or banned it. We only got here by throwing out centuries of warnings.

Of course, just like it ignores old wisdom on countless other topics, our modern regime embraces porn with absurd claims that it is healthy and normal. Sometimes, they even call it "empowering," that favorite word of those who want to trick women into debasing, humiliating, and devaluing themselves.

So if you do have a porn habit, how can you quit? I won't lie, kicking this sort of habit can be tough. By its nature, it's a very solitary battle. When you lose weight, you gain immediate positive feedback from others who notice you look better. Nothing like that is available as a motivator with porn.

When it comes to asking for help or support in an effort to better yourself, asking for support from others to lose weight is one thing. Seeking help for something like pornography can feel humiliating. People may not look at you the same way. If you've been keeping the habit secret from your spouse, you might fear damaging the relationship.

But one of the core messages of this book is that we have to *do the hard things*, and put in the effort, to create both the best version of ourselves and the best version of our country. If that means risking embarrassment to seek help from your pastor or a friend, then you have to do it.

If it means seeking help from your spouse, then that must be done as well. In the long run, building trust with your spouse, and seeking their support in overcoming sin, will make most relationships stronger rather than weaker.

And despite the challenges, there are options. One thing that makes modern porn insidious is simply how *easy* it is to find. Raising the challenge even slightly can go a long way. There is plenty of software for both desktop computers and smartphones that will block known porn websites. Much of this software can be programmed with timers and passwords to prevent it from being easily removed. Have a trusted friend set that password for you, so that you don't know it, and you have created a valuable obstacle for blocking your own weakness.

You can also consider picking up an accountability partner. If you can get over the hump of bringing this up with a friend, you'll find that porn is a problem for a lot of men. Forming a partnership or a small group where you hold each other accountable will make it far easier to quit long-term.

But this doesn't have to be a crusade for individuals alone. Red state governments can help nudge this self-improvement along, too.

Somehow, even as more and more political views get circumscribed on the constitutionally bogus grounds that they are "hate speech," we somehow without a single thought let pornography sweep the country on the grounds that it is "free speech."

The concept is ludicrous. The films dumped onto websites I shall not name are not "speech," and pornographers are not artists or activists. They are pimps who corrupt people—particularly the young—and should be treated like ones.

At a minimum, we can make it so rampant pornography is harder to access for children. Nominally, adult sites are often supposed to only be available to those 18 or older, but this is trivially bypassed, typically by the visitor simply clicking an "I'm 18" button on the site. We are not nearly as *laissez-faire* for any other age-restricted product. Bars aren't allowed to hand out alcohol to anybody who simply says they are 21, and gas stations can't sell cigarettes to anyone who says they are under 18. If a merchant breaks the law and sells alcohol or cigarettes to someone underage, they can be fined or even lose their license to sell those products. And liberals are always looking to raise the price at which one can buy a gun with sharp penalties for evading the law, even though last I checked, owning a gun was a constitutional right, while pornography was not.

We can take the same punitive perspective toward the pornography companies that blanket our Internet. Require porn sites to actually verify users' ages, for real. If they fail to do so, fine them or shut them down. If they evade those penalties, block the sites.

Or here's an idea. Accessing pornography should always require a financial transaction, even if it's as small as a few cents. The mere shame from breaking out a credit card—and the fear of a hack potentially exposing you could slash usage.

Let's strengthen our relationships, strengthen our self-control, strengthen our minds, and kill the invisible poison lurking in every American's pocket.

CHAPTER NINETEEN

Let's Get Married (and Not on an App!)

"And the LORD God said, It is not good that the man should be alone;
I will make him a help meet for him."
—Genesis 2:18

"Two are better than one . . . "
—Ecclesiastes 4:9

Leftism hates marriage, and it hates families. That's not just me being a partisan right-winger; it's right there in their own writings! In the original *Communist Manifesto,* Marx and Engels called for the "abolition of the family."[370] Mao declared that "families are the product of the last stage of primitive communism, and every last trace of them will be eliminated in the future."[371] In 2022 Sophie Lewis, a visiting scholar at the University of Pennsylvania's (brace yourself) Feminist, Queer and Transgender Studies Center, wrote a book titled *Abolish the Family: A Manifesto for Care and Liberation.* The same year, the left-wing magazine *Current Affairs* published a 6,000–word essay "Why We Should Abolish the Family."

I'll grant that, at least at the moment I write this book, *most* self-identified progressives don't want the family abolished. But there is also a clear positive relationship between weakening the family and empowering the left. The family, as a social unit, is the premiere defense against Woke indoctrination, collectivism, and social engineering. It is the natural immune system against Woke cancer, hence their desire to remove it.

When America was at her peak, American families were at their peak as well. In 1960, sixty-five percent of adult American women were married.[372] A large share of the rest were widows; only a handful were divorced. But that year was the apex of marriage in America. Today, less than half of American women are married. Marriage has particularly collapsed among the poorest Americans, who would benefit most from it. Only a quarter of black women are married. Those without a high-school diploma were the *most* likely to be married in 1943, with a 63% marriage rate. Today, that same group is married only 27% of the time.[373]

In 2019, the millennial generation ranged in age between 23 and 38 years old, meaning half of them were over thirty. As a generation, they'd had plenty of time to settle down and start families. But it wasn't happening. As of 2019, only 30% of millennials were living in what we might call the basic family unit with two married parents and at least one child.[374] When they were at the same age, 40% of Gen-Xers were married with children. For Boomers, the number is 46%, and for the Silent Generation, it was 70%.

In the place of families, we've gotten atomization, failure to launch, and chaos. One in eleven millennials lives completely alone. One in seven lives with his or her parents. One in eight is a single parent.

Why has marriage declined? All kinds of reasons. With greater economic prosperity, getting married is no longer essential to basic survival. Government support for single mothers makes it easier to raise a child without a partner.

But one of the biggest reasons is that, simply, the culture has tolerated it. The sexual revolution means that sex before marriage is routine, as is living together without marrying. It has become far more socially acceptable even to have a child without marrying ("bastardy," we used to call it), and though it's still frowned on for men to skip their obligations as a father, the pressure has lessened significantly as the era of the compelled "shotgun marriage" is long gone.

Whatever the causes of the decline in marriage, the outcome is clearcut, a tremendous win for the left, for statism, and for wokeness. Because as anyone could have predicted, the decline of the family hasn't liberated people or empowered them, but rather enslaved them. It has created more vulnerable people who can be preyed upon, and easily indoctrinated, without a mother and father to protect them. Without a supportive family around them, people look toward the state for support instead.

"Democrats' new superpower: Single parents like me are a growing political force." So read an op-ed headline in *USA Today* a month before the 2020 election.[375] The author was correct. Single mothers are not a political battleground. They're a political bloodbath. In 2012, Barack Obama won 75% of the single mother vote and single mothers were six percent of the entire electorate.[376] Do the math, and Barack Obama's advantage just among single mothers provided almost all of the five-million vote margin that he beat Mitt Romney by. And it's not just a matter of single mothers being more female or more black:

> Obama lost to Romney among white voters, 59 percent to 39 percent. But among white single mothers, Obama bested Romney 56 percent to 43 percent. Lower-income voters are another good example. Obama took 60 percent to Romney's 38 percent in all households making $50,000 or less a year. Among under-$50,000 households that included a single mother, Obama took a whopping 79 percent to Romney's 20 percent.[377]

It's not hard to grasp why single motherhood naturally leads to voting for more statism and less freedom. Single mothers are more dependent on a large government to support them. They lack stability in their lives and look to the government as the only thing that can provide it.

However, stable marriage isn't just important when it comes to reducing the number of single mothers trying to make ends meet. Even without children, marriage makes both partners more conservative. The "gender gap" in American politics is for the most part just a marriage gap. Married men and women vote quite similarly, while unmarried women are vastly more liberal than unmarried men (who are still more liberal than married men). Why is that the case? There are plenty of theories. Marriage makes people happier, and as we've discussed, misery breeds leftism. Unmarried women might be more vulnerable to the lie that easy access to abortion is the single most important issue for their freedom and happiness.

But while it's easy to blame wokeness, the left, liberalism, Marxism, modernism, or any other number of social and ideological trends for the decline of the family, the truth is that any time we speak about that we had better make sure there's a mirror in the room because we should start with ourselves. Because frankly, conservatives have easily played their share in the collapse of marriage. Decades ago, we were largely inert while divorce laws became more liberalized. Then, when divorce became normalized, we were nearly as enthusiastic about it as Democrats. Today, more than 40 percent of Republicans who have ever married have also divorced. While Republican divorces are less than the figure for Democrats, they're not far behind.[378] There are fewer qualms than you'd think among conservative elites, and even pastors, about getting yourself a younger, second wife, for the fun of it. Too often, even where marriages survive, they are unhappy ones.

HOW TO GET MARRIED

We like to think of ourselves as more enlightened or honest than previous generations but we have taken many steps back in terms of our romantic honesty. Over the last few decades, as people have gotten less embarrassed to talk about sex, they've become embarrassed to talk about love and a desire to be married and start a family.

Still, in my time as leader of Turning Point, I've heard more than enough questions and anecdotes to know that young conservatives still overwhelmingly want to find a partner, get married, and have children, yet I also know that a lot of them are struggling greatly with it. Something that was just a basic part of life for their grandparents has become an ordeal, and they aren't sure what to do.

I was one of the only men on stage during Turning Point's Young Women's Leadership Summit in Dallas last summer. Thousands of women were there, almost all of them unmarried, and one of the things they most wanted to ask me about was "Charlie, how do I find a conservative husband?"

The following draws heavily on what I told them. The advice I gave them was meant for women, but almost all of it applies well to men also.

Dating to get married means dating *seriously*. We take school seriously, we take our careers seriously, and heck, many of us take our hobbies seriously. Finding a spouse should be more serious than all of those things. That doesn't mean looking for a spouse can't be enjoyable. But it must not be done aimlessly. Dating isn't a hobby. It's not a pastime. It's not something you do mindlessly, to mindlessly pass an evening, or to get a free dinner.

Contrary to popular belief, dating also is not something you get better at by doing more of it. Endless low-effort dating gets us addicted to the momentary thrill of courtship and romantic pursuit. It keeps us stuck at the level of desiring romance's early stages of infatuation, crushes, and puppy love. It makes us obsess over variety and the pursuit of perfection rather than finding the person who is the right match on what really matters.

Dating should be aimed at its final result, marriage. Date with the intent to marry. With every relationship you enter, start immediately discerning whether this person is marriage material. Don't coast for months or years without thinking about it. Dating casually and mindlessly is how countless conservatives get themselves stuck in problematic situations. It leads to getting emotionally tied up with people they don't share basic values with. It leads to squandering years on relationships that are never going to work, or it leads into ill-advised marriages that eventually fail. If you aren't looking ahead from the start towards getting married, then don't start dating at all. You aren't ready yet.

But don't tarry too long. Because the best time to enter the serious dating pool is early—ideally, no later than when you're 23. If you're in college, there will not be a single better time in your life to look for a spouse. You're in an environment where almost everyone around you is another unmarried young person. Despite how liberal colleges are overall, the sheer number of young people present makes them a great place to meet someone who shares your values.

Why date seriously early? It's pure economics. The most valuable goods don't linger on the shelf, they get snatched off the market. It's the same with potential spouses. Your pool of potential mates starts off large and dwindles with each passing day.

This is all particularly the case for women. This is a book for honest truths, not comfortable lies, so I'll say it. One of the chief assets a woman has for winning a quality spouse in our current culture is physical attractiveness. A woman's physical attractiveness peaks in her early 20s, and after that time gradually declines. A woman who only starts serious husband-hunting when she is 30 will find that she is already past her peak physical appeal. Meanwhile, a man's economic incline, combined with a slower erosion of his physical attractiveness, usually puts his marriage market peak at his mid-30s. For the men reading this, here's another football analogy: If women are like running backs, peaking earlier, but declining quickly, men are more like quarterbacks, peaking later and declining more slowly, potentially having a much longer career on the market. Tom Brady was still playing in the NFL at 45, and a single man can still play the dating field at 45 with far more cultural acceptance and more success at finding a solid partner than a woman can.

Nevertheless, even for men, I recommend seeking marriage early. Getting married young means you will likely start having children younger, which makes being an active, involved father easier. Plus, the need to provide for a family pushes a man to be *more* successful in his career. Also, married men are simply happier than unmarried ones. We should all want to spend more of our lives married.

THE APP THING

Overall, I don't like app dating. Almost everything that was bad about modern dating became magnitudes worse with the arrival of dating apps engineered to be addictive for their users. I think it is no coincidence at all that marriage has been in freefall as app-based dating has spread.

What makes dating on an app harmful? Lots of things, but in short, online dating takes certain normal aspects of dating but drives them to extremes. It's normal for women to be the ones who carefully weigh suitors, while men have to take a chance on approaching a woman to win her over. That's fine, but online dating takes this dynamic and toxically supercharges it.

On the male side, men who once pursued a smaller number of potential romantic partners within their social circles instead have to get used to being rejected hundreds or even thousands of times for every date they actually go on. Sifting through so many women causes men to view them as borderline interchangeable. It encourages the use of psychological tricks to woo women, for the sake of efficiency. As they pursue more and more women, they like these women less and less. Grinding through so many rejections doesn't necessarily toughen men up so much as deaden them until they just view women as manipulatable sex objects.

On the flipside, women have gone from evaluating a manageable number of real-life suitors to sifting through a functionally infinite number. And with such a huge number of men trying a variety of tricks and manipulation tactics from men to help them stand out from the crowd or draw a woman's attention, it stops women from being able to see men who are worth getting to know, and makes them skeptical and wary of men as their standards grow more and more unrealistic to protect themselves from waves of emotional manipulation and unsolicited pictures of male genitals in their app inbox. Whether we like it or not, this has a psychological effect. Women are encouraged to be wary, skeptical, and a perfectionist in what they look for, but they end up chasing a phantom.

See, in the online dating world, women only see the number of men swiping right on them, viewing their Instagram stories, and trying to get that DM train going. They see that these men are after them and, being human, it flatters them. Maybe a bit of smugness sets in. The problem, however, is the women are only seeing the numerator but not the denominator. They don't know how many other women these men are also trying to flag down, or how many other women are interested in the men they mark as the best options. In other words, the women see these men chasing them and think they'll surely end up with some great guy because the ball is totally in her court. But it isn't. Instead, what routinely happens on dating apps is that a legion of women pursue the same men, and almost all of them end up losers. The psychiatrist and writer Rob Henderson described things this way:

> Relationships used to begin with courtship, meeting families, spending lots of time together, etc. and then finally sex. Today, relationships among young people commonly begin with sex, then turn into a "situationship," then "seeing each other," then perhaps a discussion about monogamy ("are you seeing anyone else?") then maybe exclusivity. But a lot of relationships don't even go that far. They get stuck in a holding pattern of casual sex,

which guys often enjoy. Girls don't want to seem vulnerable so they don't bring up the possibility of commitment and hope maybe the guy will like them enough to raise the topic themselves.

As the author Louise Perry has written, "we see young women advised to work on overcoming their perfectly normal and healthy preference for intimacy and commitment . . . Guides with titles like "Here's What to Do if You Start 'Catching Feelings' and 'How to Have Casual Sex Without Getting Emotionally Attached.'"

A 2022 study found that after casual sex, women, on average, report high levels of loneliness, unhappiness, rejection, and regret."[379]

Modern dating apps, mixed with post-sexual revolution norms, have created a disaster of unhappiness. It's no wonder so many young women end up as the most rabid adherents of wokeism.

It's a very old-fashioned attitude to have these days, but I believe sex is best saved until after marriage. Treating sex as a sacred bond between a husband and wife, and not some form of flippant recreation, is the path to the happiest possible life, particularly for women.

If you share my commitment to this ideal, you have to be even *more* intentional with your dating than everyone else. The truth is, waiting for marriage isn't the norm today. If you try to venture out in the general dating pool without making your expectations very clear, you're likely to run into problems. Instead, you should be direct about your intentions from the start. Men who aren't on board with that from the start aren't worth your time. Be wary as you begin dating with the intent to marry, as there are also plenty of men willing to say they have the same priorities as you, but are not only lying, but will ratchet up the pressure for sex as the relationship progresses.

And this all applies even more to apps. Despite all I just said, I know people who have successfully married on apps, and I am not categorically opposed to using them. But they have to be used correctly and carefully. Like guns, they are tools, and can be dangerous ones if not used responsibly.

Communicate firmly from the start what you are looking for, and don't waver on the essentials. Don't let yourself be sucked in too deep by someone you are long-term incompatible with.

BECOMING A PERSON SOMEONE WANTS TO MARRY

At the same Young Women's Leadership Summit where I gave my attitude on dating, I asked the crowd of women in attendance whether they were disappointed in American men. They responded with applause, but not for American's Y-chromosome possessors. Instead, it was applause of relief, that somebody was standing up to tell them the obvious, that men are not making themselves into good relationship or good marriage material.

And they're right. Compared to the men of the past, men today have a lot of problems, sometimes problems they themselves aren't even aware of.

If you're a young man, how do you show that you are marriage material? Here's some tips:

1. **Get a career that will provide for a family**—If you have dreams of being a musician or a writer or an artist, that's fine. But far too many young people spend their entire youth chasing a long-shot goal with nothing to fall back on. Even if you're chasing a dream, make sure you also have the skill, the means and the potential opportunities to have a good career. Women appreciate stability, and your career success will be the core thing that can provide that.

2. **Be fit, clean, and put-together**—Most single men live like slobs. Don't be most single men. Learn to keep a clean and orderly living space. Throw away what you're finished with or don't need. Learn how to buy and wear clothes that fit, real clothes that you can wear to serious events, not just T-shirts with video game characters on them. Exercise regularly. You don't have to be a jacked muscle god, but you should at least look like a man who can handle himself in a fight.

3. **Be a man that others rely on**—Being single isn't an excuse to be un-involved. Be an active member in your church and any social organizations

you're a part of, but don't just show up. Be a person who helps organize things and takes on leadership roles where available. Women admire men that can be counted on, and they are attracted to men that other men look towards for leadership. Be the man who knows what he's doing.

4. Live cleanly—Most women are fine with some drinking or a little vice here or here. But any kind of addiction or uncontrolled substance abuse is a major red flag to women. So be honest with yourself about how you are currently living. Do you binge drink regularly? Do you use illegal drugs? Is there *any* kind of activity you are sufficiently addicted to that keeps you from living your best life? It's time to address those problems. Defeating these habits will make you a more appealing man.

5. Live in the real world—Women prefer a man who is present in the real world. Spending hours a day playing games online is a turn-off to most women. So is being a bad or distracted conversationalist who is constantly distracted by his phone.

And if you're a woman?

1. Stay thin and in good shape—Men care about appearance. Even good men do. If you want a good man, making the most out of your personal appearance is crucial. Someone who tells you to find a man who doesn't care about your physical appearance is not only giving you bad advice, but they're lying in another way, because letting yourself go and becoming a fat slob is *itself* a sign of imperfections on the inside.

2. Don't get tattoos—Tattoos are more popular than ever for young women. Why? I can't say, but what's indisputably true is that it's one of the most aggressive ways to lower one's perceived value as a partner. A 2012 survey in the U.K. found that 37 percent of men rated tattoos as their number-one turnoff in women, and 78 percent put it in the top five.[380] So unless you want to willfully turn a huge proportion of men off, just don't get one. I assure you, a butterfly on your shoulder does not show you are free spirited and independent.

3. Keep your life in order—Men have learned to be wary of women who don't quite have it together. Do you show evidence of bad decision-making, like spending impulsively and piling up credit card debt? Is your friend group a source of constant drama instead of genuine support? Such a life won't just make you less appealing to good men; it will attract manipulative and dangerous ones, who hope that the latest bad decision in your life will be sleeping with them.

4. Be active in seeking out a man—Too often Christian women expect the man to do all the work in courtship, especially in meeting men. And sure, a man should ask a woman out. But don't be too indifferent! In places with desirable men, like church, women need to not be afraid to be the one to initiate conversations with men. Find out his interests, offer to help him out with a project or something he's working on. Ask him the kind of question you wish a man would ask you. Take a friendly and polite interest and right off the bat he knows you're friendly, inquisitive, and easy to talk to. Work on making his barrier to asking you out, or courting you, as low as possible. Don't act like a princess trapped in a faraway castle, where a man has to slay a dragon and cross a moat of lava just to talk to you. Many women need to understand that obstacles, problems, and drama will happen on their own in the conversations and decisions that lead to marriage. You do not need to create more of them.

5. Be feminine—Modern feminism encourages women to act like men, but most men aren't interested in men. Where a man is "assertive," a woman is "bossy." Where a man is reserved, a woman is "cold." The simple truth is that warm, feminine, and nurturing behavior is very appealing to most men, and it comes naturally to a good portion of women.

6. Be mature— Remember, almost all human "relationships" are really a kind of conversation. You'll free yourself from a lot of the bad dogmas, habits, and immature games surrounding "dating" if you think of it as a conversation and act accordingly. You're an adult and you should be respectful and deserving of respect. If you wouldn't treat a friend a certain way, why would you want to treat your future husband like that? Keep it all in the context of a conversation and it'll help you with things such as patience, politeness, and good expectations, and away from gambits and drama.

AFTER MARRIAGE

"Husbands love your wives, even as Christ also loved the Church."
Ephesians 5:25

So, if you're already married, do you get to pat yourself on the back and take this chapter off? *No.* Building up marriages isn't a solo quest, but the job of whole communities. If you have friends who are unmarried, you have the serious job of helping them change that. Ask them what they're looking for and how you can help. Engineer introductions. Do the work of pairing people off that was once a routine fact of life before the modern age. Don't abandon them alone on the gruesome battlefield of app dating.

But in addition to that, actually getting married is of course just the first step to the lifelong challenge of living a successful married life. Take your marriage's health seriously, and take the health of your friends' marriages seriously, too. Remember that marriage is not about you. It's about you merging your life with another person. That most rapid way to a successful marriage is for you to each put the other one first.

The most important thing after that is to have kids! I know a lot of older couples, and the two biggest regrets that I see are 1. Not having children, and 2. Not having *more* children.

Over and over, I run into the sentiment that, "Man, I thought I was at the limit, but in hindsight I should have just had one more kid." For most of us, children are the way we leave a mark on the world. They are our legacy after we die, as we are our parents' legacies right now.

Will that legacy be a good or bad one? That comes down to how you raise them. In truth, too many conservative parents are weirdly distant or hands-off with their kids. I've met many who don't like to bring up politics with their kids, as it will seem "preachy." Others may take their children to church, yet otherwise see their children's spiritual journey as their own affair. This is a disastrous attitude, to say the least.

Forming your children into right-thinking, right-behaving individuals is the single most important task in your life, and a task I believe we will all be judged for when we die. But how do you make sure that your children turn out right? That's a question for our next chapter.

CHAPTER TWENTY

Pull Out of Public Schools

I've spent a lot of time in this book mentioning things that conservatives should do to improve public schools. I stand by all of it. But in my opinion, the single best thing that parents can do, if they are able to, is to not send their kids to public schools at all. Send them to a private school that you *know* is in close alignment with your values, or else educate your children yourself at home.

This isn't hypocrisy, any more than it is hypocrisy to move out of crime-ridden blue cities, while still doing everything we can to make those cities safer for those left behind. We want our public schools to be as non-toxic as possible, but we can also recognize that, as they stand today, they are rotten, and the best way to avoid any poison is to not touch it at all.

This is obvious from even a little bit of thought. The only relationship in your child's life that you have absolute control over is the one they have with you. No matter what the laws are, no matter what your own community's political makeup is, whenever you send your child into a public school, you are placing them in the care of somebody hired by other people, based on criteria that likely have nothing to do with creating the future adult you want to raise. Every time you send a child to public school, you are taking a chance that they might be educated by someone like this:

A teacher in Baltimore, Maryland, celebrated "indoctrinating" students while dancing in a post on TikTok.

"Put the taxes in the bag," the teacher's post on TikTok said, as the middle school Spanish teacher jovially danced. The teacher was responding to criticism of using a song in which she lip-synched "f--- up on your b----" in a video adorning her classroom in pride materials.

Fox News Digital identified the teacher as Alexa Sciuto, who works at Pine Grove Middle School in the Baltimore County School District.

Sciuto responded to a user, who said, "None of this is what education is supposed to be about. Reading. Writing. Arithmetic. Why are you so f---ing hellbent on indoctrinating our children?"

She said, "I just got fired for indoctrinating my students."

"Sike," the next clip showed.

"Still employed," she said. "Put the taxes in the bag."

"Y'all will never take me alive," she added.

The clip also featured a gif of money falling, and an arrow pointing to it which said, "Your taxes."

Sciuto has, on another occasion, claimed that "professionalism is a patriarchal and White supremacist myth."[381]

Teachers who brazenly gloat about the power they hold over their charges are anything but rare. In Texas, Fort Worth math teacher Kelsey McCracken bragged on TikTok that she was "indoctrinating the youth" by identifying as "non-binary" and making them call her "Mx. McCracken."[382] Brenna Woods, a Massachusetts kindergarten teacher sporting the standard Insane Liberal blue-green haircut, was caught bragging on a Zoom call about teaching her kindergartners about white privilege, and mocked parents who complained about it.[383] For approximately infinity other examples, just subscribe to the Twitter account @LibsofTikTok.

Remember, for every Alexa Sciuto or "Mx." McCracken flaunting their extremism in your face on TikTok, there are hundreds or thousands who do so more quietly, but with no less conviction.

It's not that all of America's 3.2 million teachers are like this. But a great many are, and the number is growing. In 2021, The Heritage Foundation surveyed teachers about their beliefs on several basic questions intersecting with the current left-wing ideological consensus. While teachers as a whole were not in lockstep with liberals, they were still significantly to the left of the general public. Fifty-nine percent of teachers said that "white supremacy" was a "major problem" in America. Thirty-three percent said, explicitly, that the government and corporations should engage in racial discrimination in hiring for the sake of greater "equity." Thirty-seven percent supported teaching Critical Race Theory in the classroom, and 40 percent favored teaching the 1619 Project.[384]

Your child will have several dozen different teachers by the time they finish high school. The odds of at least a few of them being left-wing ideologues is prohibitively high.

From the moment your child is born until they turn 18, 157,788 hours will pass. Of those hours, they'll be awake for about two thirds of them, which is about 105,000 hours. Now, do the math on how long your child will be at a public school, if you choose to send them to one. The average American child spends about a thousand hours in school per year, not counting any after-school programs, clubs, sports, or anything else. Multiply that by 12 grades, add another 500 for a half-day kindergarten, and your child will spend, at minimum, around 12,500 hours in class. That's nearly 12 percent of all their waking hours in their formative years, being molded in an institution designed by liberals, controlled by liberals, using curricula written by liberals, and mostly staffed by liberals.

Or, instead, you can take control yourself, with a curriculum chosen by you, and taught by either you or someone you can completely trust.

Homeschooling is not new, and it's also not backwards. According to the late British historian Paul Johnson:

> It is notable in the early 19th century how many boys, as well as girls, were educated in effect at home, and in isolation from other children. Victor Hugo owed all his early education to his mother. Edward William Lane, later to be the leading authority on Egypt, was given a superb classical and mathematical education at home, mainly by his mother Sophia Gardiner, a niece of Gainsborough; when he went up to Cambridge he found he could do all the maths Tripos, and so did not stay. . . . W. E. Forster, born in 1818, the son of Quaker missionaries, "learned to discuss grave social and political questions with his father and mother before he had learned to play with children of his own age." . . . Most boys, given the choice, preferred education at home. Edward Bulwer Lytton was taught English, mathematics, and

Latin by his adoring mother and, two brief experiences at school proving objectionable, successfully petitioned to have a private tutor at home.[385]

Is homeschooling difficult? Sure. But it's also much easier than it was 40 years ago, and is getting easier by the day. As homeschooling itself has grown in popularity, so have homeschooling co-ops, where multiple homeschooling families cooperate toward their shared objectives. That might mean rotating where kids learn each day, so that homeschooling isn't a full-time job. It might mean pooling money for a tutor on a specific subject. Or, it could simply mean having a way to get your child the friends and socialization that so often are the only viable arguments in favor of public schools. If you live even remotely near even a medium-sized city, I can guarantee homeschooling co-ops already exist, you just have to look for them. And if you can't find one to your liking, you can always start your own. You'll be surprised how many other parents are interested.

There are also more options and resources than ever for building up your own curriculum. Groups like Abeka and BJU Press have been producing Christian homeschool materials for ages, and now they've been joined by options like Classical Conversations, The Well-Trained Mind, or The Good and the Beautiful. For tough subjects like math, engineering, or physics, there are specialized options like Life of Fred (a series of Christian math books) or TeachEngineering. If you have a gifted child you want to cultivate to the best of their abilities, you can use Art of Problem Solving (a favorite of future U.S. Math Olympians) and Singapore Math (the curriculum that trains Singapore's world-class civil service). None of these options is brutally expensive; many offer large amounts of material for free.

If you need more options, though, they're all just a short web search away. Check out a website like CathyDuffyReviews.com, or simply look around YouTube for a practically infinite number of parents offering their own thoughts on different options. The key point to remember is successfully homeschooling is just a matter of whether you care enough about your children to put in the effort.

If homeschooling simply isn't an option, the next best path is to find a private school closely aligned with your values. I'm favorable to Peachy Keenan's advice in her recent book *Domestic Extremist*, "I always tell people to look for a school with the word "classical" in the name or description: it's a dog whistle for anti-wokeness." The Association of Classical Christian Schools has grown from ten schools twenty years ago to more than 500 schools today. As I write this, they have members in every state but Connecticut, Rhode Island, Vermont, and New Hampshire (but seriously, if you still live in New England, why?). The Chesterton Schools network of Catholic high schools has grown to more than 40 members, emphasizing a Catholic education that isn't just in name only.

Nearly two centuries ago, French writer Alexis de Tocqueville praised Americans for their spirit of can-do self-organization.

"Americans group together to hold fêtes, found seminaries, build inns, construct churches, distribute books, dispatch missionaries to the antipodes," he wrote. "They establish hospitals, prisons, schools by the same method. Finally, if they wish to highlight a truth or develop an opinion by the encouragement of a great example, they form an association."

Remember, you are not alone in hating what is happening to this country. Millions of other parents feel the same, and they are banding together to create the schools our children need. Don't be an onlooker. Be a participant.

CHAPTER TWENTY–ONE

The Spiritual Dimension

*"The Christian . . . imagines the better future of the human species . . .
in the image of heavenly joy.... We, on the other hand,
will have this heaven on earth."*
—Moses Hess, *A Communist Confession of Faith,* 1846

*"We must picture hell as a state where everyone is perpetually
concerned about his own dignity and advancement,
where everyone has a grievance, and where everyone lives
with the deadly serious passions of envy, self-importance, and resentment."*
—C.S. Lewis, *The Screwtape Letters*

I open this chapter with the two above quotes because the first one describes where liberalism was supposed to go, and the second describes where it actually went.

Wokeness promised heaven and gave us hell. The deep unhappiness that young people feel is shown time and time again in studies and in the explosion of pathologies. Some of these have never been known, others like transgenderism have been dormant since the last days of pagan Rome. They have been amped up into a moral frenzy, and been left with a disorienting moral and spiritual void.

Throughout this book, I've emphasized the power of small marginal changes, made by many people, to change the world. We can't just wait for a man on a white horse to ride into the White House and redeem the country. Instead, we need to be involved with our city councils and our school boards. We need to change our attitudes so that we can be more assertive and robust in the face of left-wing attacks. And at the individual level, changing ourselves (by developing better skills and better habits) will make us more able to change our communities. But there is a step that comes even before making ourselves more physically fit or improving our self-discipline. That step is achieving a *spiritual* awakening from within ourselves.

I firmly believe that the battle we are engaged in is *not* merely a political one. It is a spiritual one, and it has a profoundly religious component. As the Apostle Paul wrote, "our struggle is not against flesh and blood, but against the rulers, against the powers, against the world forces of this darkness, against the spiritual forces of wickedness in the heavenly places."

Consequently, I believe that defeating woke is not simply a matter of winning the right elections, implementing the right policies, or holding the right attitudes. Long-term victory *will* require some kind of spiritual rebirth as well.

In a letter to the Massachusetts state militia in 1798, John Adams wrote that "Our constitution was made only for a moral and religious people. It is wholly inadequate to the government of any other." More recently, the great Russian anti-communist writer Alexander Solzhenitsyn said this in his 1983 acceptance speech for the Templeton Prize:

> More than half a century ago, while I was still a child, I recall hearing a number of older people offer the following explanation for the great disasters that had befallen Russia: "Men have forgotten God; that's why all this has happened."
>
> Since then I have spent well-nigh 50 years working on the history of our Revolution; in the process I have read hundreds of books, collected hundreds of personal testimonies, and have already contributed eight volumes of my own toward the effort of clearing away the rubble left by that upheaval. But if I were asked today to formulate as concisely as possible the main cause of the ruinous Revolution that swallowed up some 60 million of our people, I could not put it more accurately than to repeat: "Men have forgotten God; that's why all this has happened!"[386]

Solzhenitsyn was correct, and Adams was correct before him. What could more perfectly articulate the escalating moral failures of our leaders than that our nation and its people have forgotten and abandoned God?

I know that not every conservative in America is Christian or even religious. You might be non-religious yourself. So, am I telling you that if you are serious about pushing back wokeness, not just delaying its victory but actually defeating it, you should become Christian?

Yes. Yes I am.

Three thousand years ago, the poet Homer wrote that "All men have need of gods." Homer didn't know it, but in a single sentence he encapsulated why wokeness has been so successful in recent years. The religious impulse in man is natural and hardwired. Americans may have abandoned churches in droves, but their craving for a metaphysical belief system has not waned. They still desire to be a part of something that gives their lives order, meaning, structure, and purpose.

When I was growing up in the early 2000s, the big thing on the left was "New Atheism." Writers like Chris Hitchens, Richard Dawkins, and Sam Harris put out high-profile, bestselling books criticizing and ridiculing religious belief, which spawned countless imitators in bookstores and on the nascent Internet. Advocates bragged that this new brash, public atheism represented a triumph of reason that would brush away superstitions and backward beliefs of all kinds.

While the damage to young people's religiosity stuck, the whole "reason" thing didn't. By 2012, left-wing activists argued that it was time for a new movement, "Atheism+."[387] In a single word, Atheism+ was about "intersectionality." You couldn't be a good atheist, they argued, unless you adopted a whole battery of left-wing beliefs like being pro-abortion, pro-LGBT, "anti-racist," and anti-gun.

The specific term didn't take off, but the ideology did. Pay close attention, and you'll see how wokeness is even more of a religion than it seemed at first. In a lot of ways, it's more of a religion than that practiced by many lukewarm Christians. For the woke, Gay Pride parades or Black Lives Matter protests have replaced public sacrifices to Zeus or a medieval procession with the relics of a saint. Sacred days and months like Pride Month or Black History Month increasingly resemble the religious calendar that the lives of medieval Christians once revolved around. Drag queens might as well be a new woke priesthood (and here's an unfun fact: At least one ancient Roman cult had priests who castrated themselves![388]). George Floyd and

Jordan Neely are new woke saints, and the more criminal or repellent they were while alive, the better. In August 2023, NASCAR suspended driver Noah Gragson for liking a meme mocking Floyd. If Gragson had simply lived in 1600s France instead he might have been punished for mocking the Virgin Mary.[389]

We still desire to have our idols, too. Have you ever noticed the hysterical way people behave at a pop or rock concert in the decades since religious belief has waned? Do you remember the messianic treatment that Barack Obama received in 2007? The hysterical screaming and panting at the performers, the belief that a Senator from Illinois was a "light worker" and "spiritual being," these are both symptoms of a people transposing religious worship and enthusiasm at human idols.[390]

In its own warped, distorted way, wokeness really does fill a hole in people's lives. It gives them purpose and direction. Instead of "original sin" and the Fall from Eden, we have concepts such as "Patriarchy," "Capitalism," "Racism," even "Climate Change." These sinister forces explain all of our troubles and unhappiness. In the woke's mind, maybe instead of eating from the Tree of Knowledge, what cursed Adam, and humanity, was Adam's taking authority over Eve and creating the Patriarchy. Or maybe it was when he became a small businessman running a small family farm. Maybe at some point he uttered a racial slur towards a group of descendants he had yet to reproduce.

Wokeness supplies a simple narrative of heroes and villains, saviors and Satans. Even if its checklist of good and evil actions can change with blistering speed ("Wait, are we pro or anti-segregation this week?"), it's still a checklist with commandments and sins.

This kind of intense belief cannot be beaten with indifference or nihilism or lukewarmness. It can only be beaten by another belief system. I believe that Christianity is that system, but truthfully, any faith tradition is better than what wokeness has planned for the world, because what sets wokeness apart is how it so roundly *inverts* the moral systems of every enduring tradition, but especially that of the Bible.

The history of the world is littered with the consequences of deep spiritual awakenings. The Protestant Reformation's emphasis on individual engagement with Scripture, and the literacy and church self-government required paved the way for America's experiment in self-government. Slavery was a normal practice all around the world, until a great moral awakening among Christians in England and North America became a fire that gradually destroyed slavery everywhere on Earth.

In my opinion, a similar such revival is necessary for any long-term American comeback to happen. It is impossible, then, to speak of the social and political problems emerging from wokeism without addressing that the heart of these problems are *soul* issues. A good tree bears good fruit, but a bad tree bears bad fruit, as Christ said. Unless we spiritually regenerate the trees that are ourselves, our fruits—our families, our cities, our country—will go bad as well.

The single greatest antibody to woke poison is a robust community centered on a healthy, confident church filled with informed, devout believers. I've mentioned how wokeness appeals to the weak, damaged, and angry. This applies to how it undercuts faith as well. When the woke worldview encounters those who otherwise have no faith, or only a shoddy, poorly understood one, it sweeps through like a virus through an immunocompromised body.

It's not just about doctrines, though. Churches also provide pragmatic value in the face of modern dangers. I've emphasized throughout this book that wokeness permeates almost every facet of American social, cultural, and economic life. Pop culture is woke, government is woke, colleges are woke, and so on. If you orient your family's life primarily toward these wider institutions, you choose to live in a world that is formed by those who hate you. But when you build a faith community, you create a barrier between yourself and the wider world.

This has to be a proud and public faith. If you say that faith is a "private matter" not ever to be shown publicly, you are subtly (or unsubtly) sending the message that it is unimportant, or embarrassing, or weak. The woke are not private or ashamed about their faith in the slightest. They are confident and make it very obvious what they believe. They can only be beaten by those who feel and act the same way, but for a more worthy set of beliefs.

Do you want to make sure your children grow up without being seduced by woke lies about the world? It's not going to be enough to lecture them at the dinner table, or even to homeschool them. You must instead make it clear that there is a different worldview, with a different and robust set of values than they'll see in society at large, that your *entire* family adheres to and takes seriously.

And make no mistake, your children are paying attention. If you claim to be Christian, but then blow off services when it's inconvenient, pick and choose which sermons you pay attention to, and give no indications that religion is important the rest of the week, *they will notice*. If you're lucky, they'll just lose some respect for you. But in many more cases, they will also lose respect for the faith you represent. It's been said that one must be convinced to convince. An insincere walk is perhaps the easiest way to lose your children to wokeness.

If you're a Christian, act like one, in public and at home. Read your Bible, both on your own and with your children. Whether you're explaining politics, morals, or family decision-making to your kids, frame it in terms of your faith, and make sure you remain consistent. Pray at home as well as at church (if you practice a faith besides Christianity, just adapt all of the above accordingly).

What about those of you who are not believers? Well, like I said, if you're serious about opposing the poisonous woke threat to civilization, I think that ought to change. But you shouldn't simply become a fake believer. What do I recommend, then?

At a minimum, I propose that you seriously examine *why* you are not a believer. Was it a choice, or did you just fall into it because your family didn't care much? Did you just drift away while you were in college? Did you get won over by smart-sounding atheist friends with slick arguments, friends who might not seem so smart now?

If you're a conservative, despite all the pressure not to be one, you clearly think truth matters, and that morality is objective. Do you think that impulse toward a moral universe is just random noise from evolution, or might it have been planted by a creator? Do you think the clear signs that religiosity makes for happier families and happier lives are just an accident, or could it be a sign that man is *meant* to believe in and have a relationship with his creator?

Consider trying a prayer, even if it's to a God you don't quite believe in yet. You might be surprised at how it makes you feel.

As for you believers, reach out to the "nones" of your life, the ones who aren't believers and don't practice a religion. Don't be an irritant, but instead, be a friend. Be interested in their lives, and if they open up to you about their frustrations and problems, be ready to gently propose that there is a God who cares about those problems. Be earnest, but also humble.

Pray not just for fellow-believers but for the heathen around you, and mean it. Do not be like the self-righteous Pharisee described in the Bible, "God, I thank You that I am not like other people: swindlers, unjust, adulterers, or even like this tax collector." Instead, perhaps pray, "Lord, open the eyes of my friends who do not believe, and open the eyes of the Woke!"

As much as woke-ism can drive us nuts, we should never get hateful or too nasty with the people involved in propagating it. If Jesus on the cross can say "Father, forgive them; for they know not what they do," then we can do the same with gladness.

I know what some of you might be thinking, "These people know what they're doing! 'Forgive them, for they know *exactly* what they do'? No thanks!" But I would seriously urge you to reconsider how you think about the woke.

Wokeness is just an obvious manifestation of a profound spiritual blindness. What other metaphor but blindness explains the evil in someone choosing to castrate a small child, or to murder the unborn?

God is sovereign, and has allowed all things, even Wokeness, to happen. As Christians, it is our duty to petition God in prayer that he would open people's eyes. And it is our duty to live righteous lives, so that we might deserve his favor and mercy.

Final Thoughts

So, there it is, my blueprint for a right-wing revolution. If you've followed me this whole way, please accept my enthusiastic thanks. It's a big-time commitment to read an entire book, and I'm grateful you found my thoughts worthy of such a commitment.

But I'll be even more grateful if you earnestly take the recommendations of this book to heart. If conservative Americans read this book, then go right back to the losing attitudes, strategies, and lifestyles that brought us and our country to this point, then this book is a failure, no matter how many copies it sells or what the reviews are. I didn't write this to get a bestseller slot or to burnish a resume. I wrote it to try and improve America.

If you've read this far, do me a favor and do something *right this instant*. Think of one simple thing you can do to fulfill the recommendations of this book. Figure out when your city's next local government meeting is, and what the agenda of it is. If you're out of shape, skip your next meal and run (or jog, or walk) a mile instead. Pick out the next book you'll read, and make sure it's something that will expand your knowledge or improve your moral character.

And then, turn that little action into a habit. Take at least one little action every day that fulfills the advice I've given, and day by day you will remake yourself. If a few million conservatives do that, within a few years we will have made a revolution.

Let's get at it.

Acknowledgments

A big thanks to Winning Team Publishing, especially Donald Trump Jr, Sergio Gor, Connor Hickey, Tina Bartley, and the rest of the team involved including photographers, designers, and editors.

My deep appreciation to everyone who has supported myself and Turning Point. This organization is a juggernaut because of you.

To my incredible team at Turning Point USA and Turning Point Action, thank you for all you do every single day. Especially Mikey McCoy, Lauren Toncich, Tyler Bowyer, Justin Streiff, Andrew Kolvet, Josh Thifault, and Stacy Sheridan. I appreciate every member of the team!

Finally, a special thanks to Blake Neff for helping with the vision of this book and the immense amount of research that went into it.

Notes

1 http://www.lukehistory.com/ballads/worldup.html.

2 https://www.thecollegefix.com/beloit-college-creates-blacks-only-space -for-students-to-study/.

3 https://www.washingtontimes.com/news/2022/apr/18/more-univer sities-holding-segregated-graduation-ev/.

4 https://www.cnn.com/2021/11/24/us/thomas-jefferson-statue-re moved/index.html#:~:text=A%20statue%20of%20Thomas%20 Jefferson,City%20Hall%20after%20187%20years&text=After%20 187%20years%2C%20a%20statue,in%20New%20York%20City%20 Hall.&text=The%20statue%2C%20which%20is%20a,removed%20 from%20its%20pedestal%20Monday.

5 https://www.npr.org/2020/12/29/951206414/statue-of-lincoln-with -freed-slave-at-his-feet-is-removed-in-boston.

6 https://www.revolver.news/2023/01/reparations-supreme-court-dem ocrats-looting-taxpayers-new-bill-will-gop-grow-a-spine/.

7 https://www.revolver.news/2023/01/you-dont-want-to-know-whats -in-san-franciscos-reparations-proposal/.

8 https://abc7news.com/sf-guaranteed-income-program-preg nant-black-women-abundant-birth-project-expanding-in-ca-at -risk/12547404/.

9   https://www.nationalreview.com/news/san-francisco-launches-guaranteed
    -income-pilot-program-for-transgender-residents/.

10 https://www.theatlantic.com/magazine/archive/2006/05/john-kenneth
    -galbraith-revisited/304935/.

11 https://www.wsj.com/articles/black-latino-teachers-collecting-835
    -million-in-discrimination-lawsuit-11657800508.

12 https://nypost.com/2023/06/17/getting-rid-of-standardized-tests-is
    -bad-for-college-applicants/.

13 https://www.nytimes.com/2021/05/15/us/SAT-scores-uc-university
    -of-california.html.

14 https://archive.is/2023.05.20-011108/https://www.wsj.com/amp/
    articles/the-new-bar-exam-puts-dei-over-competence-ncbe-family-law
    -schools-9c0dd4e8.

15 https://freebeacon.com/latest-news/seattle-firefighters-now-drilled-on
    -ibram-kendi-before-promotion-to-top-jobs/.

16 https://freebeacon.com/latest-news/seattle-firefighters-now-drilled-on
    -ibram-kendi-before-promotion-to-top-jobs/.

17 https://injuryfacts.nsc.org/home-and-community/safety-topics/fire
    -related-fatalities-and-injuries/.

18 https://ascopubs.org/doi/10.1200/JCO.22.02037.

19 https://www.nytimes.com/2020/08/25/realestate/blacks-minorities
    -appraisals-discrimination.html.

20 https://apnews.com/article/entertainment-cultures-race-and-ethnicity
    -us-news-ap-top-news-7e36c00c5af0436abc09e051261fff1f.

21 https://www.edfirstnc.org/post/the-worst-crt-training-we-ve-ever-seen
    -seriously.

22 https://www.washingtonpost.com/politics/2021/05/11/power-up
    -democratic-senators-consider-forming-bipoc-caucus-ahead-aapi
    -summit/.

23 https://blogs.extension.wisc.edu/oaic/2022/03/25/the-emergence-of
    -bipoc-what-it-means-and-how-it-is-used/.

24 https://freebeacon.com/coronavirus/food-and-drug-administration
-drives-racial-rationing-of-covid-drugs/.

25 https://apnews.com/article/tn-state-wire-race-and-ethnicity-racial
-injustice-courts-business-c95f6b6c8819a66d80219cc3fca01e0b.

26 https://www.city-journal.org/article/welcome-to-the-world-of-minority
-contracting.

27 https://www.city-journal.org/article/welcome-to-the-world-of-minority
-contracting.

28 https://www.city-journal.org/article/welcome-to-the-world-of-minority
-contracting.

29 https://www.city-journal.org/article/welcome-to-the-world-of-minority
-contracting.

30 https://www.city-journal.org/article/when-the-state-comes-for-your
-kids.

31 https://www.city-journal.org/article/when-the-state-comes-for-your
-kids.

32 https://www.pewresearch.org/short-reads/2022/06/07/about-5-of
-young-adults-in-the-u-s-say-their-gender-is-different-from-their-sex
-assigned-at-birth/.

33 https://www.reuters.com/investigates/special-report/usa-transyouth
-care/#:~:text=While%20the%20number%20of%20gender,of%20
that%20treatment%20remains%20scant.

34 https://www.hormonesmatter.com/lupron-precocious-puberty-decades
-regulatory-silence/.

35 https://nypost.com/2023/06/11/englands-nhs-wont-give-puberty
-blockers-to-children-at-gender-clinics/

36 https://www.dailywire.com/news/matt-walsh-undercover-investigation
-catches-trans-health-care-providers-falsifying-patient-info-to-fast-track
-sex-change-surgeries.

37 https://www.usbirthcertificates.com/articles/transgender-birth-certifi
cates.

38 https://www.latimes.com/california/story/2023-06-03/temecula-val ley-school-board-rejects-social-studies-curriculum-that-would-have-in cluded-harvey-milk.

39 https://www.gov.ca.gov/2023/06/07/temecula-school-board/.

40 https://www.npr.org/2021/09/27/1040904770/fbi-data-murder-in crease-2020.

41 https://tradingeconomics.com/united-states/intentional-homicides -per-100-000-people-wb-data.html.

42 https://www.city-journal.org/article/the-five-worst-prosecutors-in -america.

43 https://www.stltoday.com/online/homicides-in-st-louis-1970-2021/ table_5e4f1d5c-0808-57be-b4cf-1ad8fa7acc62.html.

44 https://www.macrotrends.net/countries/ranking/murder-homicide-rate.

45 https://www.foxnews.com/us/los-angeles-man-who-avoided-prison -near-fatal-stabbing-now-charged-with-neighbors-murder.

46 https://www.theamericanconservative.com/why-jake-gard ner-died/#:~:text=Indicted%20on%20four%20felony%20 charges,supposed%20to%20turn%20himself%20in.

47 https://www.theamericanconservative.com/why-jake-gard ner-died/#:~:text=Indicted%20on%20four%20felony%20 charges,supposed%20to%20turn%20himself%20in.

48 https://twitter.com/NebraskaMegan/status/1307882691950448640.

49 https://www.nbcnews.com/news/us-news/virginia-police-officer-fired -after-donating-kyle-rittenhouse-defense-fund-n1264783.

50 https://www.foxnews.com/media/rittenhouse-utah-reporter-condemned.

51 https://www.economist.com/the-economist-explains/2021/07/30/ how-has-the-meaning-of-the-word-woke-evolved.

52 John Simon, *John Simon on Film: Criticism, 1982–2001*. (New York: Applause Theatre & Cinema Books, 2005).

53 https://www.tabletmag.com/sections/news/articles/media-great-racial -awakening.

54 https://bigthink.com/the-present/yuri-bezmenov/.

55 Bruce Bawer, *The Victims' Revolution* (New York: HarperCollins, 2012).

56 Ibid.

57 http://www.marxisthistory.org/subject/usa/eam/index.html.

58 Eric Hoffer, *The True Believer* (Harper & Brothers, 1951).

59 https://prospect.org/features/trouble-diversity/.

60 https://www.cnn.com/2023/04/12/tech/elon-musk-bbc-interview-twitter-intl-hnk/index.html#:~:text=Elon%20Musk%20has%20laid%20off,a%20rare%20interview%20late%20Tuesday.

61 https://www.nationalreview.com/news/daily-wire-claims-twitter-canceled-deal-to-premiere-what-is-a-woman-documentary/.

62 https://www.theamericanconservative.com/lgbttqqfagpbdsm-omg-wesleyan/.

63 https://today.yougov.com/topics/politics/articles-reports/2015/05/20/hate-speech.

64 https://www.courant.com/2019/11/01/police-fbi-investigating-hate-filled-flyers-found-on-western-connecticut-state-university-campus/.

65 Eric Hoffer, *The Temper of Our Time*.

66 https://www.nationalreview.com/bench-memos/law-professor-david-bernstein-on-racial-classifications/.

67 https://twitter.com/iowahawkblog/status/664089892599631872.

68 https://www.newsweek.com/army-personnel-hit-back-tucker-carlson-calling-pregnant-soldiers-mockery-1575320.

69 https://www.stripes.com/theaters/us/pentagon-expresses-revulsion-over-tucker-carlson-s-comments-about-women-service-members-1.665369.

70 https://www.politico.com/news/2021/03/11/military-tucker-carlson-female-troops-comments-475315.

71 https://nypost.com/2021/03/15/official-marines-account-walks-back-tweet-ripping-tucker-carlson/.

72 https://www.washingtonpost.com/powerpost/republicans-joint-chiefs

-chairman-critical-race-theory-congress/2021/06/23/84654c34-d451
-11eb-9f29-e9e6c9e843c6_story.html.

73 https://www.revolver.news/2021/05/bishop-garrison-pentagon-hatchet
-man/.

74 https://www.revolver.news/2021/05/bishop-garrison-pentagon-hatchet
-man/.

75 https://www.esd.whs.mil/Portals/54/Documents/DD/issuances/
dodi/130028p.pdf.

76 https://crsreports.congress.gov/product/pdf/IN/IN11764.

77 https://web.archive.org/web/20230527182737/https://www.army.mil/
armyequityandinclusion.

78 https://diversity.defense.gov/Portals/51/ACTIONS%20TO%20IM
PROVE%20RACIAL%20AND%20ETHNIC%20DIVERSITY%20
AND%20INCLUSION%20IN%20THE%20U_S_%20MILI
TARY%20OSD011769-20%20RES%20Final.pdf.

79 https://www.wsj.com/articles/military-officers-affirmative-ac
tion-identity-politics-diversity-and-inclusion-national-security
-11629402318.

80 https://federalnewsnetwork.com/air-force/2021/03/air-force-trying
-to-diversify-its-largely-white-male-pilot-corps-with-new-strategy/.

81 https://people.com/celebrity/female-rangers-were-given-special-treat
ment-sources-say/.

82 https://www.judicialwatch.org/wp-content/uploads/2022/05/JW-v
-DOD-West-Point-CRT-records-01795.pdf.

83 https://www.revolver.news/2021/05/bishop-garrison-pentagon-hatchet
-man/.

84 https://www.judicialwatch.org/wp-content/uploads/2022/05/JW-v
-DOD-West-Point-CRT-records-01795.pdf.

85 https://apnews.com/article/military-obesity-pandemic-army-covid
-404bbc1a67408d390a7d462f1ecbef75.

86 https://www.nytimes.com/2023/04/28/us/army-flights-grounded
-crashes.html.

87 https://www.armytimes.com/news/your-army/2022/10/02/army-misses
-recruiting-goal-by-15000-soldiers/.

88 https://www.politico.com/news/2023/06/01/debt-limit-deal-pentagon
-budget-00099683.

89 https://www.newsmax.com/newsmax-tv/steve-friend-fbi-whistle
-blower/2023/05/18/id/1120407/.

90 https://www.nytimes.com/2014/06/30/nyregion/boy-scouts-make
-provocative-statement-at-gay-pride-parade.html.

91 https://www.scouting.org/about/diversity-equity-inclusion/the-boy
-scouts-of-america-introduces-new-citizenship-in-society-merit-badge/.

92 https://www.nytimes.com/2021/06/06/us/aclu-free-speech.html.

93 Yes, really.

94 https://www.newsweek.com/conservative-case-gay-marriage-70923.

95 https://www.washingtonpost.com/opinions/2021/04/22/why-i-support
-reparations-all-conservatives-should/.

96 https://italianstudies.nd.edu/news-events/news/journal-italian-culture
-dedicates-special-issue-to-joseph-a-buttigieg/.

97 https://www.independent.co.uk/news/world/americas/us-politics/
pete-buttigieg-military-us-marine-corps-2020-election-new-hampshire
-a9330501.html.

98 https://www.revolver.news/2021/07/black-rifle-coffee-new-york-times/.

99 https://www.presidency.ucsb.edu/documents/remarks-announcing
-candidacy-for-president-liberty-university-lynchburg-virginia.

100 https://www.politico.com/blogs/on-media/2017/02/cnn-anchor-apol
ogizes-for-comparing-fake-news-insult-to-the-n-word-234864.

101 https://www.ncbi.nlm.nih.gov/books/NBK519584/.

102 https://twitter.com/TeamAOC/status/1422287825521844225.

103 https://twitter.com/AyannaPressley/status/1471858295329771528.

104 https://www.foxnews.com/opinion/spoke-uc-davis-politics-leftists-responded-lies-attacks-said-words-violence.

105 https://www.revolver.news/2022/01/why-the-left-calls-everything-violent/.

106 https://www.courtlistener.com/opinion/109930/university-of-california-regents-v-bakke/.

107 https://www.heritage.org/courts/commentary/how-affirmative-action-colleges-hurts-minority-students.

108 https://www.nationalreview.com/2015/12/university-affirmative-action-admissions-policies-toxic/.

109 https://www.nytimes.com/2018/06/15/us/harvard-asian-enrollment-applicants.html.

110 https://www.medicalnewstoday.com/articles/326590#recovery.

111 http://www.trans-health.com/2013/penile-implants-guide/.

112 https://www.city-journal.org/article/yes-critical-race-theory-is-being-taught-in-schools.

113 https://twitter.com/realchrisrufo/status/1371540368714428416?lang=en.

114 https://www.espn.com/espn/otl/story/_/id/7751398/how-al-campanis-controversial-racial-remarks-cost-career-highlighted-mlb-hiring-practices.

115 https://www.nytimes.com/2020/12/26/us/mimi-groves-jimmy-galligan-racial-slurs.html.

116 https://www.nytimes.com/2020/12/26/us/mimi-groves-jimmy-galligan-racial-slurs.html.

117 https://amgreatness.com/2021/04/20/defund-the-managerial-regime/.

118 https://www.revolver.news/2021/04/sergeant-jonathan-pentland-deandre-digital-lynch-mob/.

119 https://www.cnn.com/us/jussie-smollett-loses-court-appeal/index.html.

120 https://www.usnews.com/news/best-states/articles/2017-08-14/the-kkk-is-still-based-in-22-states-in-the-us-in-2017.

121 https://www.cnn.com/2021/08/09/us/chamberlin-rock-removed-uni versity-of-wisconsin-trnd/index.html.

122 https://www.nytimes.com/2019/02/16/sunday-review/ralph-northam -blackface-friends.html.

123 https://apnews.com/article/nc-state-wire-north-america-donald-trump -us-news-ap-top-news-c7e6681046e3463aa9967a8302e5a102.

124 https://www.psychologytoday.com/us/blog/the-inertia-trap/201405/ why-every-racist-mentions-their-black-friend.

125 https://www.youtube.com/watch?v=bZ0QfLkjujY.

126 https://www.nas.org/blogs/article/where_did_we_get_the_idea_that _only_white_people_can_be_racist.

127 https://diaryofablackwomaninawhiteworld.substack.com/p/6-reasons -white-people-give-to-say.

128 https://www.google.com/url?q=https://ideas.ted.com/why-saying-i -dont-see-race-at-all-just-makes-racism-worse/&sa=D&source=docs& ust=1686545683530370&usg=AOvVaw2ANVOtit3d1iTyxO2a38kE.

129 https://www.tiktok.com/@ashanimfuko/video/72431696296805532 59?lang=en.

130 https://sph.umn.edu/site/docs/hewg/microaggressions.pdf.

131 Dorothy Healey and Maurice Isserman, *Dorothy Healey Remembers a Life in the American Communist Party* (New York u.a.: Oxford Univ. Pr., 1990).

132 https://news.gallup.com/poll/351041/americans-know-juneteenth -holiday.aspx.

133 https://amgreatness.com/2021/06/22/juneteenth-george-floyds-critical -race-holiday/.

134 https://freebeacon.com/media/msnbc-and-cnn-discussion-of-june teenth-explodes-in-2020-after-years-of-barely-mentioning-it/.

135 https://www.bostonherald.com/2020/09/26/n-y-times-owes-explana tion-for-1619-project-reversal/.

136 https://abcnews.go.com/US/fourth-july-makes-republicans-study/
story?id=13979855.

137 https://www.washingtonpost.com/politics/we-dont-want-you
-here-sen-ron-johnson-is-booed-at-milwaukees-juneteenth-cel
ebration/2021/06/20/041d2ae6-d1ff-11eb-ae54-515e2f63d37d_story
.html.

138 https://web.archive.org/web/20220901043856/http://www.census.gov/
quickfacts/fact/table/minneapoliscityminnesota/PST045221.

139 https://lims.minneapolismn.gov/Download/RCAV2/28255/PHS-8
-9-22---Gun-Violence-Overview.pdf.

140 https://www.nytimes.com/2023/05/06/opinion/omaha-jacob-gardner
-james-scurlock.html.

141 https://www.ou.edu/content/dam/budget_office/FY23%20Budget
.pdf.

142 https://www.oudaily.com/culture/ou-gender-equality-center-to-host
-first-drag-workshop-led-by-local-performers/article_9c7cf712-3ab8
-11ed-adc0-7787329430e9.html.

143 https://www.ou.edu/cas/latinx.

144 https://ou.edu/cas/csj/programs/activist-in-residence.

145 https://diversity.okstate.edu/diversity-highlights.html.

146 https://archive.fo/EM3jM.

147 https://www.revolver.news/2022/08/hello-republicans-wake-up-an
-anti-white-crisis-is-unfolding-at-university-of-tennessee/.

148 https://www.revolver.news/2022/08/hello-republicans-wake-up-an
-anti-white-crisis-is-unfolding-at-university-of-tennessee/.

149 https://admin.ks.gov/for-state-employees/ks-dei.

150 https://admin.ks.gov/media/cms/Recruitment_ Guide_20221
_2989cff9dff01.pdf.

151 http://pages.e2ma.net/pages/1807892/25007.

152 https://twitter.com/Mark_J_Perry/status/1467959926567931913.

153 https://www.heritage.org/education/report/diversity-university-dei
-bloat-the-academy.

154 https://dailycaller.com/2022/05/22/university-of-south-carolina-title
-vi-ix/.

155 https://americanmind.org/salvo/how-texas-am-went-woke/.

156 https://www.texastribune.org/2023/03/02/texas-am-system-dei/.

157 https://www.theatlantic.com/politics/archive/2018/05/reverse-migra
tion-might-turn-georgia-blue/560996/.

158 https://www.bloomberg.com/news/articles/2020-11-02/how-covid
-migration-may-change-the-political-map.

159 https://newcriterion.com/issues/2015/5/the-moral-of-caesar.

160 https://www.ministrymagazine.org/archive/1951/12/martin-luther
-and-the-end-of-the-world.

161 https://www.nationalreview.com/1955/11/our-mission-statement
-william-f-buckley-jr/.

162 Ibid.

163 https://americanaffairsjournal.org/2017/02/james-burnhams-manage
rial-elite/.

164 Francis, Sam, *Beautiful Losers* (University of Missouri Press, 1994).

165 https://thefederalist.com/2022/10/20/we-need-to-stop-calling-ourselves
-conservatives/.

166 https://www.time4learning.com/blog/homeschool/homeschooling
-over-the-years/.

167 https://reason.com/1983/04/01/home-schooling-up-from
-undergr/?print.

168 https://scholar.google.com/scholar_case?case=594703374978001271
2&hl=en&as_sdt=6&as_vis=1&oi=scholarr.

169 https://nces.ed.gov/fastfacts/display.asp?id=91.

170 http://www.gun-nuttery.com/rtc.php.

171 https://www.monmouth.edu/polling-institute/reports/monmouth -poll_us_042423/.

172 https://www.npr.org/2022/06/03/1102872199/gallup-poll-pro-choice -roe-v-wade-supreme-court.

173 https://archive.fo/ua5rY.

174 https://thehill.com/regulation/court-battles/4078821-stephen-miller -warns-schools-of-lawsuits-if-they-ignore-supreme-court-affirmative -action-ruling/.

175 https://nypost.com/2022/08/18/fetterman-sponged-off-parents-till -he-was-49-but-attacks-dr-ozs-wealth-in-pa-senate-race/.

176 https://www.cnbc.com/2020/11/04/whats-behind-trumps-leads-in -michigan-and-pennsylvania-.html.

177 https://www.nytimes.com/2012/10/07/us/politics/as-more-vote-by -mail-faulty-ballots-could-impact-elections.html.

178 https://today.yougov.com/topics/politics/articles-reports/2022/10/14/ democrats-republicans-plan-vote-2022.

179 https://www.nytimes.com/live/2022/11/08/us/voting-polls-ballots.

180 https://wsau.com/2023/06/01/conservative-group-pledges-5-million -dollars-to-wisconsin-ballot-collecting-efforts/.

181 https://nypost.com/2023/05/28/target-loses-10b-following-boycott -calls-over-lgbtq-friendly-clothing/.

182 https://www.retaildive.com/news/target-pride-month-boycott-back lash/651329/.

183 https://ag.ny.gov/press-release/2023/attorney-general-james-calls-target -support-lgbtq-community.

184 https://www.washingtonpost.com/health/2022/10/10/abortion-catholic -hospitals-birth-control/.

185 https://cdn.plannedparenthood.org/uploads/filer_public/25/ ed/25ed2675-fbbc-453b-8b35-f8ddaa025b57/281222-ppfa-annual -report-c3-digital.pdf.

186 https://www.commonspirit.org/news-and-perspectives/news/common
-spirit-health-announces-fy2022-year-end-results.

187 https://www.washingtonpost.com/politics/2020/10/16/this-summers
-black-lives-matter-protesters-were-overwhelming-peaceful-our-research
-finds/.

188 https://abcnews.go.com/US/chicago-sees-18-homicides-deadliest-day
-60-years/story?id=71150234.

189 https://carrcenter.hks.harvard.edu/publications/black-lives-matter
-protesters-were-overwhelmingly-peaceful-our-research-finds/.

190 https://time.com/5886348/report-peaceful-protests/.

191 https://www.cnn.com/2020/09/04/us/blm-protests-peaceful-report
-trnd/index.html.

192 https://nypost.com/2021/06/20/hundreds-of-nyc-rioters-looters-have
-charges-dropped/.

193 https://thepostmillennial.com/breaking-nyc-jury-finds-douglass-mackey
-guilty-in-first-ever-meme-trial-after-making-memes-that-disparaged
-hillary-clinton-in-the-2016-election.

194 https://www.foxnews.com/politics/nra-legal-fight-against-woke-pros
ecutor-alleged-roadmap-abuse.

195 https://nymag.com/intelligencer/2023/06/why-are-minnesota-demo
crats-so-progressive.html.

196 https://www.nytimes.com/1964/06/19/archives/text-of-goldwater
-speech-on-rights.html.

197 https://claremontreviewofbooks.com/digital/the-law-that-ate-the
-constitution/.

198 https://claremontreviewofbooks.com/digital/the-law-that-ate-the-con
stitution/.

199 Christopher Caldwell, *The Age of Entitlement.*

200 https://northcarolinahistory.org/encyclopedia/griggs-v-duke-power/.

201 https://northcarolinahistory.org/encyclopedia/griggs-v-duke-power/.

202 https://papers.ssrn.com/sol3/papers.cfm?abstract_id=3482015.

203 https://papers.ssrn.com/sol3/papers.cfm?abstract_id=3482015.

204 Thomas Sowell (1993), "Is Reality Optional?: And Other Essays," Hoover Inst. Press.

205 https://www.eeoc.gov/laws/guidance/enforcement-guidance-consideration-arrest-and-conviction-records-employment-decisions.

206 https://papers.ssrn.com/sol3/papers.cfm?abstract_id=3482015.

207 https://dash.harvard.edu/bitstream/handle/1/3322830/Dobbin_StrengthWeakState.pdf?sequence=2.

208 https://www.nbcnews.com/news/nbcblk/diversity-roles-disappear-three-years-george-floyd-protests-inspired-rcna72026.

209 Theodore Dalrymple, *Our Culture, What's Left of It.*

210 https://www.newyorker.com/news/news-desk/laura-kipniss-endless-trial-by-title-ix.

211 https://www2.ed.gov/policy/gen/guid/school-discipline/index.html.

212 https://www.justice.gov/opa/pr/justice-department-releases-investigative-findings-seattle-police-department.

213 https://www.seattle.gov/documents/Departments/Police/Compliance/Consent_Decree.pdf.

214 https://www.justice.gov/opa/pr/justice-department-announces-significant-milestone-policing-reform-efforts-city-seattle-and.

215 https://www.seattletimes.com/seattle-news/law-justice/seattle-violent-crime-hits-15-year-high-other-takeaways-from-new-report/.

216 https://www.the-scientist.com/reading-frames/opinion-what-the-history-of-blood-transfusion-reveals-about-risk-69105.

217 https://www.nbcnews.com/health/health-news/gay-bisexual-men-can-donate-blood-new-fda-rules-rcna83937.

218 https://www.americanprogress.org/article/5-reasons-why-section-5-of-the-voting-rights-act-enhances-our-democracy/.

219 https://www.justice.gov/opa/pr/attorney-general-loretta-e-lynch-state
ment-us-supreme-court-ruling-arizona-state-legislature.

220 https://www.cir-usa.org/case/nix-v-holder/.

221 https://www.theatlantic.com/politics/archive/2018/01/the-gop-just
-received-another-tool-for-suppressing-votes/550052/.

222 https://www.theatlantic.com/politics/archive/2018/01/the-gop-just
-received-another-tool-for-suppressing-votes/550052/.

223 https://www.revolver.news/2022/09/why-every-republican-should
-back-blake-masters-war-against-affirmative-action/.

224 https://tennesseelookout.com/2023/07/18/litigation-likely-to-follow
-ags-foray-into-business-worlds-race-based-policies/.

225 https://www.nbcnews.com/politics/donald-trump/trump-signs-execu
tive-order-punish-vandalism-against-federal-monuments-n1232322.

226 https://www.stripes.com/branches/air_force/air-force-s-top-black-gen
eral-offers-emotional-take-on-racial-unrest-over-floyd-killing-1.632658.

227 https://www.nytimes.com/2023/07/17/us/politics/trump-plans-2025
.html.

228 https://www.washingtonexaminer.com/news/alleged-whistleblower
-eric-ciaramella-was-biden-guest-at-state-department-banquet.

229 https://www.axios.com/2022/07/22/trump-2025-radical-plan-second-term.

230 https://www.jcs.mil/Portals/36/Documents/CJCS%20Memo%20
to%20the%20Joint%20Force%20(02JUN2020).pdf.

231 https://nypost.com/2020/06/01/president-trump-mobilizing-us-mil
itary-to-end-george-floyd-riots/.

232 https://thehill.com/homenews/administration/3592300-milley-vowed
-to-fight-trump-from-the-inside-book-excerpt/.

233 https://www.frontpagemag.com/next-joint-chiefs-chair-wants-white
-male-officers-to-be-a-minority/.

234 https://www.nytimes.com/2018/08/15/world/europe/hungary-us
-orban-trump.html.

235 https://www.cnn.com/2020/06/15/politics/us-embassy-seoul-blm
-banner/index.html.

236 https://www.dol.gov/agencies/ofccp/executive-order-11246/as-amended.

237 https://www.employmentlawwatch.com/2020/10/articles/employ
ment-us/executive-order-13950-on-diversity-training-hidden-traps
-for-employers/.

238 https://www.hud.gov/program_offices/fair_housing_equal_opp/part
ners/FHIP.

239 https://www.lawyerscommittee.org/smith-v-trump/.

240 https://twitter.com/RandoLand_us/status/1685310894069194752.

241 https://www.hud.gov/sites/dfiles/FHEO/documents/Press%20Re
lease%20FY2019%20FHIP%20Awardes._BB.pdf.

242 https://foundationforfreedomonline.com/bidens-national-science-foun
dation-has-pumped-nearly-40-million-into-social-media-censorship
-grants-and-contracts/.

243 https://www.cato.org/blog/federal-lands-underused-federal-housing
-affordability-tool.

244 https://www.cato.org/blog/federal-lands-underused-federal-housing
-affordability-tool.

245 https://rollcall.com/2023/06/20/trump-says-hell-restore-presidential
-impoundment-authority/.

246 https://newrepublic.com/article/61068/the-agitator-barack-obamas
-unlikely-political-education.

247 https://www.revolver.news/2022/10/scott-weiner-california-transgender
-kidnapping-bill-is-pure-evil-but-republicans-must-copy-it-in-every
-red-state/.

248 https://www.buzzfeednews.com/article/jtes/california-non-binary
-gender-identity-recognition.

249 https://www.foxnews.com/politics/newsom-signs-legislation-making
-california-sanctuary-state-transgender-procedures.

250 https://www.revolver.news/2022/10/scott-weiner-california-transgender

-kidnapping-bill-is-pure-evil-but-republicans-must-copy-it-in-every
-red-state/.

251 https://leginfo.legislature.ca.gov/faces/billHistoryClient.xhtml?bill
_id=201720180SB700.

252 https://www.nbcbayarea.com/news/local/san-francisco/new-housing
-legislation/3156118/.

253 https://therealdeal.com/la/2022/03/15/sb9-starting-to-sound-like
-prop-13/.

254 https://www.latimes.com/california/story/2019-11-21/trump-taxes
-ballot-california-supreme-court.

255 https://fee.org/articles/why-progressives-fear-hate-crime-hoaxes/.

256 https://www.dailymail.co.uk/news/article-12310887/Young-North
-Carolina-woman-sues-doctors-testosterone-age-17-saying-needed
-therapy-not-double-mastectomy-latest-blockbuster-detransition-law
suit.html.

257 https://www.dailymail.co.uk/news/article-12310887/Young-North
-Carolina-woman-sues-doctors-testosterone-age-17-saying-needed-ther
apy-not-double-mastectomy-latest-blockbuster-detransition-lawsuit.html.

258 https://apnews.com/article/2022-midterm-elections-biden-health
-lawsuits-ebc1a38fd82f65b92d27ddf8bb8ea792.

259 https://archive.ph/fXN4V.

260 https://www.vox.com/technology/2023/7/5/23784987/social-media
-government-ban-lawsuit-injunction.

261 https://nypost.com/2022/03/02/judge-tosses-ny-ag-letitia-james-bid
-to-break-up-nra-but-suit-still-moving-forward/.

262 https://www.politico.com/news/2022/09/08/steve-bannon-surrenders
-to-manhattan-da-00055427.

263 https://www.nytimes.com/2023/04/13/nyregion/trump-letitia-james
-deposition.html.

264 https://www.cnbc.com/2022/09/21/trump-criminal-referral-sent-to
-prosecutors-and-irs-by-letitia-james.html.

265 https://apnews.com/article/black-lives-matter-donations-george-floyd-protests-ddcf0d21d130a5d46256aa6c5d145ea7.

266 https://www.npr.org/2022/04/07/1091487910/blm-leaders-face-questions-after-allegedly-buying-a-mansion-with-donation-money.

267 https://www.newyorker.com/news/news-desk/the-reckoning-of-morris-dees-and-the-southern-poverty-law-center.

268 https://projects.propublica.org/nonprofits/organizations/630598743/202320469349300512/full.

269 https://www.newyorker.com/news/news-desk/the-reckoning-of-morris-dees-and-the-southern-poverty-law-center.

270 https://archive.fo/f6s0h.

271 https://www.newyorker.com/news/news-desk/the-reckoning-of-morris-dees-and-the-southern-poverty-law-center.

272 Hunter Biden, *Beautiful Things.*

273 https://www.dailymail.co.uk/news/article-10966153/Hunter-Biden-spent-30k-prostitutes-FIVE-MONTHS-documents-reveal.html.

274 https://www.politico.com/news/2023/04/24/trump-rape-trial-what-to-know-00093537.

275 https://floridaphoenix.com/2020/10/05/floridas-system-for-nominating-judges-has-become-a-partisan-tool-and-must-be-reformed/.

276 https://www.washingtonpost.com/politics/2023/06/20/gov-ron-desantis-used-secretive-panel-flip-state-supreme-court/.

277 https://www.washingtonpost.com/politics/2023/06/20/gov-ron-desantis-used-secretive-panel-flip-state-supreme-court/.

278 https://www.nytimes.com/2023/03/09/nyregion/trump-potential-criminal-charges-bragg.html.

279 https://www.youtube.com/watch?v=bnaVrL8I9eM.

280 https://twitter.com/MikeBenzCyber/status/1642233840449077249.

281 https://newsone.com/4519715/kyle-rittenhouse-civil-lawsuit/.

282 https://www.yahoo.com/video/after-a-black-protester-is-killed-in

-omaha-witnesses-claim-a-rushed-investigation-ignored-signs-of-the
-shooters-allegedly-190303877.html.

283 https://www.dallasnews.com/news/crime/2022/12/01/dallas-county
-district-attorney-ends-controversial-policy-on-misdemeanor-thefts/.

284 https://www.cnn.com/2023/06/23/politics/florida-supreme-court
-andrew-warren-desantis/index.html.

285 https://news.wfsu.org/state-news/2023-01-22/a-judge-says-he-cant-rein
state-andrew-warren-despite-gov-desantis-violating-the-first-amendment.

286 https://www.fox7austin.com/news/texas-governor-greg-abbott-signs
-hb-17-bill-district-attorneys.

287 https://www.splcenter.org/hatewatch/2023/04/03/texas-am-corps-let
-cadet-skip-training-extremist-event.

288 https://www.washingtonexaminer.com/policy/courts/twitter-trolls
-trial-delayed-after-alleged-witness-intimidation.

289 https://talkingbiznews.com/media-moves/how-not-to-gawker-yourself
-what-we-can-learn/.

290 https://www.tcta.org/legal-services/legal-issues-a-to-z/qualified-immu
nity-from-liability.

291 https://www.cato.org/commentary/republicans-kill-obamas-awful
-operation-choke-point.

292 https://www.americanbanker.com/news/ny-bank-regulator-warns-of
-reputational-risk-from-working-with-nra.

293 https://www.guns.com/news/2020/04/27/appeals-court-reinstates
-california-bullet-control-scheme.

294 https://www.ndstudies.gov/gr8/content/unit-iv-modern-north-dakota
-1921-present/lesson-2-making-living/topic-2-great-depression-and
-drought/section-2-bank-north-dakota-and-state-mill-and-elevator.

295 https://www.politico.com/news/2022/10/12/5th-circuit-temporarily
-blocks-texas-social-media-law-00061555.

296 https://corpgov.law.harvard.edu/2023/03/11/esg-battlegrounds-how
-the-states-are-shaping-the-regulatory-landscape-in-the-u-s/.

297 https://wusfnews.wusf.usf.edu/politics-issues/2023-05-03/desantis
-signs-esg-ban-jacksonville.

298 https://corpgov.law.harvard.edu/2023/03/11/esg-battlegrounds-how
-the-states-are-shaping-the-regulatory-landscape-in-the-u-s/.

299 https://www.washingtonpost.com/business/2019/04/25/nra-sues-los
-angeles-over-citys-contractor-disclosure-law/.

300 https://thepostmillennial.com/breaking-nyc-jury-finds-douglass-mackey
-guilty-in-first-ever-meme-trial-after-making-memes-that-disparaged
-hillary-clinton-in-the-2016-election.

301 https://www.nbcnews.com/news/us-news/police-other-civil-servants
-donate-kyle-rittenhouse-defense-fund-n1264343.

302 https://www.nbcnews.com/news/us-news/virginia-police-officer-fired
-after-donating-kyle-rittenhouse-defense-fund-n1264783.

303 https://twitter.com/ryanburge/status/1658447901901701123.

304 https://www.pewresearch.org/politics/2018/04/26/10-political-engage
ment-knowledge-and-the-midterms/.

305 https://kenoshanews.com/news/local/city-police-department-need
-dramatic-and-practical-reform-according-to-listening-sessions/
article_511b4a8e-e36a-5506-9986-2d622921afb5.html.

306 https://www.kenoshacounty.org/DocumentCenter/View/11827/Report
-on-the-Officer-Involved-Shooting-of-Jacob-Blake.

307 https://www.carnegie.org/our-work/article/visualizing-voter-turnout
-local-school-board-elections/.

308 https://www.livenowfox.com/news/ugliest-buildings-in-the-us-around
-the-world.

309 https://www.thepinknews.com/2015/04/27/president-obama-pokes
-fun-at-indiana-pizzeria-and-himself/.

310 https://www.washingtonpost.com/transportation/2021/11/20/single
-family-zoning-race-equity/.

311 https://www.nytimes.com/2021/04/19/opinion/biden-zoning-social
-justice.html.

312 ating-single-family-zoning-can-help-in-the-fight-against-climate
-change/.

313 https://www.gsb.stanford.edu/insights/political-polarizations-geo
graphic-roots-run-deep.

314 https://abcnews.go.com/Politics/us-facing-poll-worker-shortage-cam
paign-hopes-recruit/story?id=88243733.

315 https://www.sfgate.com/bayarea/article/SF-DA-Chesa-Boudin-fires
-attorneys-14971336.php.

316 https://www.cbsnews.com/sanfrancisco/news/boudin-district-attorney
-police-pretextual-stops-officers-denounce/.

317 https://www.npr.org/2020/04/09/829955754/son-of-60s-radicals-is
-the-new-d-a-in-san-francisco-facing-the-covid-19-crisis.

318 https://www.sfexaminer.com/news/prolific-offenders-help-drive
-46-surge-in-sf-burglaries/article_a6c9ca7e-5a99-5673-ac81-edec
-4f2a93c2.html.

319 https://www.cbsnews.com/sanfrancisco/news/lowell-high-school-merit
-based-admissions-return-sf-school-board-vote/.

320 https://educationdata.org/public-education-spending-statistics.

321 https://www.dailymail.co.uk/news/article-12292959/Uni-Florida
-officials-lied-teeth-downplaying-DEI-schemes-report-DeSantis.html.

322 https://www.pgpf.org/budget-basics/how-is-k-12-education-funded.

323 https://reason.com/2022/06/29/arizonas-new-law-funds-students-not
-just-government-run-schools/.

324 https://www.azmirror.com/2023/06/01/arizona-school-voucher-pro
gram-growth-explodes-to-900-million-for-the-upcoming-school-year/.

325 https://www.edchoice.org/media/indiana-becomes-fifth-state-in
-2023-to-enact-major-school-choice-program-expansion/.

326 Miles Taylor, *Blowback*.

327 https://www.nytimes.com/2023/01/09/opinion/chris-rufo-florida-ron
-desantis.html.

328 https://archive.fo/yUwDH.

329 https://apnews.com/article/new-college-florida-tenure-conservatives
-desantis-ce711c9169ebe84e9d062ebbb281ebce.

330 https://www.heraldtribune.com/story/news/politics/2023/01/06/
gov-ron-desantis-wants-conservative-overhaul-at-new-college-of-flor
ida/69784941007/.

331 https://educationdata.org/college-enrollment-statistics#:~:text=73.0%
25%20of%20college%20students%20at,graduate%20students%20
attend%20public%20institutions.

332 https://trustees.tennessee.edu/bylaws/appendix-a/.

333 https://boardofed.idaho.gov/board-facts/board-members/.

334 https://www.washingtonpost.com/dc-md-va/2023/05/30/youngkin
-college-degree-state-workforce/.

335 https://www.cbsnews.com/news/heres-the-nations-easiest-college-major/.

336 https://archive.fo/rkb64.

337 https://www.cato.org/commentary/love-choice-dont-federalize-it.

338 https://freebeacon.com/campus/how-the-american-bar-association
-just-radicalized-law-school/.

339 https://archive.fo/7wBpK.

340 Theodore Dalrymple, *Life at the Bottom*, p. vii.

341 https://fee.org/articles/aleksandr-solzhenitsyns-forgotten-lesson-on
-good-and-evil/.

342 https://www.thelancet.com/journals/lancet/article/PIIS0140
-6736(12)61789-9/fulltext.

343 https://www.hollywoodreporter.com/tv/tv-news/peak-tv-2022-count
-599-scripted-shows-1235298139/.

344 https://www.statista.com/statistics/420791/daily-video-content-con
sumption-usa-device/.

345 https://techcrunch.com/2022/07/13/kids-and-teens-watch-more-tiktok
-than-youtube-tiktok-91-minutes-in-2021-youtube-56/.

346 https://www.pewresearch.org/short-reads/2021/04/07/partisan-dif ferences-in-social-media-use-show-up-for-some-platforms-but-not -facebook/.

347 https://twitter.com/genericeddie/status/1659081857793769472.

348 Johann Hari, *Stolen Focus* (Crown, 2022).

349 https://usafacts.org/articles/obesity-rate-nearly-triples-united-states -over-last-50-years/.

350 https://www.military.com/daily-news/2022/09/28/new-pentagon-study -shows-77-of-young-americans-are-ineligible-military-service.html.

351 https://www.newsweek.com/cdc-map-reveals-most-obese-states-amer ica-1747122.

352 https://www.foxnews.com/media/atlantic-trump-voters-obese-drug -users.

353 https://www.dailymail.co.uk/health/article-12136287/Fat-people -officially-protected-group-NYC-Eric-Adams-signs-discrimination -law.html.

354 https://www.cancer.gov/about-cancer/causes-prevention/risk/obesity/ obesity-fact-sheet#:~:text=Compared%20with%20people%20of%20 healthy,causes%20(2%E2%80%935).

355 https://www.ox.ac.uk/news/2009-03-18-moderate-obesity-takes-years -life-expectancy.

356 https://www.outkick.com/msnbc-says-exercising-far-right/.

357 http://tuftsjournal.tufts.edu/archives/1627.

358 https://www.deseret.com/2010/4/13/20375744/ucla-study-proves -mormons-live-longer.

359 G. K. Chesterton, *G.K.'s Weekly*, June 19th 1926.

360 https://www.statista.com/chart/16959/share-of-the-internet-that-is-porn/.

361 https://sexualalpha.com/how-many-people-watch-porn-statistics/.

362 https://www.nytimes.com/2018/02/10/opinion/sunday/lets-ban-porn .html.

363 https://www.google.com/url?q=https://www.thesun.co.uk/sun
-men/9424433/half-men-under-50-suffer-erectile-dysfunction/&sa
=D&source=docs&ust=1691099111880016&usg=AOvVaw0cKBH
SQdK7-UpDb9Jl0RTN.

364 https://www.fincham.info/papers/2013pornalternativesextrabehavior
sppsfinal.pdf.

365 https://fightthenewdrug.org/research-says-married-couples-who-watch
-porn-are-twice-as-likely-to-divorce/.

366 G. K. Chesterton, "On Dialect and Decency."

367 https://lithub.com/these-are-the-10-best-selling-books-of-the-decade/.

368 https://www.dailymail.co.uk/news/article-12219343/Gen-Zs-trans
-poster-child-Milo-2016-MTV-reemerges-tearfully-regretting-hormone
-jabs.html.

369 https://www.usnews.com/news/best-states/articles/states-with-the
-highest-divorce-rates.

370 https://www.marxists.org/archive/marx/works/1848/communist-man
ifesto/ch02.htm.

371 https://endnotes.org.uk/articles/to-abolish-the-family.pdf.

372 https://www.bgsu.edu/ncfmr/resources/data/family-profiles/schweizer
-marriage-century-change-1900-2018-fp-20-21.html.

373 https://www.bgsu.edu/ncfmr/resources/data/family-profiles/schweizer
-marriage-century-change-1900-2018-fp-20-21.html.

374 https://www.pewresearch.org/social-trends/2020/05/27/as-millenni
als-near-40-theyre-approaching-family-life-differently-than-previous
-generations/.

375 https://www.usatoday.com/story/opinion/voices/2020/10/14/
single-mom-parents-children-democratic-voters-biden-harris-col
umn/3629110001/.

376 https://www.washingtonpost.com/politics/single-mothers-give-presi
dential-politics-a-new-perspective/2013/06/02/b8f85702-cb90-11e2
-8845-d970ccb04497_story.html.

377 https://www.washingtonpost.com/politics/single-mothers-give-presi
dential-politics-a-new-perspective/2013/06/02/b8f85702-cb90-11e2
-8845-d970ccb04497_story.html.

378 https://ifstudies.org/blog/red-families-vs-blue-families-which-are-hap
pier/.

379 https://www.robkhenderson.com/p/swiping-and-dating-preferences.

380 https://www.dailymail.co.uk/femail/article-2173101/Tattoos-bad
-breath-beards-bitten-nails-What-men-women-biggest-turn-offs-op
posite-sex.html.

381 https://www.foxnews.com/media/baltimore-teacher-brags-indoctrinat
ing-students-taxpayer-money-put-taxes-bag.

382 https://nypost.com/2022/11/25/texas-teacher-interviews-middle
-schoolers-on-non-binary-identity/.

383 https://twitter.com/libsoftiktok/status/1523760691999428609?lang=en.

384 https://www.heritage.org/education/report/political-opinions-k
-12-teachers-results-nationally-representative-survey.

385 Paul Johnson, *The Birth Of The Modern: World Society* (HarperCollins,
1991).

386 https://www.nationalreview.com/2018/12/aleksandr-solzhenitsyn-men
-have-forgotten-god-speech/.

387 https://www.newstatesman.com/politics/2012/08/atheism-plus-new
-new-atheists.

388 https://thehistorianshut.com/2016/12/29/the-priests-of-the-magna
-mater-great-mother-cybele-were-eunuchs/.

389 https://www.cnn.com/2023/08/05/sport/nascar-noah-gragson-sus
pended-spt/index.html.

390 https://www.sfgate.com/entertainment/morford/article/Is-Obama-an
-enlightened-being-Spiritual-wise-2544395.php.